the self-sustaining garden

the self-sustaining garden

the guide to matrix planting

Peter Thompson

Drawings by Josie Owen

F

FRANCES LINCOLN LIMITED

PUBLISHERS

(Front cover) Garden at Bowen Island, Vancouver, Canada.

(Page 2) A plant matrix on a grand scale; made up of layers of vegetation composed of trees and shrubs – large and small – and ground-covering perennials. A complete matrix forms a community of mutually supporting plants which excludes outsiders (weeds to a gardener) and is largely self-sustaining.

(Right) Detail from page 67.

(Opposite, clockwise from top left): details from pages 16, 83, 112, 13.

Publisher's note: Wherever possible botanical names are in accordance with those published in the 2005/6 edition of the *RHS Plant Finder*.

Characters portrayed in the case studies of gardens are fictional. Resemblances to persons living or dead are coincidental.

All photographs by the author except on the following pages: front cover, pages 2, 20, 76, 100, 182 (Photos: Gil Hanly)

Frances Lincoln Ltd
4 Torriano Mews
Torriano Avenue
London NW5 2RZ
www.franceslincoln.com

Published in New Zealand by David Bateman Ltd
30 Tarndale Grove, Albany, Auckland, New Zealand

A catalogue record for this book is available from the British Library

Design: Intesa Group
Printed in China through Colorcraft Ltd., Hong Kong

ISBN 978-0-7112-2718-7

9 8 7 6 5 4 3 2 1

contents

Acknowledgements

To friends, to colleagues, to gardeners I have known and to gardeners whom I have never met whose gardens or books have given me pleasure or inspiration.

To my father, whose generosity in selling Oldfield Nurseries to me at a fraction of its value enabled me to resign from the Royal Botanic Gardens at Kew and take my leave of botanical research when the time was ripe.

To Christopher Lloyd, who as a lecturer at Wye College sustained my belief that gardening lay beyond horticulture, and that the calling of a gardener was one of life's most fulfilling professions.

To Harold Nicolson, and to Vita Sackville West, whom I met once, friendly, but formidable in britches and broad-brimmed hat, whose garden at Sissinghurst first compelled me to see a garden as a composition not just a collection of plants.

To Marjorie Fish, whom I never met, for her garden at East Lambrook Manor, which first sowed the seeds of matrix planting in my mind. To Phyllis Reiss, whose garden at Tintinhull first showed me the magical effects of setting informal planting in a formal frame, and to Penelope Hobhouse for reviving the garden I had carried in my mind from earliest visits.

To Gordon Collier, former owner of Titoki Point, Jack Hobbs, curator of the Regional Botanic Gardens, Manurewa, and Alison McCrae in New Zealand; to Phoebe Noble near Victoria in British Columbia, Canada; to Mrs van Bennekom and Ton ter Linden in Holland and to a hundred other gardeners whose efforts, skill and imagination have given me pleasure and inspiration over the years.

To George Taylor, who as Director of Kew appointed me Head of the Physiology Section on its revival after a lapse of fifty years, and gave unstinting support to my proposal to set up a Seed Bank in which to conserve seeds of useful, threatened or otherwise 'save-worthy' species and populations of wild plants.

To Trish Johnson, whose heroic efforts in my garden for several years converted a forlorn hope into a promising prospect, and convinced me that matrix planting has a future.

To all those whose gardens in Britain, Holland, Canada, Chile, the United States, France, Spain, South Africa, Russia, Australia and New Zealand have been the sources of the photographs that appear in this book. Captions to the plates seldom identify these gardens. No discourtesy is intended; their locations are acknowledged and the plants displayed in them listed at the back of the book.

(Opposite) On the small scale of a richly planted border, matrices are formed by intricate mixes of foliage, stems and flowers. Well chosen mixtures not only look beautiful in themselves, but are effective self-sustaining communities.

introduction
to matrix planting

IF WE LET THEM, PLANTS COULD do much of
the hard work of gardening for us. Unfortunately, the ways we have been
taught to garden actually prevent them from doing so. This book looks at
unorthodox ways of gardening which allow the plants in our gardens to
form self-sustaining communities, similar to those in which wildflowers live
naturally – a system of gardening known as matrix planting.

Orthodox gardeners dismiss suggestions it is possible to garden without
digging or forking the soil, raking it level or hoeing weeds periodically.
Suggestions their skills could be replaced by anything as unreal as alliances
with plants affront them, and many will regard this book as an attack on the
craft and traditions which they cherish most dearly.

But a self-sustaining garden in which plants do much of the work is not
an attack on established gardening methods any more than one face of a coin
represents an attack on the other. They share a common background but have
different viewpoints. The techniques embodied in gardening lore enable us
to grow the broadest possible range of plants in the widest possible variety
of situations. Matrix planting does not attempt to make all gardens all things
to all plants. On the contrary, it is based on matching plant to place with the
reward that, when done successfully, plants replace spades, rakes and hoes as
the controllers of what goes on in the garden.

Wildflowers grow all over the world with no help from humans. They
survive by forming self-sustaining communities – broadly known as vegetation – which shelter and protect the plants within them, while excluding
outsiders. They are successful because the plants within each community
have established a balance with one another which enables each to obtain
a share of resources, living space and opportunities to reproduce.

Matrix planting is based on this natural model. It aims to set up similar
self-sustaining communities in gardens by bringing together plants which
are capable of melding one with another in a balance which enables all to
survive and flourish, and excludes weeds.

The Self-sustaining Garden is written for those who garden in temperate
parts of the world – ranging from places where temperatures seldom fall
more than a degree or two below freezing point to those where -25°C (-13°F)
is not unknown. That covers the extreme range of gardening conditions in
Britain, Western and Southern Europe, parts of the USA from New England
to the mid-Atlantic states in the east, and the Pacific coastal states in the west;
Western Canada, New Zealand, the more temperate parts of Australia, Japan
and much of South Africa.

Many factors affect a plant's ability to thrive and inevitably, across such
a range of places, plants recommended for one locality will be a disaster

(Opposite) A dozen North
American woodland wild
flowers grow harmoniously
within an area of one square
metre.

Garden plants can develop similarly balanced communities like the one at East Lambrook Manor (below), or the three-layered matrix (right) formed by shrubs, ferns and ground-covering perennials. Aloes, aeoniums and agaves thrive in almost frost-free places (opposite). Gardeners in colder parts of the world know better than to expect similar results, but frost and heat tolerance, drought resistance, vulnerability to wet conditions and other qualities critically affect the chances of establishing successful communities wherever we garden.

in another. Communities which live together in one place will be riven by incompatibilities elsewhere. Well over a thousand plants are listed by name with brief descriptions, and referred to elsewhere in this book, and gardeners can consider these suggestions, bearing in mind the particular characteristics of the places where they garden. The lists provide brief details of preferences for dry, moist, acid or basic soils, etc, and plants that are vulnerable to frost are marked with an asterisk.

Gardeners everywhere are becoming increasingly aware of the value of water as a precious resource.

Orthodox gardening looks back to an age when water was freely available in apparently unlimited quantities and uses water lavishly and without regard for economy. Self-sustaining gardening, as the name suggests, grows plants within the limits of the resources available, one of which is water. Although not specifically devised to address the problems of water shortages, matrix planting has much in common with the techniques of water-wise gardening.

Natural soil profiles, which are themselves economical in the ways they store and conserve water, are maintained and the water-holding capacity of soils is reinforced. Plants with similar needs are grouped together, the plants grown are chosen to match the conditions, and in dry locations only drought-tolerant plants would be used. Mulches are used to protect soil surfaces, and watering cans and hoses play little or no part, because their use encourages unbalanced growth of those plants best able to take advantage of additional water.

If I was an orthodox gardener faced with the prospects of reducing the amount of water I used whenever there was a drought, and its consequences – brown lawns, scraggy annuals, withered shrubs and unthrifty perennials – my first thoughts would be about changing my methods. Even if this only extends initially to parts of the garden, matrix planting and a self-sustaining garden is the alternative I would go for.

what does
your *garden* **grow?**

IF ASKED, 'WHAT DOES YOUR GARDEN
grow?', many gardeners would reply that gardeners grow plants and what
grows in gardens depends on the skills and resources of the gardener. We
are able to grow dahlias, gladioli, begonias and other tender plants in places
with cold winters by lifting them and protecting them from frost through the
winter. Some invest in conservatories: small ones when we need to count the
pennies, and gigantic, multi-domed, corridored and aisled ones for those with
more expansive tastes and fortunes. The challenge of growing plants in places
far from their natural homes is a vitally important part of gardening and
sometimes goes far beyond modest pride in homespun skills.

Louis XIV saw no reason why promenades among the parterres at Versailles
should be spoilt by the frailties of plants. Whatever the season, the Sun King
insisted the beds must be bright with flowers, and on frosty nights tender
bedding plants died in their thousands. The gardeners simply replaced them,
again and again, from countless stocks in reserve in glasshouses. But it is
not only all-powerful monarchs who pit their skills against the limitations of
their garden. For many of us half the fun of gardening lies in the challenge
of growing plants where nature never intended them to be.

Natural and garden habitats
But there is another approach – one that has become increasingly popular
in recent years – and that is to match the place to the plant. It depends on
summing up the assets and limitations of a garden, or a corner of a garden,
and choosing the plants most likely to do well in the conditions provided.

(Opposite) Plants in this
picture have been carefully
chosen to match their
natural preferences with
conditions in the garden:
flag-irises in the water,
candelabra primulas on
moist ground along the
banks, and ferns and shrubs
in the shade below the
trees. Whatever its size,
every garden consists of
a variety of settings, sunlit or shaded, moist or
dry, exposed or sheltered.
Successful planting depends
on finding the right plants to
grow in each setting.

(Below) Orthodox gardening
techniques enable us to
grow plants of very different
origins side by side, as
in this modern version
of a herbaceous border.
Successful matrix planting
depends on matching
settings in the garden with
the natural adaptations of
the plants being used.

Plants adapted to extreme conditions like hot, arid, open bush (above and opposite), cool, perennially wet, deeply shaded temperate rain forests (left), or alpine locations (below) usually demand settings in gardens which match their needs. Widely grown, amenable garden plants are more likely to be the descendants of the wildflowers of meadows, open woodlands, wetlands and similar less-demanding natural environments.

If we are to choose wisely from the bewildering array of plants available to us, we first have to learn about the conditions in which they grow naturally.

That covers an immense variety of situations from Antarctic islands and high screes on mountains, to luxuriant tropical rain forests. Gardens too exist in extraordinary variety, even when we include only those in temperate regions of the world. But, within most gardens the range is quite small. It so happens that the geological formations in the part of the world where I live are exceptionally diverse and fragmented, and in a bare half hectare my garden contains soils which vary from acidic to strongly basic. It includes dry, free-draining sunlit banks, and places bordering a stream that remain constantly moist and shaded. Depending on where I stand, the soil may be heavy clay, woodland loam, an open sandy loam or shaly fragments that scarcely resemble soil at all. But that is an unusual situation and many gardeners would respond to suggestions they should vary their planting in accordance with different habitats in their gardens with derision. 'Fine, for you,' they might say, 'but I have only one habitat – so what sort of variety would that give me?'

But shade beneath an apple tree is woodland for the plants that grow there; a lawn mimics rabbit-grazed turf on a chalk hillside; perennials and shrubs in the mixed border experience some of the problems and opportunities of wildflowers amongst scrub. Instead of thinking of different parts of your garden as a series of habitats – a rather grand term that relates more comfortably to the broad scale in which plants grow naturally – think of them as a series of settings. The smallest garden provides a variety of different settings – some are sunlit, others shady; some exposed, others sheltered; some are well-drained, others hold water like a bog. The plants likely to do best, and grow most easily, will be those found in natural habitats with similar conditions.

I am not suggesting nothing should be planted without first completing a detailed ecological survey of the conditions in which it grows naturally. Considerable progress is made just by discovering that a particular plant grows in woodland or amongst grasses in damp meadows perhaps; or in rocky, exposed places amongst small shrubs. We look for meadow flowers amongst grasses, woodland perennials in the shade and shelter of trees, and cornfield weeds – assuming herbicidal sprays have spared any – in fields of cereals. We can go further afield to screes and snowfields at the tops of mountains, to arid places where sparsely scattered plants eke out a living amongst stones and rocks, and to the deepest recesses of heavily shaded forests. Plants will be there too, but these have adapted to cope with the highly specialist conditions in which they live. Few will be amongst the tolerant, easily grown, relatively accommodating plants we rely on to fill the borders in our gardens, which are also the ones most likely to settle down happily and form self-sustaining communities in our gardens.

Many places where wild flowers grow look as beautiful as any garden – the spring flowers in the Appalachian Mountains, a bluebell wood in Britain, the brilliant displays of annuals and bulbs in Namaqualand, or the intensity of

Gardens are composed of a variety of settings, or habitats. A wall of a house may shade a narrow border for much of the day (top left), while another provides a backdrop for an equally narrow, hot, sunny border (middle left). There may be a dry, steeply sloping, sunlit bank (right) or the level, soggy margins of a pool (below left). In each case, only plants naturally adapted to grow in that setting will form a successful matrix.

colours and extraordinary shapes of the flowers on shrubs in Western Australia are a few examples amongst many, but such spectacles lack the structure and evidence of deliberate intention that reveals the designer's hand in a garden. Closer inspection can even leave an impression their skin-deep beauty overlies a tangled chaos which no gardener could live with for a day.

Wildflowers do not grow as haphazardly as it may seem. The communities they form are:

Ordered
The plants exist, one with another, in relationships based on competition through which they establish balanced communities in which every plant has its place, and from which each plant derives the support, shelter or protection it needs for survival.

Predictable
The wildflowers in any community are characteristic of the situation depending on whether the soil is wet or free-draining, acid or alkaline; the climate cold or temperate, and so on. A botanist, given a description of the situation, would often be able to predict many of the species to be found there without going near the place.

Persistent
We are taught that grassland is vulnerable to invasion by shrubs to form scrub, giving way in turn to woodland as trees establish themselves, but these transitions can be very slow. The nature of the soil, grazing pressures, climatic extremes, fire and other effects – some of which correspond to forms of garden management – can delay or entirely prevent the evolution of one type of vegetation into another.

Stable
The mixture of species in a community can remain virtually the same for long periods. A return visit to a natural habitat which we knew in childhood, such as a wood or a riverside, will renew our acquaintance with the same species – even the most insignificant ones – that we first got to know perhaps half a century and more previously.

'Order', 'predictability', 'persistence' and 'stability' are words with a more reassuring ring than the apparent chaos of untamed nature might suggest, and they provide the foundation on which matrix planting is based. If garden plants share the behaviour of their wild progenitors, they too can form long-lived, self-sustaining communities that can be harnessed to make our gardens easier to look after.

Wild plants under the skin
That may sound like a very big 'if'! Full blown hybrid tea roses, cymbidiums with spikes like gladioli, the great round heads of exhibition dahlias and the multi-coloured foliage of hostas seem far from natural. Man-made creations like these could hardly be expected to survive without our protection. But garden plants are wild plants in disguise, their cover little deeper than the surface lustre and extra vigour conferred by high living and freedom from competition, amplified by selection for larger flowers with more petals and brighter, more varied colours than their wild counterparts.

In a brown, parched land wild lilac bushes grow on low, rolling hills along the valley of the Vardar River in Macedonia. This river brings the influence of the Mediterranean deep into the Balkan Peninsula, and lilacs grow naturally in places like this where winters have the cold severity of continental Europe, and summers the torrid aridity that makes the Mediterranean a sun-baked paradise for holidaymakers. Shoots and flowers are produced during the few short weeks before the drought of summer closes a brief spring. Then growth stops and the leaves develop the heavy-duty guise they need to work effectively through long periods of hot, dry weather. They fall without delay – or time to develop autumn tints – as winter closes in, and are replaced by short, sturdy twigs carrying buds encased in scales to protect them from cold winds. Dense networks of roots just below the surface collect water in spring from melting snow, and make the most of summer showers and, if unusually severe conditions or outbreaks of fire destroy the tops, suckers are produced to rebuild new plants.

Garden lilacs are more colourful; their blooms more sumptuous and their trusses of flowers more luxuriant than those of their wild ancestors by the Vardar River. In almost every other way they are the same. Superficial disguises lead us to suppose the plants in our gardens are quite different to wild plants, and repeated, but unsubstantiated, references in books, on television and in the gardening press to plants 'having been changed by cultivation' or 'having adapted to cultivation' support that supposition.

Despite obvious changes in appearance, the hidden physiological responses, which control the ways plants react to their environments, seldom change during the process of turning a wild flower into a garden plant. Michaelmas daisies have been bred from two North American species, *Aster novae-angliae* and *A. novi-belgii*, which grow naturally in damp meadows. They are tall with quite small, pale purple daisies; their rhizomes spread vigorously amongst the grasses at ground level, and extend over large areas, eventually becoming separated so they appear to be numerous individual plants dotted over the meadow. Garden plants have been selected with larger flowers, more petals and many more colours. They range in size from dwarfs, barely 30 cm (1 ft) high to plants 2 m (6 ft 6 in) tall. The rhizomes they produce are shorter and form compact clusters of stems which compete with one another for nutrients and water.

Most gardeners would think nothing of planting lilacs and Michaelmas daisies close to each other in a border; perhaps to provide similar colour tones at opposite ends of the season. Despite their very different origins and natural adaptations, they would grow quite happily together provided the ground was well prepared and they were pruned, watered, fertilised, sprayed for diseases and cared for in other ways, because, like most plants, they can tolerate a much wider range of conditions than those they are specifically adapted to cope with naturally. But even under exemplary conditions, Michaelmas daisies are so prone to mildew in most garden settings that many people have given

Garden plants are wildflowers under the skin. Dahlias and roses (below left, top and bottom) are highly bred, exotic creations; the grevillea (below right) looks no less exotic but is an unchanged wildling. Appearances change, but the natural adaptations of a plant's ancestors live on, and hold the keys to successful cultivation. Dahlias prefer moisture-retentive fertile soils and are vulnerable to frost; roses are intolerant of shade; grevilleas thrive only on free-draining impoverished soils in sunlit situations.

up growing them. Their appearance may have changed, but, physiologically, they still depend on the moist soils they are adapted to naturally, and without them become stressed and vulnerable to infection.

Many of the trees, shrubs, perennials and bulbs grown in our gardens scarcely differ in appearance from their wild counterparts; others have been selected for trivial changes, such as variations in flower colour, increased number of petals, variegated foliage. Some are hybrids between two species, and when these species occupy different habitats their offspring may inherit the attributes of both parents. Primroses grow naturally on neutral to acid soils, cowslips on those that are well-drained and strongly basic. Hybrids between the two have produced polyanthus, which are equally happy in both conditions. More complex hybrids like roses, with a network of lineages leading back to several different species, are the inheritors of so many different responses that connections with any particular wild ancestor may be completely obscure.

Simple or complex, garden plants are the descendants of their wild ancestors. Their suitability for different situations, their compatibility with other plants and their prospects of settling down to form a community are all expressions of that inheritance. Under natural conditions wildflowers live together, filling a variety of niches. Some provide shade and shelter, others ground-cover. Some are permanent residents, others ever-ready to fill spaces that become available. Some are active during one season, others at another. Garden plants can play similar roles if only we allow them to.

So the response to the question 'what would your garden grow?' will not be a single answer. There will be areas of shade and sunshine; places where the water fails to drain in winter and others where it drains too freely in summer. There may be trees to contend with, hedges to accommodate, shrubs to be planted and particular features – a rock garden, a pool, a bank covered with heathers and dwarf conifers – which you would like to include in your repertoire. Each poses different problems and opportunities, and each provides a setting within which a different community of plants will be at home.

Russell lupins (above left) were deliberately introduced into Central Otago, New Zealand. Now they maintain themselves in a range of colours most gardeners would envy. Primulas (above right) grow like natives in a wet ditch in the mild, humid conditions of the west of Scotland. Self-sufficiencies like these depend on affinities between natural adaptations and locations.

partnerships
with **plants**

2

BUY A HOUSE, AND NINETY-NINE times out of a
hundred you buy a plot, a section or a yard as well. Whatever it's called,
whatever its size, you will quickly discover the neighbours expect that space
around your house to be turned into a garden. Your skills as a gardener may be
wanting; you may have no time to be a gardener; you may share your life with
forces that are hostile to gardens – children who play games and want to ride
bicycles with their friends; dogs and cats. You may need somewhere to park
cars, caravans, even a boat. Perhaps you have a talent for relaxing and watching
the world go by which is not conducive to gardening. You have other plans for
your plot, section or yard. Whatever the excuses, few resist the expectations of
neighbours, the conventions of upbringing and the pressures of spouses, and at
some stage most of us find ourselves mowing the lawn and trimming hedges.
We puzzle about planning and planting the borders, and lose ourselves among
a maze of Latin names during visits to garden centres. We discover that the
harder we work, the more problems seem to multiply.

   That is not because plants are difficult to grow. Many manage quite well
in our gardens with or without our help, and weeds – which like it or not,
are still plants – appear despite every effort to destroy them. Could we be
creating our own problems? Rather than repeatedly assaulting our gardens
with spades and hoes, should we try to find ways to make the superabundant
energy of plants work for us? Could we even enrol them as partners?

   Gardeners, not nature, invented the rules which govern what we grow

**(Opposite) Plant partnerships
depend on maintaining a
balance of power between
neighbours. In moist, fertile,
sunlit situations, like the one
shown, vigorous perennials
form robust communities
from which more delicate,
less thrusting plants are
rapidly eliminated.**

**(Below) Few gardeners today
have the time or energy to
cope with the demands of
rose arbours (below left)
and immaculate herbaceous
borders (below right). Most
look for more carefree ways
to garden.**

and how we garden. The more carefully contrived our gardens become, the more exclusive becomes the range of plants deemed worthy of an appearance. These few are recognised as 'Garden Plants', and war is waged on all others as weeds. The higher the state of gardening, the narrower the definitions, the stricter the rules and the harder we must work. Even today, when few have help in their gardens, and other interests compete for our time, we look back nostalgically to visions of kitchen gardens, formal rose beds, herbaceous borders, lawns, rockeries and other highly unnatural versions of garden-making. If transported on a temporal flying carpet – it might be on television or by virtual reality – to a garden of a century ago, many people would say they had seen perfection.

Our lifestyles have changed vastly, but gardeners still look for inspiration to the ways gardens were run in Western Europe at the turn of the nineteenth century. The package of combining garden flora and gardening techniques was adopted wherever European influences and traditions were predominant, spreading not only to places that were suitable, but to others where climates, conditions and traditions bore no resemblance to the lands of its origin. Identical rose beds were planted and tended with equal care in Kensington, Kashmir and Kerikeri. Herbaceous borders based on similar plans were the pride of Philadelphia, Perth and Paris. The annuals to be seen in bedding schemes in Cape Town made borders bright and beautiful on Isola Bella, in San Francisco, in Darjeeling and in St Petersburg. The vastly diverse native floras of North America, South Africa, New Zealand and Australia were largely ignored apart from a small and select band of species which were accepted into the repertoire of European gardens. In due course, cultivars of these were repatriated as garden plants to their native lands.

During the twentieth century a select – though still enormous – band of plants were awarded the honour of garden citizenship and circulated throughout gardens worldwide, forming a horticultural Pangaea. Now this continent is drifting apart. Early signs of the rift appeared in California where climate and circumstances combined to create a vision of a 'New Eden' which stimulated innovation. Later, a surfeit of the 'English Garden' in the eastern states led to the idea of the 'New American Garden'. That term may be even harder to define and have no more real meaning than the concept of an all-embracing English garden. Nevertheless, it introduces freedom to explore ways of using plants in relation to the needs, aspirations and opportunities of the location and its people, instead of following styles and techniques developed and perfected under quite different conditions.

Trees, shrubs, climbers, herbaceous perennials, ferns, cacti and other succulents, bulbs and especially grasses are being found new roles in gardens. The native plants of North America, South Africa, Australia and New Zealand and their cultivars are increasingly replacing pyracanthas, hybrid tea roses, delphiniums, daffodils and French marigolds. They are frequently not only better adapted to grow in gardens in these countries, but also introduce forms and textures, and sometimes intensities of colour too, which were seldom or never seen in the gardens of Europe.

No one who visits contemporary gardens in different parts of the world can fail to notice how plants and practices vary from place to place. The Royal Horticultural Society in Britain makes a new garden at Rosemoor in Devon in a broad wooded valley, which steadfastly maintains the planting patterns and garden features of the past, and for all one can tell the site had never been visited by the garden's designer. Meanwhile, Soka University in the Santa Monica Mountains near Los Angeles opts for a garden in which the themes and plants used are based on local plant communities of live-oak woodland, chaparral and coastal sage scrub.

Gardeners are looking afresh at long-established gardening principles and reviewing the opportunities plants offer garden designers. The introduction of proteas and their hybrids into gardens in their native South Africa – as well as in Australia, California and New Zealand – has done more than present gardeners with new versions of evergreen shrubs. The aversion these plants have to even modest levels of phosphates in soils, their sensitivity to disturbance of their roots and competition from other plants, call for radical reviews of the basics of plant husbandry. The hallowed techniques of high fertility gardening, forking between shrubs, and liberal use of fertilisers do not work for these plants and may even kill them.

The introduction of phormiums, astelias and cabbage trees from New Zealand to gardens in many parts of the temperate world has made available novel plant forms scarcely known previously to garden designers and border composers. The developing taste, especially in North America, Holland, Germany and other parts of Europe, for gardens based on the native flora growing in semi-natural communities, using plants whose natural origins are carefully matched to conditions in the garden, have led to new ways of looking at gardens and our perceptions of what constitutes a garden.

We have become accustomed to composing borders of plants of many origins brought together solely for their visual impact, with emphasis on contrasting or harmonising the colours of the flowers and, increasingly, the impact of their varied forms and foliage. We are less at ease with compositions based on plants sharing common qualities, which enable them to bed down together as communities in the particular conditions of the places where they are grown.

We are used to paying a lot of attention to details such as the impact of individual plants, and even individual flowers. Now we are learning to appreciate the interaction of plants and the overall effects of the subtle signals of visual logic. The harmonies or contrasts between one section and another reveal patterns and rhythms based on repetitions of colour, texture and form. Unlike traditional garden plants whose survival depends on the gardener's skill and attention, the survival of these plants depends on their ability to fit into and contribute to the communities in which they grow.

Ferns and variegated ground elder provide an undemanding border for a house (top right). Bromeliads and monsteras create a woodland stage set (left). The special needs of proteas and related plants force us to change traditional approaches to cultivation (bottom left). The spiky accents of cordylines, astelias and grasses stimulate imaginative combinations of forms and textures (bottom right).

The concept of matrix planting is a decisive departure from the creed under-lining orthodox gardening, which enables gardeners to grow almost any plant almost anywhere, despite the natural preferences of the plants themselves, and which I – in common with so many gardeners – learnt in the earliest days of my gardening apprenticeship.

The Creed of the Orthodox Gardener

- I believe in the turning of the soil and the incorporation of humus.
- As a virtuous gardener I will frequently and repeatedly sprinkle fertilisers so that my plants shall not lack for nutrients. And, my hand will be ready ever to reach out to separate seedlings, space plants and eliminate all forms of earthly competition.
- I shall rest not from hoeing nor weeding by hand; so that no weed may be seen amongst my plants. Nor refrain from pesticidal sprays and the scattering of slug pellets.
- Neither shall I abstain from frequent watering, during dry days and in fine so that each plant may receive an abundance of its life-giving powers.
- In the dark days of winter I will raise up plants in houses of glass, or within the comfort of frames. Nor plant them in the earth till all danger of frost be past.
- Through the sure and certain knowledge that all has been done and nothing left undone, so that every plant shall grow bigger and better, lies the salvation of my garden.

Multi-tiered combinations of trees, shrubs and perennials form the strongest matrices (top left). Roses grow through ground covering perennials (top right). Hydrangeas and fuchsias grow through spring-flowering woodland perennials to form an upper tier of the matrix later in the season (bottom left). Bulbous woodlanders, like trilliums and bluebells, star briefly in springtime, before rodgersias develop a vigorous weed-excluding canopy in summer (bottom right).

The creed's guiding principle resides in the hands and on the hard work of the gardener, on which everything depends. Matrix planting's guiding principle resides in the plants, which will do much of this work if we allow them to. Then most of the operations referred to in the Gardener's Creed become unnecessary, or even counterproductive.

Why matrix planting?

A natural plant community is composed of networks of roots, entanglements of stems, mosaics of foliage and an abundance of flowers which occupy the ground and the air above it to the exclusion of intruders. Matrix planting is based on choosing and managing plants in ways which enable them to form similar matrices in the garden.

Because it is modelled on the ways plants grow naturally, matrix planting is sometimes narrowly regarded as a way of managing native plants or wildflowers, and conversely, as unsuitable for garden plants in more ordered garden settings. That is not so. Garden plants are wild plants under the skin, and there is no reason why the principles should not be applied to almost any plant in almost any garden setting. The aim is to enable the plants to occupy the ground and the space above it so effectively that no space is left for intruders (that is, weeds) and to do this in ways that are decorative and sympathetic to the setting of the garden.

These aims make well-tried methods or tools redundant. Hoes, rakes and forks have no part to play in disturbing soil between plants. The spade is no longer the inevitable, or even a desirable, means of preparing ground before planting. The use of fertilisers before and after planting, and control of pests and diseases with pesticides, are frequently harmful activities. Plants and the communities in which they grow – rather than the tools of the gardener's trade – become the agents through which control is exercised, and a great many different plants are referred to in the pages which follow.

Plant names always present problems. Vernacular names are imprecise and open to misinterpretation, especially when used in an international context. Latin names are precise but can be intimidating and may look stilted or pretentious to some readers. Wherever appropriate, vernacular names have been used freely in the text, and are identified in the index by their Latin equivalents to resolve any confusion. So where there is doubt, as perhaps with the word 'cowslip', reference to the index will show the plant intended is *Primula veris*, following British usage and not the American *Caltha palustris*. Elsewhere, Latin names are the rule.

Few plants are described in detail, and some readers may feel they are being offered a feast of good food in cans – without a can-opener. No one need rise hungry from the table. Descriptions would have submerged the message in the book, and references to virtually every plant mentioned can be found at whatever level of detail is needed in countless encyclopaedias, monographs and manuals.

Other garden writers have provided personal and often graphic descriptions and impressions of a host of plants:

Reginald Farrer – vividly
Gertrude Jekyll – artistically
E A Bowles – eruditely
Marjorie Fish – beguilingly
Christopher Lloyd – elegantly
Frederick McGourty – humorously
Beth Chatto – naturally
Rosemary Verey – perceptively
Anne Lovejoy – intuitively
Penelope Hobhouse – familiarly
Graham Thomas – authoritatively

What untapped qualities of wit or wisdom could I hope to bring to a field already so well supplied?

control
in *the* garden

3

Plants are the vocabulary we use to express our dreams or create atmosphere in gardens. Plants picked up impulsively at garden centres are no more likely to express what we want than words chosen at random from a dictionary. A quick unplanned tour might yield a golden-leaved hosta and a dahlia with crimson foliage and bright red flowers bought on impulse; three pots of aubrieta going cheap after their flowers have faded, or a conifer taken away on the promise it is the perfect thing to screen us from a neighbour's view. Skin-deep eye-appeal, inability to resist 'bargains', and belief in promises of quick solutions – that is how we all start buying plants. Finding places for this little collection in the garden is akin to creating a sentence from 'elephant' because we like the word; 'iridotomy' because the sound intrigues us, even though we are baffled by its meaning; and 'manufacture' and 'bread' because they sound reassuringly useful.

We use qualifying or linking words to connect collections of nouns and verbs like these together and define the relationships of one with another.

(Opposite) Competition is the balancing mechanism through which successful matrices are established Here, moderately vigorous, free-growing perennials flanking an informal path form a robust community in which every plant has its place. Some play leading roles, others weave amongst them, filling the spaces which otherwise would provide entry-points for weeds.

(Left) This border, planted exclusively with mono-cotyledons resembles a sentence composed of nouns and verbs. Each plant contributes equally to the display and plays the same role in the community, inviting weeds to play subordinate roles.

Plant communities are also formed in structured ways. Some plants play prominent parts, while others are unobtrusive fillers of spaces. Some come and go with the seasons, others are permanently visible. The prominent, eye-catching plants are chiefly responsible for immediate impressions, but those that weave between them are no less essential for the long-term success of a community or the atmosphere of a garden.

Matrix planting aims to construct a syntax in a garden unlike, for example, herbaceous borders where plants arranged perhaps by size or colour all contribute equally to the impact of the border, without the lesser plants that fulfil linking and qualifying roles by occupying spaces, extending the season or providing a background to the display.

What plants we choose to grow depends on where we garden, and our inclinations and interests. However, many parts of the world – and many different gardeners – share a broadly similar vocabulary, based on relatively amenable plants which can be cultivated without special skills or the need for elaborate or specialised facilities. These lingua franca plants are broadly referred to as 'good garden plants'. They are the mainstay of the 'vocabulary' used in this book, supplemented occasionally and where necessary with 'dialect' words drawn from the more rarefied lingos familiar to those dedicated to more specialist subjects including alpines, orchids, cacti, succulents and the mysteries of xeric gardening.

Successful planting depends on an equation which in its simplest terms can be expressed as follows:

People x Place = Planting

'People' is us (domestic harmony improves when the family is included), and what we need. Neighbours may expect every plot to be a garden. Convention may suggest a lawn, a patio, a border here, and a carefully placed small tree there, not forgetting a screen for the dustbins. Your spouse may insist on a pergola, yearn for a conservatory or a pool, and demand space for the children to play. In no time at all the space around the house has become a garden of a familiar kind following a general and civilised view of what a garden should be. Before that happens reflect on your individual needs,

limitations, or temperament, and your right to do what you like within that space, as long as it falls within the law, and, hopefully does not outrage neighbours to the point of conflict.

'Place' is where the garden is and the opportunities and limitations governing its use, and the plants that could be grown in it. You can, at your peril, ignore these pointers and insist on growing the plants you want irrespective of their natural needs. After years of trial and error, sweat, tears and damning frustration, you might triumph at last and enjoy the spectacle of blue poppies flowering beside the Mediterranean, or burst with pride as friends admire your tree ferns arching gracefully over the Hudson River. As an alternative, you can try matrix planting, matching the conditions in your garden with the places plants grow naturally in order to create a garden with established plant communities which come up, year after year, with few demands on your time or efforts.

The essence of successful gardening lies in control. Orthodox gardeners measure success by visible evidence of the gardener's hand. Judges in gardening competitions expect lawns to be trim with well defined edges, and hedges to be immaculately formed and closely shaved – with extra points for being imaginatively embellished by being shaped into peacocks, pyramids or poodles. They like shrubs to be neatly pruned, paths and borders to be scrupulously weed-free and empty ground to be dug over to maintain a neat and tidy appearance. They look for evidence that the hoe is regularly used between plants – because this destroys weeds , but also because finely tilled soil creates a reassuring impression of authority.

When these controls are relaxed, gardens appear unpleasantly neglected. Weeds grow, quickly followed by the disappearance of most of the garden plants. Clearly, if we abandon orthodox methods we must find alternative methods of control, such as the self-sustaining matrices which enable plant communities to survive under natural conditions. In brief, we can rule our gardens directly through the spade, hoe and shears, or indirectly by encouraging plants that are compatible with one another and with the conditions in which they grow to form self-sustaining communities.

The penalties of interference

Gardening fashions ebb and flow, driven by whim, novelty and expediency. When the beach, or holidays abroad or the squash club beckon, we ditch the delphiniums and plant easy-care day-lilies instead; avoiding hours of staking, tying, dead-heading, forking and slug hunting. When someone points out that astrantias, geraniums, lady's mantles and hellebores also have certificates of proven self-sufficiency, we add them to the day-lilies. But, conditioned by our dependence on familiar, traditional methods, we start to fuss over them and tend them like the delphiniums, phloxes, sidalceas and lupins which they replaced. We set them out singly, or group them in three's and five's. We maintain *cordons sanitaire* of hoed earth round every plant. When they meld together we dig them up and subdivide them to keep them in order. If the soil looks dry after three days without rain we feel compelled to water it. We spray the plants with insecticides against nameless, imaginary pests, and sprinkle artificial fertilisers between them as offerings to the gods of gardening. In no time at all, we find ourselves paying so much attention to our 'easy-care' plants we are faced with resigning our membership of the squash club, foregoing

Orthodox gardening depends on returning periodically to bare earth. Displays of bedding plants (top) are maintained by careful spacing, incorporation of humus and fertilisers and annual digging. Even in the more relaxed setting of a mixed border (bottom) the ground between the plants is forked over annually, and from time to time the perennials are dug up, divided and replanted.

visits to the beach and curtailing our holidays. We might as well have stuck with our delphiniums.

We have discovered that any plant can make excessive demands on our time and attention when we manage the garden in ways that require constant care and attention. Our fear of the dire consequences of relaxing control creates a 'Triffid' complex, which leads to the ruthless use of garden tools as weapons of counter-insurgency whenever plants – cultivated as well as weeds – threaten to make themselves at home without needing our support.

It is not enough simply to invest in a random selection of easy-care plants. We must also provide the three crucial elements which will enable the plants themselves to do the work of spades and hoes.

- The first is the plant *mix* composed of plants with compatible needs, which are suited to the soil, climate, exposure, etc, of the site itself.
- The second is *time*, needed to enable the plants to form communities based on mutually balanced matrices of roots, stems, leaves, etc.
- The third is *competition*, which is the mechanism which eliminates incompatible or unsuitable plants and enables the survivors to establish harmonious, balanced communities.

Harnessing competition

Parkinson's Law states that work expands to fill the time allotted to it. A similar principle applied to gardens states that *plants expand to consume the resources at their disposal.* Plants in straitened circumstances make do with limited resources. Trays of annuals left unplanted long past their sell-by date, starved, barely watered and neglected, still contrive to produce a meagre display of flowers, and eventually a few seeds by recycling minimal resources. Each one planted out at the right time, widely spaced in fertile soil, hoed and watered, would have been more productive than the whole starved trayful together.

Orthodox gardeners reduce competition between neighbouring plants so each one can fulfill its potential. This might be a sound way to grow a giant cabbage or produce a prize-winning flower on a hybrid tea rose. It is a recipe for disaster when attempting to encourage the development of a community.

Matrix of trees, shrubs, perennials, ferns and bulbs.
A natural woodland community provides the basis for the planting in this garden. The layered effects of plants growing above, beneath or through their neighbours create vital, constantly changing communities. The deep, three-dimensional matrix of trees, shrubs and perennials seen here ensures that there is always something new every day. In this view the layers are made up by:

a) an overhead canopy of kanukas.

b) a sub-canopy of immature kanukas, lancewoods and pittosporums, supplemented with planted deciduous trees like the young Norway maple.

c) climbing plants including *Hydrangea petiolaris.*

d) tall deciduous shrubs and small trees like Japanese angelica, flowering cherries, smoke bush and flowering nutmeg.

e) evergreen shrubs including rhododendrons, hebes, schefflera and viburnums.

f) perennials at ground level include paeonies, euphorbias, epimediums, tellimas and tiarellas, and shifting, self-sown carpets of forget-me-nots.

g) numerous woodland bulbs such as bluebells, camassias and daffodils appear before the lilies.

h) ferns and mosses.

The yellow archangel (*Lamium galeobdolon*) is a notably invasive plant, but its variegated forms provide precisely the effect of dappled shade on a woodland floor longed for by those with dim corners. Sometimes we kid ourselves that we need it in our gardens, but we would be wiser to leave this archangel in the woods where it belongs, unless we do not mind seeing our smaller shrubs and precious woodland plants reduced to mounds beneath its shrouding foliage. Yet, within its woodland home, this is not a rampaging monster but a plant that is rather vulnerable to disturbance. It is a natural occupant of shaded corners in my own woodland garden amongst native stitchworts, wild roses and red campions, weaving amongst plants from further afield – amongst them tellimas, goatsbeards, dicentras, pulmonarias and bright blue navelworts. It does not smother its neighbours and each spring I welcome its pale yellow chamois leather coloured flowers. It fails to achieve its full potential because it has to share resources with other woodland herbs, and the oak trees beneath which it grows.

The resources which plants need to function effectively and for which they compete are:

Light – from which plants derive energy. The more they receive, the more actively they photosynthesise and the more energetically they grow. Chlorophyll is the essential pigment in this case, but a variety of pigments which respond to other wave bands in the visible spectrum control plant development in other vitally important ways.

Nutrients – a dozen or so inorganic chemical elements are essential for healthy growth and development. Limited supplies in the soil are shared between members of the community.

Water – plant tissues function effectively only when hydrated. Competition for water is a major factor affecting the vigour, variety and nature of plant communities.

Oxygen – the fuel of respiration and the utilisation of energy in all plant tissues. It is available more or less on

demand to aerial parts of plants. Below ground level, the condition of the soil, the activity of worms and other fauna, and the presence and density of plant roots have considerable effects on availability.

Carbon dioxide – combines with water during photosynthesis to produce sugars – the source of energy. Like oxygen, it is more or less freely available to the leaves and in gardens is seldom a competitively limited resource.

In matrix planting competition becomes the balancing mechanism through which neighbours share resources. My geraniums, day-lilies and dicentras growing with the archangels are natural inhabitants of deciduous woodlands. In sunlit borders in fertile, well-watered gardens each of these plants can grow impressively large. In the shadow of the oak trees they compete for and share limited resources. All survive as part of an integrated carpet of relatively small plants.

Geraniums, day-lilies, dicentras and archangels share similar life cycles and seasons of activity, and compete directly for resources. However, plant communities are usually much more complex than that. Numerous different species complement one another; some grow actively at one season, others at another; some exploit soil at deeper levels than their fellows. The result is a garnering and partitioning of resources that ensures a widespread distribution, and also uses what is available efficiently by diversifying peak demands over the seasons.

The ground flora compete one with another, but largely avoid direct competition with the oak trees below which they grow. Their cycles of active root growth and development in late summer and autumn occur when the roots of the oaks are least active. Their foliage is at its best when the oaks are leafless, and they flower in late spring before being overshadowed by the developing canopy after the oaks come into leaf. The oak trees moderate, but do not overwhelm them, and provide shelter and protection throughout the winter.

But what has all this to do with the millions of gardens which bear no resemblance to a wood? To understand that, we need to look at analogies between familiar garden settings and the places where wildflowers grow naturally. Many gardens have lawns, some have meadows and the affinities of both with natural grasslands are obvious. Herbaceous borders seem to be giving way to so-called mixed borders – a combination comparable to the communities of shrubs, grasses and herbs known as scrub. Rockeries provide modest imitations of alpine peaks. Gravel gardens, garden pools and herb gardens introduce elements of mountain screes, wetlands and the Mediterranean garigue or Californian chaparral, and the shaded space beneath a tree brings woodland into a garden.

Even the smallest garden has room for one tree and, when carefully chosen, for several. Neighbours' trees which overshadow boundaries and defeat attempts to grow plants in borders become assets when the space is filled with woodland plants. The pergola above the patio, the hedge along the boundary, and the sides of the garden shed create strips of 'woodland' edge within their shadows which, as far as the plants are concerned, are scarcely different from the woodland garden beneath my coppiced hazels and standard oak trees.

Weeds

Cowslips growing in a flower bed by my back door attracted the attention of a friend. He examined them attentively, then as though venturing to express a forbidden thought, turned to me and said, 'Aren't those things weeds?'

Proper gardeners maintain two mutually exclusive lists. One bears the names of plants which figure in regular gardening books and qualify for approval as 'Garden Plants'. The other is a catalogue of the damned. It includes numerous recognised weeds, anything which grows wild, anything which has not been seen before, and anything which crops up spontaneously and causes surprise. Lumped together and labelled 'Weeds', good gardeners blush when caught in their company.

Then one day they find themselves making excuses. They say, 'Yes! Perhaps it is a weed but don't you think it's really rather pretty? I thought I'd just leave it for now. It seems to be doing no harm.' Excuses for accepting plants which hitherto were condemned gradually become more frequent and more ingenious.

One plant after another slips from one list to the other or hovers uneasily between the two, until the schizophrenic situation seems to be resolved by the aphorism: 'A weed is a plant in the wrong place.'

Any plant growing where we happen to like it, whether we put it there or it just appeared, is deemed to be growing in the right place. It is not a weed and can (should) be left where it is.

Any plant we object to for any reason – it might be a garden plant which has outstayed its welcome – is in the wrong place and should be destroyed. Weeds somehow seem less of a threat when their existence depends on such whims.

So far so good, until we notice that scarcely has the undear departed been dumped on the compost heap when its space is filled by another plant, and we have to decide whether that is 'right' or 'wrong'. Many happy hours can be spent, year after year, destroying 'plants in the wrong place' as generations of weeds occupy the spaces we have prepared for them.

Somehow the cycle of space creation and space occupation has to be broken. Mulches fill gaps and exclude weeds, and under the high input/high return conditions of a kitchen garden can be economical and productive as a regular, permanent method of weed control. In less intensive situations mulches are better used as stop gaps pending the development of a complete plant cover.

Eventually we recognise that spaces are open invitations to 'weeds' – however we define them. The recognition that our gardens will continue to be weedy as long as there are spaces to be filled by plants we do not want is the key to successful weeding. We must replace plants we do not want with those we do, and as one hand stretches out to pull up a weed, the other should be holding an approved successor to take its place.

Often conditions will be unfavourable or we will not have a suitable replacement. Sometimes the season and conditions may be just right for planting and we will have a suitable replacement, but even then an opportunist, piecemeal approach like this can create more problems than it solves. More radical and more purposeful approaches serve us better.

The woodland flowers (left) form a matrix within which prominent perennials grow in a competitive balance and forget-me-nots occupy spaces which would otherwise be filled by weeds. In another garden (above), an orthodox gardener uses herbicides to prevent weeds occupying spaces between the plants.

Choose your weeds

We can tear weeds out by hand. It takes a long time and considerable effort and dandelions, ground elder, couch grass, onion weed and oxalis seem to find it rather stimulating. We can make for the tool rack and arm ourselves with a hoe. Hoes are pleasant to use, and if we possess several different kinds we can experience several different pleasures; unfortunately the fine tilths left in the wake of hoes make comforting beds for seedlings, and a familiar green haze will cover the surface soon after the first shower of rain. We can resort to chemical warfare – after all, paraquat has been dubbed the chemical hoe. We can even combine an instantly effective herbicide with another that acts residually, and watch as the weeds that first attracted our attention curl up and shrivel in a few days, while enjoying the satisfaction of knowing that for weeks or even months any others that germinate will be dead before we even see them.

These are stop-gap solutions. We must use the time we have gained more constructively, or when the curtain opens on Act Two of Operation Weed Control it will just be a repeat of Act One.

Every garden knows its own weeds. My first was a sea of annual mercury, known locally by the curious name of butcher's bacon weed, and the plant has never bothered me since. Elsewhere I have met groundsel, ground elder, shepherd's purse, popping weed, dandelion, creeping thistle, and other members of the international brigade which crop up wherever ground is regularly turned over. I have had to contend with more specialist plants like nipple wort, creeping buttercup and hairy vetch and once, to my astonishment and discomfort, with the Roman nettle. This alien annual infested my kitchen garden in Scotland. Dealing with it was an unpleasant, painful experience until, to my delight, my particular colony of this rare plant followed others that had grown in Britain down the path to extinction.

Weeds exist as a direct result of what has happened in the past and what we are doing today. The weeds which defy our attempts to destroy them owe their existence to our activities. A weed-free garden may be an unobtainable dream, but change what we do, and the weeds we contend with will change too.

We can hoe unremittingly for decades between rows of vegetables without apparently reducing the hordes of groundsel, chickweed, sow thistles and fat hen seedlings that need to be destroyed each time. But those weeds will all disappear if we make a lawn where the vegetables once grew. Their seeds still lie in the ground, but none grows amongst the turf covering the soil. The respite will be short-lived. Within a few years, hoary plantains, hop trefoils, white clovers that attract bees to sting bare feet, daisies, the ferny eruptions of yarrow, brown and yellow tufts of field woodrush, cocksfoot, Yorkshire fog and mosses will find congenial homes amongst the grasses in the lawn. If we find these blemishes disturbing, we can let the grass grow long, and the plants that were happy under the mower's rule will disappear. Ribwort plantain,

birds' foot trefoils and buttercups, hawkweeds, red clover and moondaisies, field scabious and lady's bedstraw will take their place. Crested dog's tail, timothy and other meadow grasses will replace the fescues that made the lawn and in time we have a meadow. Plant trees in the meadow to make a spinney, and their shade will gradually suppress the grasses and wild flowers. Brambles and wild roses will appear from seeds dropped by birds, and old man's beard and honeysuckle will drape the young trees. Stinging nettles will make an unwelcome appearance. Eventually, ground elder, foxgloves, red campion, celandine and cow parsley appear from heaven knows where and, if we are lucky, primroses, sanicle, sweet woodruff and violets.

The 'vegetable garden', the 'lawn', the 'meadow' and the 'spinney'; each is an example of a plant community with its own kinds of weeds. Change your gardening and you change your weeds. The precise mix will depend on where you live, but the next time a particular weed threatens to drive you demented, remember it exists only because the way you garden provides it with a congenial home.

Not many of us would be content to design our gardens simply with the need to weed in mind. We may want to keep our vegetable gardens; we may enjoy roses growing formally in their beds; the children would protest if we dug up the lawn. But, those who find life unbearable without a lawn or potager

A garden need not be within a wood to provide woodland settings. A group of trees (above) form a spinney for the plants in their shade. An orchard (top left) provides shaded spaces separated by grassy 'rides'. Bulbs and woodland perennials flourish in the 'woodland edge' beneath a pergola (middle left), and patterns of sunlight and shadow produced by walls, structures and shrubs (bottom left) simulate a woodland glade.

– which make heavy demands on time and energy – can balance them with meadows and spinneys that can be left more to their own devices. When the demands of the garden become too pressing, and ways must be found to reduce the pressure – or move to a house with a smaller garden – the strong matrices formed by mixtures of trees, shrubs, perennials and bulbs growing together can be used to save work, and perhaps save us from having to move house too.

Garden management

The twin aims of matrix planting appear to be so simple I hesitate to write them down:

Encourage the plants you *do* want

Discourage the plants you *do not* want

They are achieved by enabling the first to compete successfully with the second. That also sounds simple, but it depends on a sympathetic understanding of the ways plants compete and interact with one another in the battle for survival.

The key to success lies in the choice of plants. Ill-judged choices result in excessive dominance by one or two species, and the disappearance of those that cannot cope. Well-judged choices lead to the establishment of persistent communities of plants which are diverse, self-renewing, resistant to invasion by weeds and look attractive. This is not simply a matter of planting and walking away. Matrices take time to develop and depend on positive, rather than neutral, management.

Management is by manipulation rather than the brute force of hoes or forks, which destroy rather than encourage the development of matrices. Only super-optimistic gardeners expect every plant to survive or every combination to perform as expected, or even for effects that looked good one year to look presentable the next. Initial plantings, however well conceived, always lead to surprises. Plants which were expected to do well will fail, others which were included on a wing and a prayer may settle down surprisingly well. Only you can decide how insistently to plant and replant those that make a faltering start; how actively to push forward

management towards a particular ideal, or, how tolerantly to accept developments. Be prepared to be flexible and always listen to what your plants are telling you.

Simply labelling one plant a weed to be destroyed and another a desirable garden plant is inadequate, especially in semi-natural garden settings like meadows, ponds and woodlands. Matrix planting calls for a more perceptive view of plants and the roles they play. They may be pernicious weeds to be destroyed; they may be desirable plants needing little attention, or they may require lavish care and skilful treatment for their survival. Some will be wild flowers we would like to encourage, others, garden plants which need to be restrained from take-over bids.

All this needs to be taken into account when deciding whether to eliminate or encourage particular plants or just leave them well alone. In my own garden this is done on a nine-point scale described below, ranging from plants which must be eliminated at all costs to those which need constant care and attention. Plants towards the centre of the scale require relatively little management, those at either end require frequent attention either to keep them under control or to ensure their continued presence. It follows that those most likely to meld into successful communities will be found towards the centre of the scale between categories three and seven.

The plants named in brackets below as examples were members of a mixed community of garden plants (planted) and wildflowers (spontaneous arrivals) in a woodland setting on a light loam, partially shaded by coppiced hazels.

1. Out-and-out weeds with vigorous powers of regeneration. Clearly not wanted.
Must be singled out for destruction, and every effort made to eradicate them as soon as possible. (Bramble; Stinging Nettle.)

2. Plants that are out of place and pose a threat to the planting unless closely controlled.
Successful methods of control needed to reduce/ eliminate existing plants and prevent their regeneration. (Dandelion, ground elder, rosebay willow herb, blackthorn, ash.)

3. Weedy, but not threateningly invasive plants, that are better out than in.

Complete control is unnecessary, but numbers should be reduced as and when opportunities occur. (Hedge woundwort, herb Bennet, hairy willow herb.)

4. Plants with attractive qualities, but an inclination to take over unless watched.

Regular attention needed to remove surplus plants and reduce seed production or vegetative renewal. (Stitchwort, betony, yellow archangel, hazel, field rose, periwinkle.)

5. Long-lived tenacious plants, appropriate to the site and largely self-maintaining.

Little or no direct attention should be necessary. (Cowslip, violet, bird's eye speedwell, bugle, foxglove, male fern, red campion, honesty, snowdrops, mosses.)

6. Plants appropriate to the situation but unlikely to survive entirely unaided.

Support needed may include very occasional replanting, reduction of local competition, etc. (Snowy woodrush, *Geranium nodosum*, grape hyacinth, lady's mantle, *Brunnera macrophylla*.)

7. Plants whose survival depends on intermittently repeated regular attention.

Some preparation of planting sites necessary, and removal of competition in early years; also replacement of failures. (*Lysimachia ciliata, Viola* 'Couer d'Alsace', *V. riviniana* 'Purpurea' , *Waldsteinia geoides, Tellima grandiflora, Valeriana* 'Phu', *Narcissus* 'Little Witch', *Geranium phaeum, G. endressii, Pulmonaria* 'Fiona', Hellebore hybrids.)

8. Plants dependent on regular attention over indefinite periods for survival.

Attention needed may include periodic pruning, feeding, long-term reduction of competition and replanting. (Hosta cultivars, *Primula vulgaris* subsp. *sibthorpii*.)

9. Plants unable to persist without frequently repeated, time-consuming attention.

May require annual replanting, frequent radical pruning or protective measures against pests and diseases. (Crown campion.)

Despite early optimism, ground elder could not be controlled in this setting and eventually spread unacceptably. It should have been treated from the outset as a Category One weed. Crown campion failed to self-sow on this site, and attempts to maintain it were soon abandoned, unlike honesty, which self-sowed freely. Hostas, initially rated at 'seven' due to slug damage in the early years, became less vulnerable as they established and were re-rated to 'six'.

Forming alliances

Botanists long ago recognised the tendencies of plants to form communities, naming these after the most conspicuous or characteristic plants present. Gardeners need not be concerned with the passionate disputes over the minutiae which distinguish one community from another, and certainly should not feel obliged to refer to the patch of heathers by the back door as an erecetum. It is enough to recognise that plants can form stable, long-lasting alliances, and that the conditions in which they grow define which plants are fit to join the club.

The most critical factors are the choice of plants and the way they have been planted:

1. Choose plants that are compatible with each other and the setting.

2. Plant them in ways which facilitate the formation of self-sustaining matrices, rather than in close-knit groups of a single kind.

3. Manage them positively to avoid disrupting the formation of a matrix.

The knack of co-existing harmoniously is the essence of compatibility. This sounds simple but is complex and challenging in practice. Until recently, few gardeners paid much attention to the natural origins of the plants in their gardens. Apart from extremes like aquatics, alpines and the frost-tender, garden plants in general would thrive irrespective of their origins, provided the soil was

well prepared and fertilised, and they were hoed or hand-weeded to eliminate competition, and dead-headed or sprayed when necessary. Without those supports, compatibility between plant and plant, and plant and setting, as well as the plants' natural origins and the ways they respond to opportunities and adversities become vitally important.

Establishment of a matrix

Unfortunately, ready-made spinneys, pools, meadows, screes or bogs are garden rarities. Most of us must make such settings from scratch if we want to enjoy them. In their early years, these are less than pale imitations of the final result. The smallest garden pond takes time to establish a balance; newly planted mixed borders favour pioneering species which will later give way to more durable alternatives; freshly sown meadows change progressively for decades; whips and maidens, supported by a scattering of standard or even semi-mature trees, are not a forest this year, nor will be in ten years.

Spaces on plans labelled 'meadow', 'woodland garden', 'mixed border', etc, reflect hopes rather than actualities, and allowances have to be made for changes in the character and composition of any planting as it develops and matures. Annuals and short-lived perennials serve useful and effective roles as fillers in the early stages but within a few years are eliminated as the vegetation matures.

Meadow seed mixtures frequently include poppies, cornflower, love-in-a-mist, larkspur and corncockle. These are cornfield weeds which have no future in permanent meadows. They contribute colour and excitement (and customer satisfaction!) in the first year, and serve as nurse plants, giving

Large groups of plants with strongly individual colour, form or texture create atmosphere, whether from the umbrella-like leaves of rodgersias (top right); the brilliantly glossy foliage of galax in a woodland setting (left); or the repetition of the plump forms of a cactus (above right).

MATRIX PLANTING

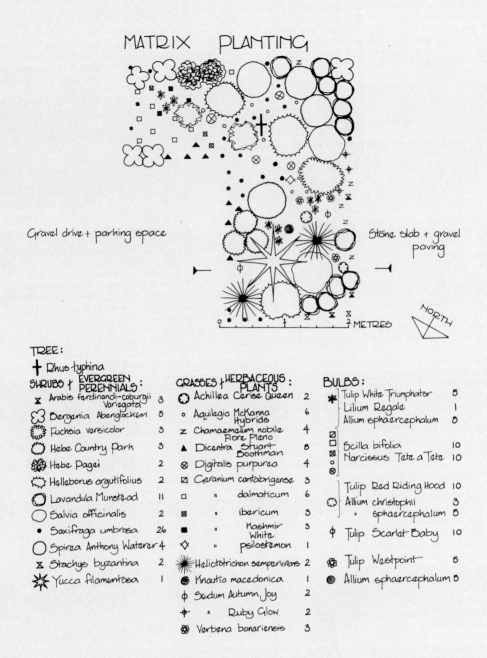

Gravel drive + parking space

Stone slab + gravel paving

METRES

NORTH

TREE:

✝ Rhus typhina

SHRUBS + EVERGREEN PERENNIALS:

Symbol	Name	Qty
✕	Arabis fardinandi-coburgii Variegata	3
✿	Bergenia Abenglocken	8
✿	Fuchsia versicolor	3
✿	Hebe Country Park	3
✿	Hebe Pagei	2
✿	Helleborus argutifolius	2
◯	Lavandula Munstead	11
◯	Salvia officinalis	2
•	Saxifraga umbrosa	26
◯	Spiraea Anthony Waterer	4
✕	Stachys byzantina	2
✳	Yucca filamentosa	1

GRASSES + HERBACEOUS PLANTS:

Symbol	Name	Qty
✿	Achillea Cerise Queen	2
○	Aquilegia McKanna Hybrids	6
z	Chamaemalum nobile Flore Pleno	4
▲	Dicentra Stuart Boothman	8
⊗	Digitalis purpurea	4
☑	Geranium cantabrigense	3
▫	" dalmaticum	6
⊠	" ibericum	3
▪	" Kashmir White	3
◇	" psilostemon	1
✳	Helictotrichon sempervirens	2
◎	Knautia macedonica	1
φ	Sedum Autumn Joy	2
φ	" Ruby Glow	2
✿	Verbena bonariensis	3

BULBS:

Symbol	Name	Qty
✳	Tulip White Triumphator	5
	Lilium Regale	1
	Allium sphaerocephalum	5
☑		
▢	Scilla bifolia	10
⊠	Narcissus Tete a Tete	10
⊙		
⊗		
	Tulip Red Riding Hood	10
◔	Allium christophii	3
	" sphaerocephalum	5
φ	Tulip Scarlet Baby	10
✿	Tulip Westpoint	5
◎	Allium sphaerocephalum	5

This planting is an open, sheltered, sunny front garden. There is no lawn and no precisely defined drive or parking space. Instead the garden is composed of gravel, stone and brick paving combined with beds and borders. These are planted in a manner which produces dynamic, constantly interesting effects. The trees, shrubs and evergreen perennials provide a permanent framework within which other plants produce shoots and flowers, change colour and come and go with the seasons. Some plants grow side by side as neighbours; others grow through each other – e.g., bulbs are planted in the same holes as compatible herbaceous companions. In this way the dying stems and leaves of early spring bulbs are concealed by developing foliage, and summer bulbs are supported and shown off by the foliage of the perennial plants. Management relies on restraint but constant attention throughout the growing season.

TRADITIONAL PLANTING

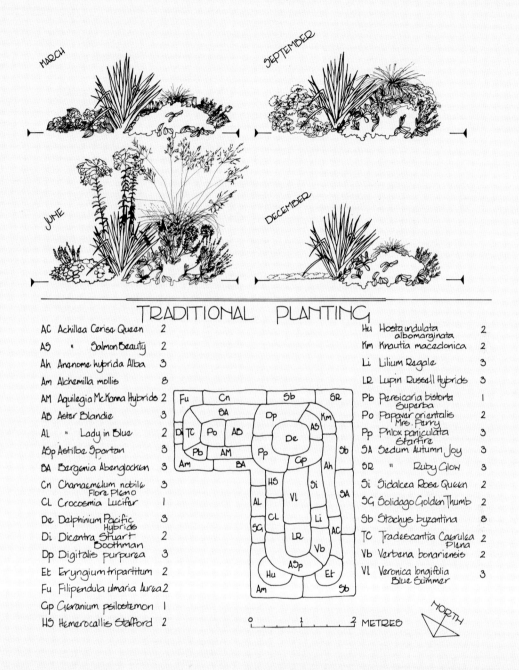

Code	Plant	Qty
AC	Achillea Cerise Queen	2
AS	" Salmon Beauty	2
Ah	Anemone hybrida Alba	3
Am	Alchemilla mollis	8
AM	Aquilegia McKanna Hybrids	2
AB	Aster Blandie	3
AL	" Lady in Blue	2
ASp	Astilbe Spartan	3
BA	Bergenia Abendglocken	3
Cn	Chamaemelum nobile Flora Pleno	3
CL	Crocosmia Lucifer	1
De	Delphinium Pacific Hybrids	3
Di	Dicentra Stuart Boothman	2
Dp	Digitalis purpurea	3
Et	Eryngium tripartitum	2
Fu	Filipendula ulmaria Aurea	2
Gp	Geranium psilostemon	1
HS	Hemerocallis Stafford	2
Hu	Hosta undulata albomarginata	2
Km	Knautia macedonica	2
Li	Lilium Regale	3
LR	Lupin Russell Hybrids	3
Pb	Persicaria bistorta Superba	1
Po	Papaver orientalis Mrs. Parry	2
Pp	Phlox paniculata Starfire	3
SA	Sedum Autumn Joy	3
SR	" Ruby Glow	3
Si	Sidalcea Rosea Queen	2
SG	Solidago Golden Thumb	2
Sb	Stachys byzantina	8
TC	Tradescantia Caerulea Plena	2
Vb	Verbena bonariensis	2
Vl	Veronica longifolia Blue Summer	3

MARCH · JUNE · SEPTEMBER · DECEMBER

0   1   2 METRES   NORTH

If the bed was planted in the traditional manner shown above – the effects produced and the management needed would be very different. In the Northern Hemisphere, from early November to early June there would be little to see. Everything would then come in a whoosh – early spring growth would be accompanied by urgent efforts to provide support. A blaze of showy summer flowering would decline into, with luck, a mellow autumn display – but more often descend into a matted, dank mass. This incites premature and overzealous clean-ups and forkings between plants and a sterile-looking winter garden, for which an impression of neatness is the only claim to merit.

shelter and protection to the perennials that replace them, and within a year or two all will be gone.

Short-lived perennials from the woodland edge – foxgloves, rose and red campions, toadflax, fringe flowers and columbines sown beneath newly planted trees provide shade and shelter for woodland perennials, and help to hold grasses at bay, until the overhead canopy of leaves starts to develop.

During the first years of the life of a mixed border, spaces between shrubs and perennials can be occupied by sun-loving annuals including cosmos, hares' tail grass, spider flowers, shoo fly plants and pot marigolds. Short-lived, self-sowing perennials including Jacob's ladder, Miss Wilmot's ghost, peach-leaved bellflowers and violettas, can be encouraged to find and occupy gaps in the matrix for many years.

The strongest matrices consist of a succession of layers of vegetation through which sunlight filters, until at ground level there is enough only to support plants that can cope with very little light. The most complete examples of such matrices occur in deciduous woodlands, but that does not mean all gardens have to become micro-forests. Effective matrices can be formed by shrubs and perennials in mixed borders. Those who believe no garden is complete without a rose bed can take advantage of the fact that roses inherit the rough, tough pioneering qualities of their wild progenitors. They are amongst the first to infiltrate meadows, in company with thorns and brambles, and prepare the way for other shrubs and eventually trees. Roses need no coddling in segregated beds but can be planted to thrust their way above geraniums, violas, lamiums, hostas, grasses and other weed-excluding perennials at ground level.

The essential quality of a plant matrix is the occupation of space. The way this is achieved takes many forms – from the multi-layered canopies of forests to single, ground-covering layers no more substantial than a spreading mat of pearlwort or mosses. The latter make fragile matrices and need special conditions to be effective, but between the two extremes we have endless options open to us. Shrubs can emerge like islands, surrounded by a sea of perennials; perennials can be planted to interlock like jig-saw puzzles, or as intimate mixtures of foliage and flowers; underplantings of bulbs occupy spaces amongst

deciduous plants during winter and early spring; tussock (bunch) grasses can be interplanted with annuals and bulbous plants; sub-shrubs and mat-forming perennials can be combined to carpet the ground on banks and rocky slopes; ferns can be used to colonise dark corners close to buildings or under evergreens.

Maintaining the balance

In an ideal world the choice of plants and the manner of their planting would be so well contrived they would inevitably form self-sustaining communities. There are situations and combinations of plants where that can and does happen. More often we have to intervene to maintain a balance. A balancing act of this kind may seem a precarious form of gardening, but is not such an unfamiliar idea as it may at first appear. Lawns are familiar examples of matrices composed of complex, but balanced, mixtures of grasses, wild flowers and mosses living together without any question of hoeing or forking between the plants. The balance is maintained by the mower. This works very effectively as a routine without even having to think about the likes and dislikes of different plants. Those that do not like the treatment disappear; those that do thrive.

Similarly, we are quite used to the idea of mowing meadows to maintain the balance between grasses and wild flowers; of pruning shrubs to limit their spread and make them more inclined to produce flowers, and dead heading or cutting back perennials to encourage renewed flowering or to give their neighbours space.

Selective cutting back is one of the most constructive tools available for the management of a matrix, and plays a vital part in balancing competition within any plant community, whether it is developing or mature. It is used to:

Regenerate the plants – resulting in a flush of new foliage, freshening the appearance and eye appeal of the plants, and helping to maintain close ground cover.

Reduce competitive effects of foliage – this is particularly important beneath trees, but the stronger grasses and broad-leaved perennials also overshadow lesser plants, and annual reductions allow closer and more diverse planting.

Reduce height – cutting back the stems of some of the late flowering daisies, including heleniums, sunflowers and Michaelmas daisies, when about half grown, increases the density of cover provided by the foliage and produces a greater concentration of flowers on shorter plants.

Prepare the way for winter mulching – the removal of mats of foliage in late autumn pin-points the positions of individual plants more clearly.

Remove blight infested foliage – to interrupt the cycles of infection; it also reduces cover for insects, etc, both beneficial and pestiferous.

Control the size of shrubs – maintaining the production of new growth, and/or improving flowering performance.

Provide a means of dead heading – preventing competition for resources between developing seeds and other parts of the plant, or preventing over-enthusiastic self-sowing by ardent colonisers.

Controlling pests and diseases

Stock of alpines in my nursery used to be grown on a rock garden and, at night, slugs emerging from crevices would dine on the shoots of the choicest. Eventually, these feasts went too far; in desperation the area was saturated with slug pellets and for several mornings we collected the corpses, quietly satisfied with our success. A few months later, Kanji, my affectionate and gentlemanly tom cat, died of kidney failure. Hedgehog droppings on the lawn became a thing of the past and, the following spring, for the first time in memory no thrush nests could be found in the hornbeam hedge. By then the slugs were back in strength, and continued so in ever-increasing numbers till nothing survived on the rock garden except the coarsest, hairiest, most slug-repellent plants.

I gave up slug pellets and insecticides and fungicides of all sorts, and for the next twenty-five years, in two quite different gardens, I have not used them at all. The shoots of my plants are seldom laden with green

fly, leather jackets and destructive caterpillars seem to be quite rare, and slugs are no more than a passing nuisance on a few susceptible plants in spring. The plants remain for the most part remarkably free from damaging attacks of any sort, and over the years it has become rarer and rarer to encounter attacks by insects or fungal infections that could justify a return to chemical warfare.

Mixed collections of plants, like those used in matrix planting, should not need the protection of poisonous chemicals to keep them healthy. Nevertheless, from time to time plants of a particular species or a cultivar will be repeatedly crippled by an insect infestation or fungal infection. Sometimes this is due to their situation – it may be too dry or too shaded – and mulching, the removal of overhanging branches or a move elsewhere provides a cure. Those that remain chronically afflicted or die are replaced with something else.

Biological pest control has become modish. We buy mites to control mites, bacteria to destroy caterpillars, eelworms to devour weevils or slugs, and even fungi to attack other fungi. Farmers, having destroyed the hedges that sheltered the predators of slugs, construct beetle banks covered with coarse grasses to serve the same purpose.

A perusal of the associated literature leaves the impression that biological pest control is a smart new idea thought up by scientists. A short walk in the countryside reveals it as something nature does all the time – without our interference. Leave well alone, and our gardens too become the haunts of predatory beetles, wasps, mites, eelworms, bacteria, fungi and other organisms which hunt, trap, ingest or otherwise destroy most pests and diseases before they become a problem. Natural balances between predators and prey are the best possible guarantee of a disease- and pest-free garden. Unwise use of poisonous chemicals interferes with the ways these function, and destroys the foundations on which natural pest control depends.

But over and beyond that, the success of a plant matrix is fundamentally dependent on maintaining the structure and profile of the soil and the well-being of the soil fauna and flora through which nutrients are recycled.

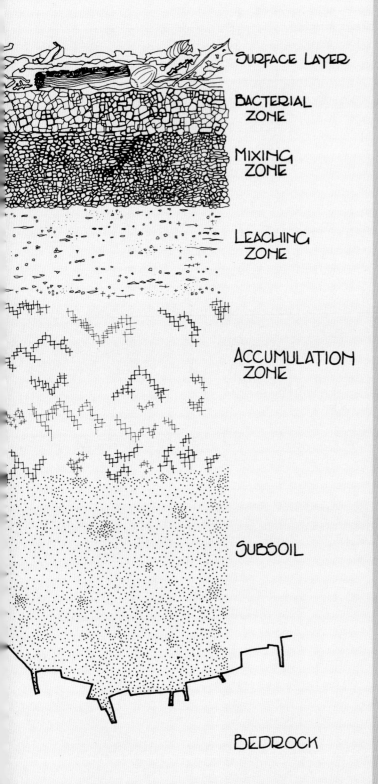

SURFACE LAYER

BACTERIAL ZONE

MIXING ZONE

LEACHING ZONE

ACCUMULATION ZONE

SUBSOIL

BEDROCK

1. Surface layer – dead and dying leaves, twigs, animal droppings etc.

2. Bacterial zone – fungi, bacteria and small creatures break down organic remains to form humus. Dark in colour with a spongy texture and high organic content.

3. Mixing zone – activity of worms and other soil fauna mix mineral components with humus washed down from above. Usually a dark loam, maybe slightly acid due to rain water.

4. Leaching zone – mainly mineral particles from which nutrients and particles of clay are lost by leaching, especially under acid* conditions – often a light colour. (*Acid conditions may develop in areas of high rainfall, because rainwater is a weak solution of carbonic and sulphuric acids. The effects are reduced by the presence of basic rocks which provide calcium, and most pronounced above acidic rocks, beneath coniferous trees, and in areas where temperatures and rainfall are low).

5. Accumulation zone – clay particles leached from above accumulate and clump together, holding nutrients and iron washed down from above. This is where the major nutrient reserves of many soils are conserved – held at a level where they are still within easy reach of roots, deep enough to remain constantly moist, and within range of worms and other soil fauna.

6. Subsoil – filled with weathered and decomposing mineral fragments – penetrated by the larger roots in search of water and anchorage, but low in bacterial activity and usually relatively infertile.

7. Bed rock – acidic (e.g., granites and millstone grits) or basic (e.g., chalk and limestones). Penetrated only by the largest roots. The nutrients derived from the rocks dissolve in ground water and percolate into the layers above – contributing to their fertility, acidity/ alkalinity and other qualities.

down to basics:
care *of the* soil

4

ANYONE WHO HAS BOUGHT a house and garden knows the feeling. The hassles and traumas of Removal Day are over – the cat did not make itself scarce before the day dawned nor escape during the journey, and the first night has been spent in makeshift fashion. In the morning, after stepping gingerly through a muddle of possessions and packing cases, the curtains are pulled aside to reveal not a garden, but a bewilderness calling for attention. All but the incorrigibly insensitive shudder, draw the curtains and return to bed.

Newly-acquired gardens demand attention when our minds are full of the business of settling into unfamiliar houses, discovering unknown districts, finding new routes to work and feeling our way towards untested relationships with neighbours. This is not the time for urgent action – it's better to dream about possibilities and turn things over in the mind. Otherwise, we plunge too eagerly into the trite and trivial. We may even fall for the tempting advertisements in glossy magazines offering computerised solutions for those seeking 'Paradise on Prescription'.

Such concoctions are as personal as cans of baked beans – space fillers that will never satisfy your appetite for a garden of your own. Wait, first, to see how the patterns of your life develop in new surroundings. Second, to discover more about the garden's limitations and assets, and how these fit in with the things you like to do, and the time you have to spare. You can be as traditional or radical as imagination, time and resources allow. You can base your garden on age-old methods of tilling the soil, or manage it by approaches that depend on understanding the natural processes through which soil fertility is conserved and maintained indefinitely.

To dig or not to dig

History relates that during the Peasants' Revolt, English yokels who had never heard of 'Here we go/here we go/here we go' chanted a moralistic little ditty about Adam delving and Eve spinning, before marching on London and removing the Archbishop's head in their attempt to establish a people's proletariat in 1381. This unlikely story illustrates the age-long link between gardening and digging. Spade, fork, digging stick or hoe, these and the plough have been the tools used to make successful gardens since memories fade into the mists of time. Forking between the shrubs in winter, regularly tickling the ground between plants with a hoe through the summer, and double trenching every patch of spare ground by dawn on the day of the winter solstice are widely accepted signs of the well-run garden.

However, there are those who will tell you these activities are unnecessary, adding that they are a waste of time and energy because plants grow perfectly well without their aid; and, warming to their theme, they will end by asserting they do more harm than good. These are fundamental issues to consider for anyone with a garden to look after. We can choose between a system that commits us to endlessly repeated cycles of hard physical labour, or much less onerous and more sustainable forms of gardening.

Once established, the matrices of stems and roots make it impossible to work between the plants with spades, forks, hoes or anything else, and other ways need to be found to conserve the soil in a condition capable of supporting the healthy growth and development of plants.

That depends on maintaining:

Fertility – a measure of the nutrients available in the soil. Under natural conditions, the level and availability of particular nutrient elements varies widely. Gardeners aim to produce soils with high levels of nutrients, all present in so-called 'balanced proportions' – implying levels at which plants are able to obtain what they want in more or less the proportions they need.

A satisfactory pH – the balance between alkalinity and acidity (referred to as the pH) of a soil is vitally important. Roots take up nutrients between relatively narrow ranges, and the availability of some nutrients is critically affected by pH. Some soils have a natural balance (they are more or less neutral) and display resistance to change, making them easy to manage. Others veer towards excess acidity or alkalinity, and need careful management to maintain healthy growing conditions.

Structure – this vitally important quality refers to the way small and ultra-small particles in the soil combine to form what are known as crumbs. Clay and silt in poorly-structured soils form layers so compact they are almost impenetrable to water and roots.

Drainage and water-holding capacity – free-draining and water-retentive are approving descriptions frequently used in relation to soils. This apparent contradiction in terms depends on a well-developed structure in which particles of clay and humus are aggregated together by physical forces to form irregularly shaped crumbs within which nutrients and water are conserved, and between which water and air move freely.

Aeration – roots cannot grow without oxygen. They obtain it from air diffusing through the spaces within the soil – the result of a good crumb structure – or the presence of large particles of sand, grit or small stones, and products of respiration like carbon dioxide and ethylene can disperse before reaching harmfully high concentrations.

Well-being of the soil fauna and flora – the soil fauna and flora, ranging from bacteria to earthworms – even slugs – are the keys to well structured, fertile soils. Their activities break down plant and animal residues and recycle them as nutrients, or build them into the soil as humus.

A perfect soil might be defined as:

A deep, homogeneous, water-retentive, free-draining neutral loam, containing a complete range of nutrients in readily available forms.

Digging, especially when practised as double trenching, is the orthodox gardener's means of attaining this ideal. It is a mechanical process intended to maintain fertility by regular additions of nutrients – organic, inorganic, or both, depending on preference – and counter tendencies towards increasing acidity by applications of lime or chalk when necessary. Crumb structure is maintained by digging-in partially decayed, usually described as 'well-rotted', organic matter each year. Aeration and drainage are promoted by turning over, loosening and breaking up the surface soil, to a depth of at least 20 cm (8 in),

Make-up of the soil

Soils are complex mixtures of minerals, organic matter, nutrients and living organisms. Their nature, condition and proportions directly affect ease of cultivation, the plants they support, and the care needed to maintain them in a fertile condition. The major constituents of soils are listed below, with brief notes on their origins and functions.

Constituent	Origin & description	Function
Minerals: including stones, grit, sand, silt, clay	Result from the weathering and breakdown of rocks. May be acidic or basic depending on origin. Soils of different types derive their properties from varying proportions of these minerals.	Responsible for the soil's major physical characteristics, including: porosity, fertility, rate of loss of nutrients by leaching, liability to erosion and water-holding capacity.
Organic residues: humus, peat, plant and animal remains	Consist of the remains of plants and animals, either close to the surface, or within the soil itself. May decay partially or completely, depending on soil and climatic conditions.	Partially decayed remnants provide nutrients and hold water. Humus is a product of organic decomposition which alone, or in combination with clays, improves soil structure and the availability and retention of nutrients.
Inorganic nutrients: nitrogen, potassium, phosphorus, calcium, magnesium, sulphur, iron, etc[A].	Apart from nitrogen, which is mostly obtained from air by bacterial activity, all are derived from the weathering and decomposition of rocks. Plants take up minerals – by a process known as cation exchange – from the soil solution through membranes in the root hairs.	Nitrogen, calcium, magnesium, sulphur and iron are tissue-building nutrients. Calcium also plays a major part in cell division. Potassium balances ionic concentrations in cell sap. Phosphorus is involved in energy transfers.
Gases: including oxygen, carbon dioxide and nitrogen.	These are obtained from the air and from the respiration and decay of living animals and plants.	Nitrogen is fixed by bacteria in nodules formed on the roots of some plants. Oxygen is taken up by roots and soil organisms during respiration, and carbon dioxide by algae and green plants during photosynthesis.
Water: predominantly from dew, rainfall or snow.	Ground-water can rise by capillarity to 30 cm (1 ft) in sand, and more than 2 m (6 ft 6 in) in silt. Water vapour condenses on the cool undersurfaces of stones.	Water is the liquid medium within which dissolved nutrients and gases are transported and absorbed by the roots of plants. It is the basis of life on which almost all living organisms depend. Without it the soil seems dead.
Living organisms: roots, worms, slugs and snails, insects [B], algae, fungi, bacteria.	The soil micro-flora and fauna forms a hidden world of mutually dependent, interacting organisms. Some live throughout their lives within the soil; others for a part of their life-cycles or during particular seasons.	They sustain a balance between destructive and constructive activities in a myriad of ways – turning over and aerating the soil mass; recycling nutrients; improving soil structure and porosity, maintaining or building up soil fertility and existing in mutually beneficial and complex symbiotic relationships with plants.

(A) 'etc' includes trace elements: manganese, copper, zinc, molybdenum and boron, which plants use in minute quantities – often as catalysts in enzyme reactions.

(B) includes many creatures other than insects, e.g., springtails, mites, nematodes, crustaceans, etc.

and to three times that depth in the gardens of the most enthusiastic delvers. The aim is to produce a growing medium independent of the variations produced by natural conditions, in which plants adapted to widely varying conditions – maize, asparagus, cabbages and lettuce, for example – can be set out side by side in rows with every hope of success.

Non-diggers, on the other hand, aim to modify and improve soils rather than change them totally. Fertility is sustained by applications of fertilisers that are generally applied in different forms, less frequently and in lesser quantities than by those who dig. Regular applications of organic matter are used in a less decayed condition and applied to the surface of the soil, relying on the activity of the soil fauna and flora to break them down and incorporate their remains in the soil as humus. Soil acidity is balanced by applications of minerals containing lime – often in forms which release it relatively slowly, rather than as an immediate boost. The overall aim is a progressive, steady incorporation of organic matter and nutrients to form a soil that is well structured and changes in character at different depths below the surface to reproduce the kind of soil profile found under natural conditions. This is very different from the homogenised product of digging. Nutrients released by decay in the upper layers move down to, and are held, in the lower layers where they are conserved and become available for uptake by the roots of plants. Fertility may seldom, or never, reach the peaks attainable by fertilising and digging, but under good management remains at more constant levels which are fully capable of supporting plant growth. Aeration is favoured by a residual layer of undecayed organic matter on the surface of the soil, and by undisturbed channels to deeper levels produced by the tunnelling of worms and the disintegration of roots. The soil fauna and flora play a major part and the lack of disturbance, and regular inputs of organic matter, encourage a diverse and active community.

Foundations of soil fertility

Plants absorb nutrients dissociated as ions in water in the soil. Insoluble forms of phosphorus, nitrogen, potassium and other vitally important nutrients are of little immediate use to most plants, although they may provide

reserves for future use. Nutrients can be carried away in water and eventually lost to rivers or reservoirs of ground water far beyond the reach of roots.

This loss goes on all the time and is known as leaching. It would have catastrophic effects on soil fertility but for the fact that most soils are able to hold nutrients by physical forces that prevent them being washed away. This is possible because nutrient minerals occur in one or other of two forms. Some – for example, calcium, potassium, magnesium, ammonium and iron – exist as positively charged cations which bind to negatively charged particles in the soil. Others – such as phosphorus, nitrate nitrogen, and sulphur – exist as negatively charged anions and are held by positive charges. Clays and humus are the vital ingredients which lock on to nutrients and conserve soil fertility. Stones, sand and silt carry few effective charges, and do little to prevent loss of nutrients through leaching.

Care of the soil

Fertile, easily managed soils are composed of sands, silts and clays combined with humus to form the rich responsive mixtures we call loams. Throughout much of Europe, the eastern parts of the United States, Japan and large parts of China, the natural soils are loams of one kind or another – originally nurtured beneath deciduous forests. These areas, so significant to gardeners, have moderate rainfalls, temperatures high enough for much of the year for effective bacterial activity, and generally fertile soils. The processes which once fashioned them into the foundation which sustained the deciduous forests continue, and can still be called upon by those who want to make use of them. Nevertheless, we abandon spades at our peril, unless the natural processes we expect to do the work for us can operate effectively. In summary these depend on:

A supply of organic matter – This can be compost, or any other organic residue, spread on the surface between the plants. The amounts needed depend on the nature of the underlying soil. Light (sandy) soils and heavy (silty) soils need heavy, repeated applications to make significant improvements. Well balanced loams, containing 10% to 30% clay mixed with sand and silt, respond to lower levels. Established plants produce annual residues of organic matter from falling leaves, decaying stems and roots which are valuable sources of humus, often sufficient to maintain well-balanced soils in good condition.

A vigorous and active soil fauna and flora — Top-dressings of compost and occasional applications of lime, when necessary, support high biological activity in soils. The presence of large numbers of worms, insects and other small animals is a good sign, and the sight of a few known or suspected plant pests should not be taken as an excuse to blunder in with poisonous chemicals which have unpredictable and harmful effects far beyond their intended victims.

Effective drainage – Most plants abhor water-logged soils and, particularly in the winter, short periods of excessive wet kill many otherwise fully hardy plants. Water fails to drain freely for two reasons:
1. It has nowhere to run to.
2. Spaces are clogged by silt or badly structured clays which prevent the movement of water.

If ditches need to be dug they should be dug before any other kind of garden-making is attempted. The traditional remedial treatment for poorly structured silts and clays is to dig in as much bulky organic material as possible. This is laborious, and better results can be obtained by spreading the organic material over the surface and relying on worms and other soil fauna to incorporate it. Both treatments lead to rapid improvements, and their effects should be consolidated after the plants are in position by repeated top dressings of compost and, if necessary lime, between the plants. Worms burrowing through the soil make drainage channels, and, even more significantly, ingest and mix together calcium, humus and clay particles. These mixtures are excreted and contribute to the open, crumbly structures which make soils easy to work, free-draining and well-aerated.

A source of calcium – Calcium is one of the agents which binds clay particles together to form the clusters which are the foundation of a good crumb structure. Soils lose calcium by leaching due to the acidity of rainfall, but in soils derived from basic rocks it is replaced by natural weathering. Neutral or acid soils lack natural sources of replenishment, and levels will need to be topped up from time to time by applications of lime, finely ground limestones or gypsum.

Calcifuge plants

Books warn us that rhododendrons are not for soils that contain lime. These plants, we read, are calcifuge. Of course, they cannot literally turn and flee in the face of lime, but their leaves go pale, diminish in size and soon cease to be produced at all. Nevertheless, many rhododendrons grow naturally on limestone formations, and when that enduring plant collector George Forrest found them in Yunnan growing out of the fissures in limestone rocks, and on screes formed from piles of lime-rich fragments, he voiced his doubts about their inability to thrive in gardens where soils contain lime. Eventually, the point was examined in a series of trials, but the results did little more than convince gardeners that, whatever wild rhododendrons might get up to, they do not do well in gardens on lime-rich soils. This remains something of a mystery, but it contains a caution about the pitfalls of interpreting the conditions under which plants grow naturally, and the dangers of applying what we think we see to garden settings.

The distinction between calcifuge and calcicole plants (those that prefer base-rich soils) is deeply rooted in the evolution of flowering plants, ferns and even algae. It can be vitally important for gardeners, too, especially in Britain where many gardens are made on soils derived from chalk and limestone, and to a lesser extent in parts of France, Spain and Italy. It is much less significant in the eastern side of the United States, where limestone formations are comparatively unusual, and is something which most gardeners in Japan and New Zealand scarcely need to think about.

In practical terms, calcifuge plants fail to thrive in soils rich in basic chemicals, amongst which calcium (or lime in gardener's terms) is usually by far the most predominant. But, like other plants, calcifuges need some calcium to stiffen their cell walls, and play its part in cell division. The trouble is caused by alkaline chemical

Calcifuge plants, unhappy on base-rich soils, include many glamorously splendid shrubs and trees, including rhododendrons and azaleas (top left), most magnolias (middle left), most proteas (bottom left) and waratahs (above).

groups associated with calcium and other bases, which reduce the acidity of water. Iron becomes insoluble as acidity decreases and calcifuge plants can no longer take it up for use as a catalyst in the production of chlorophyll.

The problem can be solved by using solutions of iron combined with organic molecules known as chelates (or sequestrenes), which maintain the iron in an available form under alkaline conditions. These are effective when watered over the soil around plants on marginally lime-rich soils – more severe cases have to be treated several times a year by spraying their foliage.

Managing acid and basic soils

Nowadays, rain in many places consists of a devil's brew of organic vapours, pollutants and fumes known as that sinister-sounding potion, acid rain. But rain has always been acid, only the scale of acidity is new and threatening. Rain from the cleanest, most unpolluted skies has never been pure water, but extremely dilute carbonic acid – not detectable to our tongues, but powerful enough to have been one of the great shapers of our landscapes.

Limestone and chalk, both calcium-containing minerals and amongst the most widespread building materials of mountains, are dissolved by carbonic acid, which destroys their structure and washes them away in solution. Long after the rocks disintegrate, soils made from their remains continue to lose nutrients as rain leaches calcium and other bases out of the upper layers, moving them down into lower levels of the soil profile where they are bound on to particles of clay which prevents their total loss. The consequence is that the surface layers of natural soils become progressively more acid, particularly when a covering of vegetation supplies a steady input of organic matter, which itself produces acids as it decays.

Under natural conditions, leaching of calcium from the surface layers enables rhododendrons, heathers and other calcifuge plants to grow immediately above limestone rocks – their shallow roots confined to the acid surface layers of the soil. This can happen in gardens too, where digging is replaced by other forms of

soil-processing, allowing calcifuge plants to be grown above soils that are, potentially, too replete with lime for them to thrive. But, unless that is a deliberate intention, or you garden on basic soils with a pH above c.7.5, with natural reserves of lime, you may need to counter steadily increasing acidity from time to time with dressings of ground limestone, chalk or other minerals containing calcium.

Effects of acidity on soil fertility

Acidic rocks tend to contain fewer nutrients than basic rocks, and available levels of some elements – including phosphorus and manganese – are further reduced as acidity increases, because they are converted into insoluble compounds unavailable to most plants. However, some acid-loving plants, including lupins and members of the protea family, secrete citric acid from their roots, which enables them to obtain phosphorus from these less soluble forms. Plants of many kinds form symbiotic associations with fungi, through which they have access to phosphorus absorbed by fungal hyphae.

As acidity increases many bacteria and fungi cease to function effectively, and in very acid conditions the recycling of nutrients from the remains of animals and plants slows down, supplies become restricted, and production may even almost cease. Reduced bacterial activity inhibits the production of humus from organic remains, and these remain partially decomposed. Peat is a familiar example, but leaves of trees may also hang in a limbo of unfulfilled decay.

Lack of humus, with its high cation exchange capacity, leads to the loss of nutrients from silty and sandy soils by leaching. Clays, deprived of calcium and humus, degenerate into poorly structured minerals that restrict the movement of water and air.

This catalogue of ill-effects could lead to an unbalanced view of acid soil as a problem which any gardener could do without. That is not usually the case at all, as most people with gardens on acid soils who enjoy the pleasures of growing rhododendrons, camellias and heathers will testify. Many acid soils are light and easy to work, free draining and rewarding to garden, but they also have their weaknesses and particular problems.

Base-rich soils

Heather and azalea addicts cast by fate into gardens with lime-rich soils are one of gardening's sadder sights. At first, an inconsolable refusal to accept their loss leads to explorations of the possibilities of making peat beds, or growing their darlings in containers. Desperate efforts follow, including rebellious sallies, and surrendering to the impulse to plant or be damned, or resort to potions of iron sequestrene to restore green leaves to the plants they love so dearly. Despair lightens as winter-flowering heaths appear in neighbours' gardens, and the realisation dawns that there are heathers able to thrive in this damned soil. As the seasons bring renewed light and warmth, the diversity of the plants that fill the gardens comes as a revelation to those previously enthralled by heathers and dwarf conifers, and the flamboyant but limited charms of rhododendrons. They discover that the flowers which grow naturally on soils containing lime are at least as rich and varied an assembly as those to be found on acid soils.

The limestone floras of the world are rich in:

- *Silver-leaved plants*: including many species of Anthemis, Artemisia, Argyranthemum, Helichrysum, Lavandula, Santolina and Phlomis.
- *Herbs and shrubs with fragrant foliage*: Calamintha, Cistus, Hyssopus, Origanum, Ruta, Salvia, Rosmarinus, Satureja and Thymus.
- *Bright and vigorous alpines*: Achillea, Alyssum, Arabis, Aubrieta, Campanula, Dianthus, Erysimum, Gypsophila, Pulsatilla, Saxifraga, Sedum and Sempervivum.
- *Striking shrubs*: Ballota, Buddleja, Caesalpina, Clematis, Coronilla, Daphne, Genista, Halimiocistus, Helianthemum, Iberis, Psoralea, Punica, Spartium, Syringa and Viburnum.
- *Attractive meadow wild flowers*: amongst the flora of short grasslands in well-grazed situations, on thin soils above chalk and limestone.

Calcicoles are plants that in the wild grow only on limestone formations and almost all are tolerant enough to grow on acid soils under the protected conditions of a garden. They may grow less well where soils are acid, and many are more susceptible to adverse conditions, usually cold or wet, but they can be grown. Nevertheless, they are naturally adapted to base-rich conditions and this may show in the freedom with which they grow and flower, their longevity and their air of well-being, and the success with which they can be induced to form sustainable communities.

Some natural indicators of acid and basic soils in Europe

Wildflowers are useful indicators of soil acidity. The table on the next page lists some conspicuous plants characteristic of acid or base-rich soils in

Western Europe. Similar lists, often including closely related plants, would have equal significance in other parts of the temperate world.

Coping with clay soils

Clays exist in a world almost beyond imagination, where seemingly infinitely small particles dance in a complex of physical forces, separating or combining one with another in ways which almost defy representation in familiar terms.

Sands and silt particles are more or less rounded, more or less impervious, more or less stable and more or less inert. Clays are none of those things. Clays have scarcely more substance than electrical charges, but, arranged in layers stacked one upon another and cemented together like bricks in a wall by calcium and humus, their particles form the large and vitally important structures referred to earlier as crumbs. Water molecules sandwiched between these layers cause clays to expand when wet and contract as they dry out. Clays are not inert but super-active, and the most vital part of the complex material we call soil or dirt.

Clay soils have:

Natural high fertility – due to their ability to retain nutrients, and prevent their loss by leaching.

High cation exchange capacity — making them very receptive to treatments intended to increase fertility.

High water-holding capacity — relieving the effects of drought on the plants that grow on them.

Loams based on clay can be fertile, open and a pleasure to work, though many gardeners may be surprised to read this. They deteriorate rapidly if neglected, and the sins of omission weigh heavily. As the crumb structure collapses, particles of clay fill the spaces between the coarser grains of sand, impeding the movement of water and air. Caps form on the surface, restricting drainage after rain, while the soil below lies water-logged and airless. The recycling of resources, and the production of humus, is reduced as poor aeration inhibits biological activity, leading to further deterioration in soil structure. Roots grow less vigorously, accentuating the effects of reduced fertility, leading to restricted plant growth, and a downward spiral in the rate of accumulation and recycling of organic matter and nutrients.

Keeping on top of clay

A ride on Barry Brickell's railway into the hills above Coromandel in New Zealand is an entertaining way to discover the rewards and problems of managing clay soils. Originally designed to transport clay to his pottery, the home-made trains of Driving Creek ascend a steep,

Indicator Plants

Acid soils: pH<6.5	Base-rich soils: pH>7.5
Aruncus dioicus;	Anthyllis vulneraria;
Athyrium filix-femina;	Campanula glomerata;
Calluna vulgaris;	Cirsium vulgare;
Campanula barbata;	Cistus salvifolius;
Cytisus scoparius;	Clematis vitalba;
Dianthus deltoides;	Cornus mas; Cornus
Digitalis grandiflora;	sanguinea; Dictamnus
Digitalis purpurea;	albus; Fragaria
Erica tetralix; Lavandula	vesca; Galium verum;
stoechas; Osmunda	Geranium sanguineum;
regalis; Oxalis acetosella;	Helianthemum
Potentilla erecta;	nummularium; Lactuca
Potentilla sterilis; Primula	perennis; Lathyrus
vulgaris; Pteridium	aphaca; Lavandula
aquifolium; Raphanus	angustifolia; Ligustrum
raphanistrum; Rumex	vulgare; Lotus
acetosella; Saxifraga	corniculatus; Muscari
granulata; Spergula	botryoides; Origanum
arvensis; Stellaria	vulgare; Plantago media;
holostea; Rhododendron	Primula veris; Scabiosa
ponticum; Trifolium	columbaria; Silene
arvense; Vaccinium	vulgaris; Sorbus aria;
myrtillus; Vaccinium	Trifolium campestre;
oxycoccos; Viola canina.	Tussilago farfara;
	Viburnum lantana.

narrow-gauge track between the shuttlecocks of tree ferns, and trundle on trestle bridges over deep, shaded gullies as they zigzag up his clay mountain. Alongside the track, and all over the hill, thousands of trees have been planted and it is hard to believe that, following the logging of the kauri and rimu trees and the burning of the rest of the bush a century ago this was farmland for many years. During the first years of restoration, kauri tree seedlings were planted into holes laboriously dug in the clay, and summers were spent struggling to bring them water. Most were dead by autumn. Now kauri seedlings are lightly dapped into heaps of decaying vegetation piled on top of the clay. They are no longer watered, but they flourish.

Digging is the time-honoured way to add organic matter and lime to clay soils. Alternatives which are at least as effective in the long term improve clay soils bit by bit, starting with the parts that are most accessible to the roots; taking advantage of their high water-holding capacity, and thriftily conserving the reserves of nutrients which they hold. Organic matter is not dug in, but spread over the surface – the place where it is found naturally. This creates conditions which lead to progressive improvements by:

- Encouraging the activity of the soil fauna and flora.
- Providing an absorbent surface that does not cap, and avoids loss of water and nutrients by run-off.
- Preventing the development of surface cracks by maintaining the water content of clay particles.
- Restoring and improving soil structure by providing a source of humus.
- Conserving nutrients by restoring effective soil structure and reducing loss by leaching.
- Suppressing weed growth.
- Maintaining aeration by protecting the surface of the soil from compaction by trampling or the effects of the weather.

Results depend on the generosity with which these surface layers of organic matter are spread. In new gardens and on unplanted beds they should be applied lavishly – 30 cm (1 ft) of farmyard manure is not too deep – and layers of compost, bark, wool waste, grass cuttings, or whatever is available, should be spread as thickly as can be afforded. Plants are set out directly into these top dressings, and as worms and other creatures carry humus and recycled nutrients into the clay layers below, the plants' roots follow.

The leaves, shoots and roots of the plants themselves provide a source of humus as they decline and decay, and this can be supplemented by annual or less frequent applications of organic matter, with additions of lime if needed. A great many perennial plants – especially woodland perennials and bulbs – benefit from dressings of organic matter spread over their tops while they are dormant during the winter. Fallen leaves, compost, farmyard manure, etc., can all be applied in this way to ensure the long-term maintenance of soil structure, and the health and vitality of the plant communities that depend on it.

Management of sandy soils

Those whose houses and gardens are built on sand, struggle to conserve water and maintain fertility. The most positive way to do both is to follow much the same guidelines as for clay. Light, open-textured, sandy soils can be dug with less effort than solid clays, but surface dressings make better use of organic materials and are more economical than digging them into the ground. There are differences in degree; for example, the surfaces of sandy soils are not easily compacted and mulches have little effect on aeration. Nor will organic matter increase the rate of water movement through the soil – on the contrary, it will help to retain water and counter too rapid loss. Humus does not combine with sand in alliances that build up structure and retain nutrient ions as it does with clays, but humus itself retains nutrient ions and prevents their loss by leaching.

Sandy soils are infertile because nutrients are easily and rapidly lost from them by leaching. But their infertility is more fundamental than that. Often they consist of almost pure silicon, the last remnants of rocks which never contained more than low levels of the elements that contribute to plant nutrition. Unlike soils which contain stones and rocks, let alone clays, they hold practically no untapped reserves of nutrients. Applications of organic materials help build up nutrient

levels. The addition of humus to the soil reduces losses by leaching and more efficient recycling of dead leaves, roots, etc., by an enhanced soil fauna and flora conserves nutrients more effectively. Even allowing for these benefits, sandy or gravelly soils are much more likely to need regular additions of fertilisers than more balanced loams containing significant proportions of clays.

Effects of adding fertilisers

We add fertilisers to our gardens to make them more fertile, but they also affect:

pH of the soil – especially when applying calcium. Lime and chalk reduce acidity, which can adversely affect calcifuge plants. Less active forms, including ground limestones, break down slowly and result in smaller changes over longer periods, and calcium, applied as gypsum, has little effect on soil acidity. Sulphates, widely used as sources of ammonium (nitrogen), potassium and magnesium, increase acidity. This is often beneficial, but when soils are already acid it can lead to losses of calcium and other bases, reduced rates of humus formation, deterioration in the structure of clays, and reductions in overall fertility by increased leaching of nutrients, or their conversion to unavailable forms.

Structure of the soil – may respond to changes in pH, and increases or reductions of calcium levels in the soil. Chlorides, sometimes applied as economical sources of potassium, can adversely affect the structure of clays.

Soil fauna and flora – plants and animals respond in complex, often obscure, ways to changes in pH and nutrient status, and the presence or absence of particular chemicals. Calcium is essential for worms as a digestif of organic residues.

The relative proportions of nutrients in the soil – these are directly affected by those applied in fertilisers. They have beneficial effects when used to increase levels of nutrients which are deficient, but a build up of high levels of individual nutrients can reduce the availability of others. For example, liberal applications of potassium reduce the uptake of magnesium.

The nutrient status of plants – which is governed by ion uptake from the soil. Plants take up nutrients selectively and can function effectively despite widely varying levels in the soil, but high levels of nitrogen, in particular, result in unbalanced, excessively luxuriant growth.

Orthodox gardening aims at maximum productivity, based on intensive systems of management, something entirely different from the more passive approaches of matrix planting, when abundant fertility can become a problem. Plants can grow too well! A self-sustaining community depends on a competitive balance between its component plants, and the vigorous growth made possible by heavy applications of fertilisers can produce specimen plants that are little emperors, overwhelming weaker neighbours.

Increased fertility may have other, less obviously undesirable consequences. For example, many species are naturally adapted to cope with infertile sandy soils. In similar garden settings, successful matrices are more likely to be achieved by using well chosen, appropriate plants than by attempting to change the soil to accommodate a broader range. Before adding fertilisers to infertile, free-draining, sandy soils or gravels, we should ask ourselves:

- Is high productivity – as in a vegetable garden – a priority?
- Is the aim optimal growth of individual plants?
- Are we aiming for high maintenance planting in which success depends on constant intervention?

Only when those questions are all answered in the affirmative should fertilisers be added at an early stage and replenished regularly, most quickly and easily by dipping into a bag. In that case, irrigation will almost certainly be needed during dry spells, and any thought of matrix planting should be abandoned.

When balanced communities of plants rather than maximum individual performance is looked for, and when a low level of interference by the gardener is intended, much more specific use of fertilisers from a bag is appropriate, accompanied by reliance on deep-rooted, drought-resistant plants that do not need or – like ceanothuses and Californian live oaks – can even be killed by ill-advised attempts to water them. It may even be possible to rely almost entirely on natural sources of nutrients based on the bacterial and fungal associations with roots through which many plants obtain nitrogen from the air, and phosphorus from otherwise unavailable sources. These associations are most familiar in plants of the pea family, but also occur extremely widely amongst other plants. These are situations where matrix planting, in which lack of disturbance favours symbiotic associations, may be the preferable form of management.

setting up

5

MY BROTHER ONCE HAD A DOG called Fido – a scrap of a thing – but, like other Jack Russell terriers, size meant nothing to him and on his outings he would court disaster by assaulting every large dog he met. His suicidal assaults failed because his 'victims' refused to take him seriously, fending him off with their chests, or kneeling on the squirming Fido until he was quiet. Eventually, while maintaining his right of way down the white line in the middle of a road, he met his match in a car which shared his lack of awareness of size but also lacked a sense of humour. Gardens, too, are sized by attitude not area. They are small when time is ample rather than when space is limited, and grow large – whatever their measurements – when we cannot control what goes on inside them.

That applies whether the garden is a new one on a so-called 'green field' site – though there are likely to be precious few traces of green fields after the builders have finished their work – or a mature garden with its quota of well established plants. The latter can be dubious bargains. They beguile purchasers with promises of off-the-peg convenience, but what we buy is somebody else's garden, never our own. Our predecessor may have been a manic rhododendrophile, or a dedicated plantsperson whose pernicketty, aristocratic beauties make demands beyond our skills. Perhaps we succeed a lawn addict who erased every crinkle, displaced daisies and dandelions and preferred to rake moss rather than go fishing. Sometimes, the trees and shrubs in the garden we buy have grown old and tired together. Their skin-deep beauty barely hides the need for drastic facelifts to restore vitality and balance.

Other people's gardens, like other people's clothes, seldom fit. Sooner or later we have to accept the finery is not for us, before discarding it – bit by bit, or in one dramatic disrobing – and replacing it with something we can slip into more comfortably.

The vision and ability to recognise when changes are needed, and the confidence to make them are amongst the less widely regarded skills of gardening. Never assume anything is where it is wanted, or should be left, just because it is there. Nothing, not even a tree, should be sacrosanct because of a feeling that 'the previous owner must have had a reason for putting it there'. At best, most of the garden can be left as it is, and be made to fit with a tuck here, or a gusset or two there. At worst established gardens are assets to be stripped.

First steps

Plants are the stars of television programmes about gardens, and in the alluring photographs we find in magazines, because they make wonderfully attractive pictures, and we are left with the impression gardens are places for plants.

(Opposite) The entrance to a garden frames a world which reflects the personality, dreams, idiosyncrasies and individuality of the gardener. Plants, paths, pergolas, pools and everything else stem, almost inevitably, from decisions made and actions taken during the first days of the garden's creation. This the time to choose between exercising control with spade, hoe and rake or through partnerships with the plants, where they will do much of the work for you.

Plants are fine when they are wanted but – first and foremost – gardens are places for people. Places to sit or stroll around, places to play or work, places to entertain friends or relax, to ride a bicycle, fly pigeons or breed rabbits, even places to do a spot of gardening. What you and the family want from the space around the house that we call a garden should have priority, then the plants can be fitted in according to your needs.

The starting point in most gardens will be the area close to the house; making a place to sit out and enjoy a cup of coffee, or where children can play; somewhere for breakfast in the morning or a G&T, a chardonnay or a Fosters in the evening. First thoughts are likely to insist the space must be sunny, but shelter from the wind, and shade in hot weather, are just as important for comfort, and lead to thoughts of screens and cover overhead – perhaps a trellis or a pergola – on which climbing plants can be grown.

Warm places near the house provide settings for plants that would not survive elsewhere in the garden; somewhere to grow the tender perennials whose colourful flowers fill patios and terraces with colour for months on end during the summer. The shade beneath a pergola provides a woodland setting, and many of the woodland plants that are evergreen in winter and flower in spring will do well there, complementing the summer displays of the tender perennials.

Next, think of the garden as a playground, for children certainly, but for adults too. Plants and play make an incompatible combination unless carefully contrived. Sand-pits and paddling pools create local wear and tear. Their contents spread out and toys accumulate in and around them. Ball games involve lethal missiles, flailing legs, hurtling bodies and dogs in hot pursuit, during which fragile, tender or special plants are destroyed. More ambitious thoughts like a basketball pad, a tennis court or a swimming pool need ample space, and freedom from unwanted nuisances like falling leaves or shade at the wrong times of day.

These activities become sources of friction when imposed on finely tuned gardens. They need to be taken into account by choosing plants which are resistant to damage from balls. Oleasters, many kinds of eucalyptus or, in warm climates, Moreton Bay figs planted close to a swimming pool, quickly reveal what a nuisance falling leaves, twigs and fruit from trees can be! Bright and cheerful displays from plants in flower are likely to be less satisfactory than carefully placed, well-chosen evergreen, dense and compact shrubs and small trees. That should not involve sacrificing all that makes a garden attractive, as many of these lend themselves to strong structural effects, and can be used to form weed-excluding matrices with little help from the gardener.

Lawns are popularly regarded as the indispensable resort of children at play, and adults at rest. But other features in a garden serve these purposes as well, or better, and many lawns are never used in these 'indispensable' ways. Quiet, open, horizontal spaces from which to view the surrounding planting, and complement the vertical forms of buildings, hedges and walls can be

Lawns in gardens are quiet horizontal spaces which complement neighbouring vertical features. Paving, gravel, or a pool need less maintenance, offer more scope to the imagination and are often at least as effective.

provided in other ways. Paving, or gravel – even a broad path down the centre of a garden – are less demanding options, needing less maintenance, and when well designed can stir the imagination more seductively. Materials can be varied or combined; plants can be used between paving, in walls or planters, or in other ways to create shade, localised spots of colour or contrasts between textures and effects. Surfaces of this kind avoid the problems of wet or frozen grass in winter, and do not become dessicated apologies for a green sward in hot summers. Pools and garden ponds are another way to introduce horizontal surfaces, with all the imaginative possibilities they bring with them.

Privacy is valuable in a garden and, judging by some of the boundary hedges and fences to be seen, many people are prepared to pay a high price for it, aesthetically if not financially. Field hedges can still be exciting places, even today after half a century of herbicidal sprays have done their worst, where shrubs, some with flowers, some with berries, some with glowing autumn foliage, combine with wildflowers growing in their shelter. How many garden hedges display such interest and variety? Too often they are mere screens, planted without considering their effects on the garden, their demands on maintenance or the alternatives available. The hedge bottom is written off as sterile space beneath the sterile foliage of 'Castlewellan Gold' or scarlet-leaved photinias, and the possibilities of hawthorn, blackthorn, dogwood and wild rose beneath which primroses, violets, wood anemones and other spring flowers will thrive are simply not considered.

It is perverse to disregard the opportunities these mixed communities offer

Boundaries and entrances provide opportunities to enhance a garden. A gateway can be a decorative link between one part of a garden and another (above left); a trellis (bottom right) covered with clematis, honeysuckles and other climbers, makes a stimulating backdrop to a mixed border. A boundary fence (top right) planted with a vertical matrix of shrubs, climbing roses, bamboos, ground covering perennials and ferns is more rewarding than the monotony of a hedge.

Busy lizzies (above left)
coexist colourfully with ivies,
periwinkles and ferns during
the summer. The bottom of a
hedge should not be sterile
space. Spring flowering,
woodland perennials (above
right) are at home amongst
the roots of blackthorn,
hazel, dogwood, hawthorn,
hornbeam and other
hedgerow shrubs.

for changing effects throughout the year and instead choose to surround our gardens with dull monocultures; a perversion carried to extremes when every boundary around a garden is uniformly treated, irrespective of aspect, situation or viewpoint. Boundaries form the backdrops to planting, and, in small gardens in particular, are too conspicuous and occupy too much precious space to be wasted by irrelevant regimentation which diminishes the impact of everything within the garden. Hedges, fences, trellises and arbours, groups of shrubs and carefully sited trees can all be used to vary the boundaries in ways which complement the planting and contribute to the matrix of the community.

My earlier comments belittling the importance of plants in gardens were made tongue in cheek, disregarding the fact that plants and how to make the best use of them is the main interest of readers of this book. Places to play and places to sit are all very well, but once provided for it is the plants and how best to use them that fill our minds with anticipation.

Orthodox gardening techniques are heavily based on bare earth as an essential element in the processes of control. Growers of vegetables, annuals and bedding plants start and finish, and then start again with bare soil. Herbaceous borders and other less ephemeral forms of gardening depend on periodic renewals and a return to bare soil. The ground between roses and shrubs is hoed or forked according to the season. The mounting complexities of the mixed border are once in a while resolved by wholesale clearances and new beginnings to reduce the power of the strong and encourage the weak. Only lawns and meadows are managed without periodic resort to open ground, and even in these the option to destroy and start again from scratch is often the first response to serious problems.

Yet most of us garden in places where bare earth is a rare and fleeting natural phenomenon. The tight sward in communities of meadow grasses may open up after flowering, especially during droughts to let in seedlings. Mole hills, ant heaps and worm casts also provide opportunities for colonists. Spaces appear each spring amongst plants on the woodland floor or provide points of entry for a tiny proportion of seedlings to grow and replace their parents, but most are reclaimed as the foliage of established plants develops. Land-slips, floods or windblown trees expose ground, which is quickly occupied by new plants, and in time develops a cover which is indistinguishable from the surrounding vegetation. Regularly recurring expanses of bare earth are characteristic of parts of the world where intense droughts and periods of rain succeed each other seasonally or at more erratic intervals. Only in such places do natural events follow the gardener's traditional cycle of germination, maturation, destruction and resurrection from the seeds of the previous generation.

The Mediterranean basin and lands to the east is one such area. Annuals emerge with the first rains of autumn from expanses of bare soil burnt by the summer sun; they grow, flower, produce fruit and then die, and drought and sun return the spaces where they once were to bare soil. Orthodox gardening started in these parts of the world and has stuck faithfully to the cycles of growth, death and renewal ever since. If, on the other hand, we had learnt to garden in the oceanic conditions of Western Europe, where bare earth is a rare and ephemeral condition, would we have developed entirely different techniques?

Perhaps so; then matrix planting which starts with bare earth, but aims to establish long-lived communities that knit together to exclude unofficial outsiders, would be both orthodox and traditional.

Baring the soil

Digging destroys established soil profiles and structures, and disrupts natural balances within the soil fauna and flora. In gardens where borders have been dug for many years, a final flourish of the fork, a last delve with the spade, in a fond farewell to digging, will do no further damage. But it is not necessary, and in other situations is a backward step. The soil beneath a meadow, and even under lawns, will have horizons and structures that may be embryonic or very well developed. Soils beneath established trees may be infertile and dry – one of the bogey areas of gardening – but often have a good structure. The same goes for long established, neglected or overgrown borders and shrubberies. In every case, rather than destroy them, it is better to build on the structure of the soils, and the integrity of their fauna and flora. This is done by:

Clearing the surface – unwanted garden plants should be lifted and moved elsewhere, and perennial weeds destroyed with herbicides, or in other ways – sheets of black polythene used as covers can be very effective when time allows. Standard and worthy advice to destroy every fragment of perennial weeds should be followed, but it is dangerously optimistic to act as though that were the end of the matter. The seeds of the unwanted plants will still be in the ground, and they will return, if allowed, to plague you later. Outbursts of annual weeds may shame conscientious gardeners into their removal, but these have no long-term future. Conversely, it will always be necessary to maintain a sharp look out for intrusive perennial seedlings, and their destruction is a vitally important ploy in the development of a successful matrix.

Supplying organic matter – in order to improve the soil structure, regenerate the soil fauna and flora and assist newly planted plants to establish themselves. This is essential for success in most situations, but especially when attempting to establish plants beneath trees. Anything that breaks down into a source of humus can be used, spread in as generous a layer as can be afforded (in material and financial terms) over the surface.

Boosting soil fertility – may be urgently necessary, or something that can be pursued gradually. The former calls for applications of either organic or inorganic fertilisers out of the bag. The latter may be satisfied by using sources of humus, including garden compost, farmyard manure and other animal derivatives, cocoa shell, etc., which contribute significant quantities of nutrients.

Adding calcium – either to bring acid soils closer to neutrality, or to provide for the needs of earthworms. The most readily available source of calcium is agricultural lime. Alternatives are chalk which, depending on the size of particles, becomes available more gradually, or ground limestones, including magnesium limestone, which release calcium steadily over periods of several years. These raise the pH of acid soils and can pose hazards for calcifuge plants, which can be avoided by using gypsum.

Planting patterns and rhythms

Placing the first plant in a new garden or flower bed deserves celebration with champagne, the cutting of ribbons or discreetly muted fanfares of trumpets. It is our last chance to discard most of what we have been taught to do when planting a border, and think about the ways plants form communities when growing under natural conditions. It is still almost standard practice to set out groups of plants in discrete blobs, though a few follow the Jekyllian principle of planting in narrow drifts. Tall plants to the back, short to the front is the general rule, but one which may be broken in the interests of added excitement. How many of us can resist packing in as many different plants as possible? We rationalise the diversity by paying attention to colour theming, harmonies and contrasts, and we excuse excess with the plea of a prolonged flowering season.

An oft-repeated gardening dictum admonishes us to plant in threes and fives. The source and sense are equally obscure and it is dubious advice even when applied to traditional patterns of planting. But plant matrices are not formed by plants growing in threes, or fives, or even fifteens. Small plants grow naturally under, and weave amongst, larger ones. Relatively few kinds, but large numbers of each, will combine better than extreme diversity, and the ability to thrive in a particular setting is more critical than contrasts, harmonies and colour theming.

Matrix planting draws inspiration from the ways plant grow together natu-rally but it is not a mere imitation of nature, any more than maps are copies of the countryside they represent. Map-makers adapt reality by simplification

Mulches fill spaces simply and effectively. A pond has been dug out during the construction of a garden (top, left), and the soil used to build up beds elsewhere. Thick layers of fresh, strawy horse manure have been spread over beds in the foreground, and between newly planted roses in the middle distance. Trees and shrubs (top right) are thickly mulched with dried pea haulms until they grow large enough to provide shade for woodland perennials. Vegetables can be grown in deep layers of annually replenished hay or straw (bottom).

and organisation, accentuating some features and eliminating others to produce a comprehensible, serviceable and agreeable result. The same landscape can be represented in a hundred different ways depending on the intended use of the map and the art of the cartographer. Similarly, the success of a garden depends on visual logic, and intentional compositions of colours, shapes and textures melding together to form enjoyable, even inspiring, impressions.

A newly planted border possesses no matrix of any kind, and invites occupation by weeds. However skilfully plants are chosen, and however effectively they will combine eventually, stop gaps are needed at first, either in the form of weed-excluding mulches, or as short-lived plants to fill spaces between more permanent residents.

Trees and shrubs can be grown to produce canopies so dense that no perennials – weeds or otherwise – can survive beneath them, but this is usually the mark of neglected gardens, or badly conceived public parks. Much more attractive effects are obtained when overhead canopies are open enough for perennials and bulbs to thrive in their shelter and make their own contribution to the garden. Whatever the ultimate aim, perennials are likely to be the main matrix-formers during the first few years, and underestimating the contribution of perennials was the crucial, strategic error of the mid-twentieth century gardener's retreat into the shrubbery.

In traditionally managed gardens, the plants – no matter how chaotic or lacking in rhythm the mishmash may be – appear beautiful to most observers, especially when the effects are sanitised by mown grass, clipped hedges and freshly turned soil. In more relaxed situations, the familiar cues identifying a place as a garden are absent, and more easily misinterpreted. The planting itself has to provide the visual logic, and the rhythm and coordination that make a garden. The most effective ways to achieve this are by well-placed, repetitive use of particular plants, and bold combinations based on relatively few kinds.

Undisturbed soils develop a complex structure which is destroyed by digging. Recently cleared woodland (top left) was not dug over or even mulched before planting shade-tolerant perennials. Two years later (top right), the plants had formed an intricate matrix, almost completely covering the ground.

First and future colonists

Annuals might seem an obvious starting point when building up a matrix, and so they can be. Many perennials – especially those naturally associated with grasslands – tolerate and even benefit from their presence, and grow strongly as the annuals decline and die. But annuals used in this way are playing the part of weeds. They are more decorative and enjoyable than fat hen and annual nettle, but compete nonetheless for water, light and nutrients. Unless there is good reason for a display of flowers during the first year, better results are likely, and life is simpler, without the annuals. It is usually preferable to use mulches to fill temporary spaces, exclude weeds, conserve water and provide a source of humus and some nutrients.

The vivid displays of annuals that attract people to places like Springbok in South Africa and Morawa in Western Australia – and colour the landscape round the Mediterranean and in California each spring – seldom initiate a succession leading progressively to a closed community of shrubs and perennials. More often, the gaps they occupy between long-lived shrubs and perennials become vacant year after year.

The Tontine effect

A matrix composed of annuals may seem an oxymoron, since matrices are usually associated with plant communities capable of holding their own in a sustainable, semi-permanent fashion. But under natural conditions annuals, more than most plants, depend on finding a roothold and establishing themselves, and frequently do this by forming matrices. These are short-lived in the sense that each lasts only during the short life-span of its members, but permanent in that they recur annually in the same locations

Annuals form temporary matrices of seedlings (top left), many of which die before maturity, but yield their space and nutrients to the survivors. This tontine affect goes against the grain for gardeners accustomed to thinning out plants to give each one space, but can be used in gardens – especially in dry situations – to form annual meadows (top right).

Short-lived plants – like verbascums (opposite, left) – filling gaps amongst perennials and shrubs, self-seed on well drained, calcareous soils in open, sunny situations. Foxgloves (opposite, right) are more likely to oblige in humus-rich, neutral to acid soils, in lightly shaded parts of the garden.

year after year. Most of our garden annuals grow naturally in places where periods of adequate rainfall alternate with drought. The latter destroys much of the existing vegetation – an effect often accentuated by mankind's reduction of the more permanent plant cover – so large areas of bare ground are available for colonisation by annuals at the start of each rainy season. Seeds of the annuals growing in these places fall to the ground beneath their parents at the end of each growing season. Months later, at the start of the rainy season, they all germinate almost simultaneously, producing masses of seedlings. The numerous seedlings produced by each species occupy space, denying it to others, and conserve nutrients in the upper layers of the soil which might otherwise be lost by leaching during the wet season. As weaker plants die, they bequeath their space and nutrients to others until eventually – as in a tontine – the survivors inherit the resources once shared amongst a large number.

Similar processes can be harnessed to make annual 'meadows' in gardens by departing from the orthodox gardener's insistence on giving every plant ample space to develop. Sowing, pricking and thinning out are time consuming, but essential chores when large specimen plants are required for formal bedding. In more relaxed situations, especially when filling spaces between more

permanent plants – whether in gardens in dry areas where such spaces are annually recurring features, or in more temporary situations – the natural abilities of annuals displayed in the tontine effect will produce a successful result with much less effort on the gardener's part. Mixtures of seeds of annuals can be sown thinly in rows, or broadcast over the spaces to be occupied and, apart from the removal of weeds, can be left to develop with little other attention.

In gardens on fertile soils in well-watered situations, spaces for annuals are likely to be transient at best. In drier settings, annuals, biennials and short-lived perennials capable of sowing themselves successfully year after year are a colourful way to fill gaps – between unsociable shrubs and tussock grasses, for example – at seasons when these would otherwise be occupied by weeds.

The plants that can be used vary from one garden to another depending on soils, situations and climates. The following are a few examples of suitable short-lived plants: columbines, red orache, larkspur, quaking grass, marigolds, squirrel and hare's tail grasses, candytuft, poached egg plant, Moroccan toadflax, crown campion, honesty, foxgloves, forget-me-nots, evening primrose, poppies, Jacob's ladder, Our Lady's thistle, nasturtiums and pansies.

The Gardens
C A S E *S T U D I E S*

Starter Pack for a Small Garden

This back garden of about 300 sq m (350 sq yards) is part of a development of small detached houses near High Wycombe in southern England. The soil is a light woodland loam, overlying chalk. Summers are usually cool, winters are seldom severe, and spring frosts are unusual, but the site has little shelter from the prevailing westerly wind. The owner is in her mid-thirties and practises locally as an architect. She has a nine-year-old daughter, who goes to school nearby. The mother likes gardening and has a smattering of the principles of garden design, and quite a good general knowledge of plants picked up from her parents who are keen gardeners and live nearby. She has little spare time, and insists she does not want to spend too much of it doing the garden. The daughter finds gardening 'dead booooring' and has no intention of becoming involved.

Review

A. Building activities have left the ground in a bad state. The first priority is to reinstate surface drainage, and start on the restoration of the structure of the soil.

B. The soil has a high pH, and moderate fertility, which needs boosting before planting begins.

C. Privacy and shelter are urgently needed to give the garden a more relaxed ambience.

D. There are no plants, paths or features of any kind. The sooner a start can be made on doing something about this, the better.

E. Much of the initial work can be done by contractors, but after that the aim is for an easily maintained, low-maintenance garden.

Outcome

A. & B.

- The surface was thoroughly forked over to remove builder's rubbish and restore surface drainage and a more or less level working surface.
- A top-dressing of inorganic fertiliser made up of equal parts of sulphate of potash, sulphate of ammonia and superphosphate was broadcast over the soil at the rate of 100 g/sq m (3 oz/sq

yard). No lime was added as the soil already contains ample reserves of calcium from the underlying chalk.

- The garden was then covered with a 7.5 cm (3 in) layer of mulch. Farmyard manure was avoided for fear of upsetting the neighbours; mushroom compost was unsuitable because of its chalk content, and was available only in inconveniently large bulk loads. The owner disliked the coarse appearance of wood chips or stripped bark, and quotations for composted bark exceeded her budget. Eventually, sources of shredded bark or composted town refuse were found at more or less the same price. Her 'green' tendencies favoured the town refuse and this was used for the initial mulching. Bark was preferred subsequently because of its greater staying power.

C.

- The owner was determined to avoid the boxed-in effect of fences and hedges along the boundaries, and used carefully sited trees, trellises and arbours with short lengths of fence and groups of shrubs to give shelter and privacy.

D.

- Six months after laying the mulch, the paths and other surface features were dug out and beds formed for plants. Top soil excavated from

The design and style of planting in this garden avoids a 'fenced in' feeling. Low, shade-loving plants run under and through taller, open-branched shrubs and trees. This produces layered effects which are more lively than hedges or fences fronted by a mass of shrubs.

The appearance of the boundary changes around the garden – trellis panels merge into weathered old floorboards that give way to strained wire on which trained fruit trees and climbers grow. Elsewhere shrubs, trees and evergreen perennials provide informal screens.

The management of the planting relies on observation and interpretation of the ways plants grow and relate to their neighbours. It becomes a much more creative and imaginative form of gardening than the outdoor housework involved in keeping hedges trim, shrubs confined to their allocated spaces and herbaceous plants uniform, upright and neat.

the paths was used to make raised beds close to a small terrace behind the house, providing changes in level and contributing a comfortable sense of enclosure.

- More fertiliser was broadcast over the beds and raked in, using a mixture of two parts of ammonium sulphate to boost nitrogen levels and one part each of superphosphate and potassium sulphate in preparation for planting.
- Trees and shrubs were planted first and a 5 cm (2 in) layer of shredded bark was spread between them. Perennials and bulbs were planted through this mulch.

E.

- In the interests of low maintenance, no lawn was laid and short-lived plantings of annuals, etc, were restricted to one or two easily managed raised beds close to the house.
- Paths and areas of paving and gravel were designed to make every part of the garden accessible and to form spaces amongst the densely filled beds.
- Gaps between the plants were kept topped up with shredded bark until they had grown into a more or less complete ground cover.

The Plants

Plants were used to form weed-excluding matrices of two kinds. Parts of the garden away from the house were planted with a mixture of bushy trees, shrubs and shade-tolerant perennials to form strong three-dimensional matrices, which also contributed shade and shelter. Sun-loving, unsociable shrubs interplanted with a close carpet of evergreen perennials overlying numerous bulbs were preferred around the house. A few trees were used to provide height amongst the shrubs, including *Aesculus parviflora*, *Clerodendrum trichotomum* var. *fargesii* and *Hippophae rhamnoides*, all pruned to two or three main stems to develop tree forms. Structures along the boundary were covered with climbers, especially hybrids of *Clematis viticella*, for the ease with which they can be controlled by hard pruning, and one or two more burgeoning species like

Akebia quinnata for rapid cover, grown with climbing roses, backed by ivies such as *Hedera colchica* 'Dentata Variegata' and 'Sulphur Heart' to form a dense screen and provide shelter in winter.

Gregarious shrubs planted amongst the trees included *Buddleja* 'Lochinch', *Deutzia* x *hybrida* 'Mont Rose', *Forsythia giraldiana*, *Leycesteria formosa* and *Viburnum farreri*, supplemented by the evergreen shrubs *Choisya ternata* and *Viburnum tinus* 'Eve Price', with others towards the boundaries. Small, shade-tolerant evergreen shrubs like *Sarcococca hookeriana* var. *digyna*, *Viburnum davidii* and *Ribes laurifolium* were used to reinforce the matrix close to the ground.

Shade-tolerant perennials were planted in mixed groups and drifts to develop into a ground covering matrix beneath the trees and shrubs. Amongst them were: *Aegopodium podagraria* 'Variegatum', *Brunnera macrophylla* 'Hadspen Cream', the long-flowering *Geranium* 'Johnson's Blue' and *G.* x *riversleaianum* 'Russell Pritchard', amongst others, and pulmonaria species and cultivars, *Dicentra* 'Langtrees', a number of hostas, *Fragaria vesca* 'Multiplex', *Tellima grandiflora* 'Purpurea' and *Waldsteinia ternata*.

Unsociable, mostly evergreen shrubs, many with fragrant foliage were planted near the house and on sunlit margins of borders; cultivars of *Lavandula angustifolia*; *Rosmarinus officinalis* 'Sissinghurst Blue'; *Ruta graveolens*; *Salvia officinalis* 'Icterina' and 'Purpurascens'; *Santolina chamaecyparissus* 'Oldfield Hybrid' and *S. pinnata* 'Edward Bowles'; and *Satureja hortensis*. Spaces between them were filled with drifts of carpeting evergreen perennials such as *Acaena novae-zelandiae* and *A. buchananii*, *Artemisia schmidtiana* 'Nana', *Dianthus* 'Pike's Pink', *Origanum vulgare* 'Aureum' and *Thymus citriodorus* and *T. serpyllum* with occasional upright plants of *Verbascum chaixii* 'Album' and *Digitalis ferruginea* for contrast.

Bulbs were used throughout the garden, with several species of cyclamen and cultivars of narcissus in lightly shaded parts. *Allium cristophii*, *Crocus chrysanthus* cultivars, and *Tulipa kaufmanniana* hybrids were used in the more sunlit spaces.

The Captain's Little Love Nest

This sheltered garden around an Edwardian villa at the bottom of a high hill in Bishop Auckland in County Durham, England, lies in a frost pocket and suffers from late frosts in spring and early ones in autumn. The soil is a poorly drained, poorly structured clay loam overlying limestone. The owner, formerly a merchant seaman and master on container ships operated by a company registered in Cyprus, now shares his house and his retirement with the two women who each expected to be his sole companion. After initial ructions, the *ménage a trois* has settled for a wary truce. One 'wife' takes care of the garden; the other of the house, and the two have developed a mutual respect bordering on fondness for one another. The captain at first congratulated himself on an arrangement which looked likely to revolve around his every need, but now has second thoughts, as two capable and stubborn women rule the roost, leaving him little choice but to fall in with what they suggest. One problem about which they cannot agree is what to do with a row of three large flowering cherries dominating half the back garden. He complains they earn their keep only for about ten days a year when they are in flower, and wants to remove them. The 'wives' regard them as one of the glories of the neighbourhood and are determined to preserve them.

Review

A. The short burst of flowers from the cherries is poor value for the ground they occupy. Over the years their shade has progressively suppressed shrubs, roses and miscellaneous garden plants that once grew beneath them.

B. The ground has been neglected for years, even the fallen leaves from the cherry trees which provide the one source of humus have been carefully swept up every year. It lies wet all winter with a slimy surface, and ranges from damp, to bone dry during the summer. The soil is infertile and, despite the underlying limestone, has become very acid. Before it can be replanted, lost humus and nutrients must be replaced, and the soil structure and fertility improved.

C. The cherries' roots lie almost on the surface. Digging or forking the ground would damage them and lead to a profusion of suckers.

D. Attempts to plant annuals in the spring have been miserable failures, and delphiniums and lupins optimistically proposed by an assistant at the local garden centre did no better. Ivies are now spreading over the surface which at least provides a green carpet, but one thing they all agree on is they would prefer something more interesting.

Outcome

A.
- His plea to do away with the cherries was brushed aside by his wives' declaration that if the trees went, he would follow them! They decided to take advice about making the ground beneath the trees more amenable to plants.
- As a start, the lower limbs of the cherry trees were removed to let more light reach the ground below them. This was done in spring to minimise risks of infection from bacterial canker.

B.
- The ground was top dressed with ground limestone broadcast at 500 g/sq m (1 lb/sq yd) then covered with a 20 cm (8 in) deep layer of mushroom compost to provide humus and more lime in the form of chalk.
- During the late summer 7.5 cm (3 in) of good quality topsoil was spread over the remains of

'A' shows the three cherry trees before their lower limbs were removed. The ground beneath them is uninviting, even hostile, to plants and not readily accessible to gardeners.

In 'B' the lower branches have been carefully and cleanly cut off, making it more comfortable to move about beneath the trees, and allowing light and rain to reach the ground beneath them. Substantial improvements to the surface layers of the soil and careful choice of suitable shade-loving, woodland plants make it possible to transform the space under the trees into a very inviting part of the garden.

the mushroom compost, and a general purpose fertiliser – 7:7:7 – was broadcast over it at 100 g/sq m (3oz/ sq yd) and lightly raked in. This was then covered with a 5 cm (2 in) deep layer of shredded bark through which the plants were set into the top soil below.

- Gaps between plants were filled with mushroom compost, leaving many of them partially buried, an effect which was reinforced when the leaves of the cherries dropped soon afterwards, and were left where they fell.

C. & D.

- Early the following spring 150 g/sq m (5 oz/sq yd) of blood, fish and bone manure was scattered between the plants. The following autumn after the leaves had fallen, a repeat mulch of mushroom compost 7.5 cm (3 in) deep was spread over the bed, again partially submerging many of the plants.

- There were plans to repeat these applications of blood, fish and bone and a mulch (mushroom compost, rotted stable manure or shredded bark depending on cost and availability) annually but by the third year the bed had become almost self-maintaining, needing virtually no further attention.

The Plants

This situation represents a garden spinney. Apart from its darkest, driest corners, ground-covering woodland shrubs and perennials find the conditions tolerable with a little help, provided plants which would suffer from the prevalent spring frosts are avoided. Bulbs establish easily and do well, and a great many were put in during September, about a month before the other plants.

The fully developed roots and canopy of the cherries formed a dominant overpowering matrix which made it difficult to establish plants beneath them. This was countered as described above, and the border planted with shade-tolerant plants including lots of winter-greens, amongst them pulmonarias and hellebores, in mixed groups; alternating with drifts or clumps of a single kind.

Preference was given to plants with persistent, decorative foliage and textures that harmonised or contrasted attractively, and some of the more striking forms were planted in large drifts for bold effects. Some clumps of *Ruscus aculeatus* had survived and these were left to emerge above the rest of the planting. More procumbent evergreen shrubs, to form a pattern at ground level and enfold perennials, included *Cotoneaster* x *suecicus* 'Coral Beauty' chosen for its bright berries, and *Euonymus fortunei* 'Dart's Blanket' and 'Emerald 'n' Gold' for their foliage. *Lonicera pileata*, in spite of some sensitivity to spring frosts, was used for its fresh spring foliage and to provide slightly bolder clumps, and varieties of *Vinca minor* were planted amongst small-leaved, variegated ivies for foliage effects and flowers in the darker, drier recesses.

A few perennials were also used in these 'difficult' areas, mainly large groups of *Asarum europaeum* and *Lamium maculatum*, interplanted with the broad glossy leaves of *Iris foetidissima* var. *citrina* and 'Variegata'. In lighter areas towards the edges, *Campanula poscharskyana*, *Epimedium pinnatum* subsp. *colchicum* and *E.* x *versicolor* 'Sulphureum', *Convallaria majalis*, and *Viola riviniana (labradorica)* 'Purpurea' were planted around clumps of ferns. These included forms of *Dryopteris affinis* and *Polystichum setiferum* 'Acutilobum'; the latter home-grown by the gardening 'wife' from buds produced on its fronds. *Aquilegia vulgaris*, *Digitalis grandiflora*, *Lychnis coronaria* and *Myrrhis odorata* were included in the original planting as self-seeders to plug gaps in the matrix.

The bulbs included large numbers of *Scilla bifolia* intended to form drifts beneath the trees – unfortunately, many turned out to be the dirty pink form rather than the blue. They also planted *Galanthus nivalis* 'Flore Pleno', *Hyacinthoides hispanica*, *Camassia cusickii* and *C. leitchlinii* 'Alba' as well as daffodils including 'Beersheba', 'Dutch Master', 'Golden Harvest', 'Ice Follies' and 'Mrs R. O. Backhouse'. Both women insisted on these large and florid hybrids rather than the smaller species hybrids preferred by the captain.

Garden Take-away in Auckland

A 1000 sq m (1100 sq yd) section around a cream and blue painted wooden house in Birkenhead, on the North Shore of Auckland harbour in New Zealand, owned by the former head of a large company's public relations department, who has recently retired. Following an enjoyable day out, at the first Ellerslie Flower Show in spite of the queues, she decided the garden was in need of a face-lift. She lives with her father, formerly a gardener in the city's parks department, who also helps his wife with the family's Indian take-away restaurant at weekends and in the evenings. The garden has been his baby, and almost all of it had been turned into lawn which he tended with great pride, totally absorbed in a perpetual cycle of mowing, edging, rolling, feeding, watering, sweeping and a dozen other tasks. He acceded to her plans, 'provided there were no shrubberies and absolutely no aciphyllas!'.

Review

A. The owner's father was secretly pleased by his daughter's interest. He was beginning to find the garden hard work, and was not unwilling to allow her a small part in its care.

B. Winters are practically frost-free, summers tend to be hot and sometimes humid, and droughts are unusual. It is possible to grow an unusually wide variety of plants. But the favourable conditions encourage weeds to grow with exceptional vigour and persistence more or less year-round.

C. The stricture on 'shrubberies' is an echo of old rivalries within the city's parks department, and was not be taken too seriously. This is just as well, since shrubs of some kind and trees too, are almost essential here as part of a strong, weed-resistant matrix.

D. A visit to the Regional Botanic Garden at Manurewa drew her attention to the hitherto unsuspected possibilities of native plants, revealed in collections of coprosmas, pseudopanax, manukas and phormiums, amongst others. These provided plenty of choice for matrices formed by dense, evergreen, weed-excluding plants.

Outcome

A.

- The father's hopes of restricting his daughter to a few beds tucked away in a corner proved to be unrealistic. She had not worked in public relations for nothing, and quickly persuaded him to let her do things her way.
- Trees and shrubs were planted to mask the boundaries of the garden, and provide a setting for a much reduced lawn, flanked by an ornamental pool.

B.

- The structure of the soil beneath the lovingly maintained turf was excellent, and could only have been damaged by digging.
- Instead, the positions of new beds were marked out on the grass, sprayed with glyphosate to kill the turf and then covered with 10 cm (4 in) of shredded tree fern mulch.
- Bonemeal was broadcast over the surface of the mulch at 150 g/sq m (5 oz/ sq yd) before planting.

C.

- Trees and shrubs were planted through the mulch. The father suggested planting them through sheets of woven plastic, to reinforce the effects of the mulch following the practise he had used on roadside plantings of native trees and shrubs.

- His daughter vetoed this idea, preferring to keep spaces mulched with organic matter. She supplemented the mulch with annuals to brighten up the garden while filling spaces. This was fine for the first year but, the following year, an unusually severe drought reduced the annuals to a less than exhilarating performance.

D.

- After heavy rain in the autumn of the second year, blood, fish and bone meal was broadcast over the ground at 100 g/sq m (3 oz/sq yd) before planting shade-tolerant, ground-covering perennials and ferns beneath the developing canopy of trees and shrubs.

The Plants

Nearly all the trees and shrubs used were evergreens. Amongst the former were fast growing native pioneer species like *Knightia excelsa* and *Leptospermum ericoides* to provide a quick impression of height and cover. These were combined with other fast-growing, but ultimately moderate sized exotics: *Agonis flexuosa*, *Callistemon salignis*, *Embothrium coccineum*, *Michelia x foggii* 'Touch of Pink' and the Australian frangipani – *Hymenosporum flavum*. Small groups of cultivars of *Cordyline australis* and *Griselinia littoralis*, with a single plant of *Meryta sinclairii*, were included for their contrasting foliage textures and forms.

Few conifers were used, but an existing pair of *Agathis australis* was given a prominent role in the design, and a *Podocarpus totara* was used to screen a corner. Several tree ferns, including *Cyathea dealbata* and *Dicksonia squarrosa* were planted to add variety to the treescape.

Shrubs provided dense evergreen cover between the trees, carefully composed to make the most of the boldly variegated glossy leaves of coprosmas like 'Kiwi-gold', 'Coppershine', 'Pride', 'Beatson's Gold' and *C. repens* 'Pink Splendour', with contrast provided by the broad foliage of *Macropipum excelsum* 'Variegatum', the dark leathery leaves of *Pseudopanax* 'Adiantifolius' and *P. discolor* 'Rangatira', and the soft greys and crimsons of *Brachyglottis repanda* 'Purpurea'.

Other shrubs included several cultivars of *Camellia japonica* because, as her father said, 'they perform too jolly well, not to have some, somewhere'. *Hebe albicans, H.* 'Inspiration', 'Snow Cover', 'Wiri Charm' and 'Wiri Dawn' provided rapid front-of-border substance, and *Leptospermum scoparium* 'Crimson Glory', 'Martinii', 'Rosy Morn' and 'Wiri Joan' were chosen for their masses of deep crimson, pink or white flowers during late winter and spring.

The dense evergreen foliage of the shrubs afforded few opportunities to plant perennials, grasses or bulbs beneath them. Some, like *Astelia chathamica*, and cultivars and hybrids of *A. nervosa*, a couple of groups of *Cortaderia richardii* and clumps of agapanthus were planted where spaces could be found to contrast with the shrubs. The peppermint-scented *Pelargonium tomentosum* and *Arthropodium cirrhatum* were set out in drifts in semi-shaded parts, and *Acaena inermis* and forms of *A. microphylla*, and other species and cultivars, carpeted more open spaces. As overhead cover developed, groups of ferns were planted, using amongst others, *Blechnum capense* and *B. penna-marina* in the less shaded spaces, and *Asplenium bulbiferum*, *Polystichum vestitum*, *Blechnum discolor* and *B. fraseri* in shadier settings.

The old man finally rebelled, and delivered the firmest possible veto, when his daughter proposed to plant freesias and sparaxis in what was left of his lawn.

variations
on grassy themes

6

A VISITOR TO MY GARDEN drew me aside as she was leaving and with an encouraging smile whispered confidingly, 'Of course, I can always tell a proper gardener by his lawn.' She then got into her car and drove off, leaving me wondering whether this splendid assertion of the pivotal role of mown grass had been a barbed comment or had she simply failed to notice my garden lacked a lawn of any kind?

A million gardens, large and small in Britain and New Zealand, and the summer-long rattle and whirr of contractor's mowers crisscrossing the private prairies around houses in the countryside of the mid-Atlantic states of the USA, testify to many gardeners' fixation with lawns. Patch or prairie, lawns cloak matrix-planting in a familiar guise. Whether a choice selection of fine-leaved, low-growing grasses on bowling greens, or a score or more mixed wildflowers and grasses in a rough sward, they are examples of tight-knit, sustainable communities of plants maintained by highly developed systems of management and control which teach valuable lessons about matrix planting in general:

1. Where we garden and what we do are more critical in matrix planting than in traditional forms of gardening. The situation, climate and pattern of use – as well as management – decisively affect the composition of the species that eventually form the matrix.

2. It is extraordinarily difficult to forecast precisely which species will form the matrix. Whatever the seed mix originally used, within a few years all lawns develop their own flora. In this, as in other applications of matrix planting, the gardener must view alliances with plants as cooperative ventures in which developments may take unexpected turns.

0

(Opposite) Communities of grasses are mainly of two kinds: some form densely interlocking swards, others grow as individual clumps. Both have their place in gardens. Even in situations where grass blankets the surrounding countryside, trees, shrubs and other plants flourish within the protected conditions of a garden.

(Below) Lawns are examples of matrix planting. Irrespective of the grass mix originally sown, every lawn quickly develops its own flora, dependent on its situation, previous history and the frequency and height of cutting.

0

Not long ago even the most avid lawn enthusiasts were less than enthusiastic about grasses met elsewhere in the garden. Attempts to disentangle couch grass from clumps of herbaceous plants, the all-investing, surface nastiness of annual meadow grass, or the penalties of falling for the seductively variegated foliage of gardeners' garters, had instilled a deeply embedded distrust of the entire breed. Recently, a growing recognition of the decorative possibilities of grasses and their cousins – sedges, reeds and rushes – has led to increasing awareness that not all are baddies and those that are good can be very good indeed.

Grasses are free spirits. Their wind-born motion transforms the atmosphere of a garden, but the traditional suspicion of the orthodox for the free has some justification. Marram grasses may be priceless to those who contend with shifting sand dunes, and Gertrude Jekyll may have recommended lyme grass for its striking silvery-blue foliage, but she and her clients employed gardeners to restrain its wanderings. Most of us should be deeply wary of, or ban totally, those grasses – including some bamboos – whose insinuating, pervasive rhizomes invade territory unseen beneath the ground.

Apart from these space-eating rhizomatous infiltrators, grasses can be divided into two main groups:
Some grow intermingled as well-knit swards
Others develop as independent tussocks

Swards – flowers in lawns and meadows exist in close-knit matrices, dominated by grasses, and management of the latter defines which flowers thrive and which die out. Change the frequency or height of mowing, and conditions within the matrix change too, leading inevitably to additions and subtractions amongst the plants that live amongst the grasses. Meadow wildflowers are also a great source of perennials for our gardens; brought to us from wet meadows and dry, salt marshes by the sea, and alpine grasslands high in the mountains, they grow side by side in borders wherever gardens are made. Divorced from their natural association with grasses, and free from their competition, they flourish in open, sunlit, fertile borders, where the natural preferences that restricted them to particular niches in particular habitats are rendered largely redundant by the gardener's care and the undemanding conditions. We will return to them later.

Tussock, or bunch grasses – these also often dominate their communities under natural conditions. However, gardeners tend to use them as accent plants, either to create effects on the grand scale of bamboos, pampas grasses, cultivars of miscanthus and *Arundo donax*; or more modestly within the framework of a border, where stipas, chionochloas, helictotrichons, digitarias, fescues, themadas and poas introduce a change of texture or focal point. When grown in borders like this, the growth cycles and management of the grasses have much reduced effects on the plants that grow with them.

When tussock grasses are used in gardens as they grow in nature – where plants are sometimes arranged so evenly that they might have been set out by hand, and cover enormous areas – the spaces between them are filled with a bright variety of flowering herbs and bulbs. But the grasses are dominant elements within the matrices. The bunch grasses of the American prairies and Russian steppes, or the tussocks of New Zealand and South Africa, could be used much more in dry gardens, including those in colder, more exposed situations where the grasses not only shelter the plants between them from wind, but also from cold in winter.

Natural grasslands

In parts of the world where grasses stretch from horizon to horizon (or at least, would do so without mankind's interference), it is often assumed woody plants would not grow well. But that is not necessarily so. The mixtures of grasses and attendant herbs extending over country-sized expanses of steppes and prairies do not depend on rainfall alone, but develop as the result of alliances between rainfall, wind and fire.

Decreasing rainfall favours transitions from forest, to savanna, to prairie – a process in which fire and wind are allies of the grasses. As tree and shrub cover is reduced, air movement increases and with it the dessicating effects of wind on the landscape. Dryer conditions and increased wind speeds boost the frequency and intensity of fires started by lightning or other causes, destroying remaining trees and shrubs. The grasses, with well-protected ground-level buds, recover quickly after fires. As the grasses take over, their dry stems and leaves, and increased air movement, accentuate the effects of fire

Meadow grasses and wild-flowers grow in intimate mixtures (top left). On the other hand, tussock grasses grow individually (middle left), separated by spaces often occupied by bulbs or annuals or – as here – by astelias, celmisias and other clump-forming perennials. Grasslands (bottom left) can persist indefinitely in places like this, maintained by wind, fire and drought which prevent the regeneration of woody plants. Nevertheless, given shade and shelter, trees and shrubs may grow perfectly well in gardens in these situations.

to the further benefit of the grasses, which gain from the recycling of nutrients, elimination of plant litter and removal of overhead shade.

Even in places where grasses dominate the landscape, trees and shrubs may actually be able to grow quite well, so long as they are protected from fire. Woody plants in gardens made in such situations reduce wind speed, reversing the desiccating effects which favour grasses, and creating oases of forest and scrub. These can even attract woodland birds and insects unable to survive in the surrounding grasslands.

Garden grasslands

Selected forms of fine-leaved grasses are the pride of those who seek the perfect lawn, because of their appearance and resilient acceptance of wear and tear. Their narrow leaves resist damage, and rapid growth repairs worn areas. Nothing serves better than the traditional lawn in situations exposed to daily use and abuse. Other grasses and broad-leaved flowering plants can also form very attractive communities in less demanding situations, roles that would make any self-respecting greenkeeper weep, but can be very attractive and rewarding to less dedicated graminophiles.

'Weedy' lawns

My grandfather would pay me threepence (pocket money for the week was tuppence) per hundred plantains removed from his lawn during World War II, when the garden lay neglected due to lack of labour. Today, a quick tour of garden centres' shelves laden with herbicides, lawn sand, fertilisers and every kind of sward cosmetic confirms that the jealous preservation of turf from contamination by wild flowers survives as a major gardening preoccupation.

Yet, my grandfather's lawns consisted almost entirely of 'weeds', and if every plantain had been removed, speedwells, buttercups, field woodrush, mouse ears, medicks and white clovers would still have far outnumbered the grasses. Butterflies, bees, burnet moths and other insects attracted to their flowers throughout the summer made them much more lively and interesting places than pure swards of fine-leaved grasses could ever have been. Those lawns grew on

perfectly drained calcareous loams above deep beds of gravel and when mown they developed a sward not unlike that on the Downs of Southern England, where intensive grazing by sheep or rabbits produces a close turf of fine-leaved grasses, herbs and orchids on thin soils above chalk.

Lawns on free-draining soils, whether acid or alkaline, are almost impossible to maintain in dry weather without lavish watering. But during droughts green patches of deep-rooted clovers, which survive

Plants for floriferous lawns on well-drained calcareous soils

Numerous plants associated naturally with short grass will form well-knit matrices in sunlit situations. The essentials of success include excellent drainage and generally low levels of fertility. Occasional sparing applications of fertiliser, containing little or no nitrogen, may be necessary and on neutral soils regular applications of ground limestone.

Achillea millefolium: Colonises dry, infertile sites on free draining soils. Drought-resistant with attractive ferny foliage. Flowers are now available in various pastel shades.

Anthyllis vulneraria: A deep-rooted species, tolerant of drought and heat, with many forms ranging from pale yellow through ochre yellow to apricots and brick reds.

Bellis perennis: One of the most characteristic wildflowers in lawns. Shallow-rooted with little drought-tolerance, it spreads rapidly by seed to colonise gaps on damp, poorly drained sites.

Festuca ovina: An excellent, drought-tolerant grass, providing good conditions for matrix formations with other plants.

Festuca rubra: Low-growing, very fine-leaved perennial grass, available in a wide variety of selected strains for different situations.

assaults by most lawn weedkillers, may stand out amongst the shrivelled remnants of grasses burnt crisp by sun and dry weather. Such settings are ideally suited for garden versions of downland (base-rich) or heathland (acidic soils) communities of grasses and wildflowers. These can be encouraged to develop by abandoning herbicides applied in futile attempts to maintain grass-only swards, and forgetting about the standards by which good lawns are judged. Then worms become allies, because their casts are places in which seeds germinate, and can be deliberately seeded with suitable wildflower mixtures. Regular applications of lime can be used on already neutral or slightly basic soils to accentuate the alkaline conditions many downland plants need to compete successfully with grasses. The blades of the mower can be adjusted to raise the cut a little higher than a purist would approve for a well turned out lawn, and in early summer the interval between cuts can be extended to allow the plants more time to produce flowers.

Helianthemum nummularium: This and other species and cultivars of rock roses thrive in sunlit sites on dry soils thinly covering calcareous rocks. Notable for their flowers in variously coloured yellow, orange, pink, white or terracotta.

Koeleria cristata: A tough, rather stiff, little grass, unloved by lawn aficionados, which forms open swards that associate well with herbs on dry, base rich soils.

Linum catharticum: A slender annual, with dainty white flax flowers, self-sows amongst grasses in open swards on well-drained, infertile soils.

Lotus corniculatus: Colourful, vigorous leguminous plant able to establish and reproduce itself even in competitive situations. Rich in nectar. Bacterial nodules in the roots fix nitrogen.

Medicago lupulina: Tolerant of close mowing and an effective coloniser of open to moderately dense swards on dry, well-drained sites. Another nitrogen-fixer.

Pilosella officinarum: Many hawkweeds and cat's ears are excellent colonists of thin grass swards on well-drained soils. Produce prolonged successions of small dandelion-style flowers.

Plantago media: Spreading rosettes of leaves establish readily from seed in open or thin swards on well-drained soils. Produces numerous pale but attractive spikes of flowers with prominent stamens.

Polygala vulgaris: Several forms, with conspicuous blue or white flowers, maintain themselves successfully amongst grasses on dry, sunlit sites

Primula veris: Easily established on fertile, base-rich meadows and open swards on thin soils above calcareous rocks. Produce trusses of fragrant, yellow or rust-coloured cowslips in spring.

Prunella grandiflora: Adaptable species, growing in semi-shaded and sunlit sites, preferring moist, or even seasonally wet conditions, in mixed communities of grasses and herbs.

Sanguisorba minor: Deep-rooted, drought-resistant plant for hot sunny slopes amongst fine-leaved grasses.

Thymus serpyllum: Forms intimate mixtures with fine-leaved grasses on exceptionally free-draining, sunlit sites. Colourful white, pink or purple flowers are rich sources of nectar for bees.

Trifolium pratense: Variable and adaptable species associated with grasses in rich, moist meadows and on thin soils. A nitrogen fixer and excellent source of nectar.

Trifolium repens: Drought-resistant species, very tolerant of close-cutting and adaptable to a wide range of conditions. Another nitrogen fixer.

Viola hirta: Able to grow amongst other broad-leaved plants in open grass swards in sunny well-drained situations.

Plants for floriferous lawns on sandy or acid soils

Plants for growing amongst grasses in acid conditions may form more open communities than those on calcareous soils. Most depend on very good drainage to do well, and top dressings of sand and peat laced with seeds of suitable species encourage their development.

Acaena inermis: Several of the smaller, less invasive acaenas are suitable. Their burrs can be exceedingly objectionable and kinds which produce smooth heads are preferable.

Agrostis alba: An attractive, markedly drought-resistant small grass, spreading by underground stems to form colonies. Can invade neighbouring flower beds.

Arctotheca calendulacea*: This strongly drought-resistant plant produces attractive bright yellow flowers over a long period. Self-sows, sometimes too freely.

Blechnum penna-marina: A small fern, tolerant of many situations. Will establish and run gently amongst grasses.

Calluna vulgaris: Good coloniser of dryish or wet, infertile acid sands. Forms a dense, wear-resistant, ground-hugging sward when mown.

Campanula rotundifolia: Several forms are available, all with attractive blue bells in late summer; too upright for close-mown swards. Forms of *C. carpatica* are also sometimes successful.

Dianthus deltoides: Numerous named forms with flowers in shades of magenta, or white, form spreading mats of deep green foliage; capable of self-sowing into open swards.

Erigeron philadelphicus: This and *E. karvinskianus* (in drier conditions) will form spreading colonies.

Festuca ovina subsp. *glauca:* Low growing, tufted grass with glaucous foliage. Numerous horticultural forms have been selected, varying in vigour and the intensity of blue tones of the foliage.

Geranium molle: An annual with tiny, fugitive flowers. The soft-textured, round-lobed foliage is its main attraction. Short-lived but self-sows freely.

Hieracium pratense: Invaluable for its small yellow 'dandelions' from mid to late summer.

Houstonia caerulea: Bluetts form scattered, low, tufted clumps of usually pale blue, occasionally white flowers, in early spring.

Leptinella perpusilla: A mat-forming perennial with rounded flower heads, and fern-like grey, sometimes brown, leaves.

Oxalis purpurea*: Large purple, pink or white flowers carried low above shamrock-style lobed foliage.

Petrorhagia saxifraga: A little tall and lightly built for close swards; particularly suitable for sunlit, well-drained situations, especially on sunny banks.

Pratia angulata: Closely infiltrating, mat-forming plants with tiny leaves spangled with star-shaped white flowers followed by conspicuous scarlet or cerise berries, also *P. pedunculata* and *perpusilla*.

Primula vulgaris: Old-fashioned, unimproved primroses co-exist with grasses in open or even moderately close swards much better than brightly colourful modern strains.

Soleirolia soleirolii: Forms dense mats of tiny, almost moss-like leaves. Can be extremely invasive, but also can form luxuriant swards in damp, shaded, mild situations.

Veronica filiformis: Invasive, but very beautiful. Can transform a lawn into a pool of shimmering blue.

Viola tricolor: Very variable flower colours and forms, ranging from pale yellow to deep purple; does better on open swards, especially on well-drained banks, than in closely mown situations.

* Note: plants marked with an asterisk are vulnerable to frost in cold locations.

Meadows

Prior to the the advent of the tractor and its tremendous horsepower, intractably heavy land was managed as permanent pasture. This avoided teams of horses becoming bogged in the mud in wet weather, and development of brick-like surfaces that were impossible to cultivate in summer droughts. Annual crops of hay, followed by grazing, made full use of the great reserves of fertility possessed by many clays, accessed by deep-rooted herbs which tapped minerals from the lower levels. Dense mats of grass roots close to the surface maintained the structure and natural profiles of the soils, conserved their fertility, and perpetuated drainage channels which disposed of surplus water.

Gardeners faced with the problems of coping with heavy, poorly drained soils replete with clay and silt might look to these meadows for a solution to their problems. But old meadows have characteristics which are not quickly or easily achieved in many gardens:

- They are composed of communities of plants which have become precisely adapted to the conditions over a long period.

Meadows are diverse and exciting plant communities. The simplest are composed of cornflower weeds in fields of cereals (top). Varied and beautiful mixtures of wildflowers grow in long-established hay meadows (lower left), especially on moist soils. Alpine meadows, like this fragment bright with mountain flowers (lower right), are surely amongst the hardest to reproduce in gardens.

- A balanced distribution of the resources available has been achieved, particularly nutrients, which have often been depleted by the annual removal of grass as hay, over many years.
- They possess an established soil structure, and well developed soil profile appropriate to the composition of the soil and the situation.

Newly sown meadows possess so little of the self-sustaining balance of established grassland communities they can scarcely be described as meadows at all. Well-endowed garden soils do not provide easy conditions for meadow-making because their fertility favours takeover bids by coarse grasses and vigorous, weedy wildflowers. It is much easier to establish a balance between grasses and attractive wildflowers when water or fertility, or both, are seasonally or even perpetually limiting.

Lawns sometimes turn spontaneously into meadows when the mower breaks down and sits idly in the tool shed while the grass grows long. That would probably have happened with my grandfather's 'neglected' lawns. But, apart from notably dry or infertile situations, it is better practice to kill existing swards by spraying with glyphosate, then sow or plant the colonists, which will eventually combine to form the meadow, into the remains of the dead turf.

In a meadow, control by mower – the chief instrument of control in a lawn – is largely replaced by control from within the community of plants itself, supplemented by mowing. This change of emphasis leaves the gardener much less power to dictate what goes on. The composition of the community, and the relative success of different members, depends on the timing, frequency and height of successive cuts, and the use or non-use of fertilisers of one kind or another. Any bit of ground left more or less to itself and mown only from time to time will give rise to a matrix of some sort eventually. The gardener's part is to guide these developments in a direction which produces an attractive mix of species.

Everything possible should be done to:

Select species which match the physical and climatic conditions of the site.

Combine those likely to be compatible in terms of vigour, one with another.

Blend together species whose various growth forms provide the essential components of a matrix. This includes a mixture of grasses, bulbs and broad-leaved herbs; a variety of flowering seasons and periods of growth; and ability to occupy ground or to infiltrate and occupy spaces as they become available.

Meadows lack the in-depth matrix of woodlands, nevertheless, they present formidable obstacles to the successful establishment of invading plants, and only those well adapted to cope with the conditions are likely to gain entry or persist. Apart from gaps produced by mole and ant hills, and damage to the sward by the feet of large animals, the matrix of an established grassland can be nearly impenetrable for much of the year. It may appear to be ragged and open to invasion after winter weather and storms, but seedlings germinating in the spring face immediate competition from established grasses and perennials, whose well-developed roots and reserves of storage compounds give them an immense advantage. In mid-summer, vigour declines as the grasses and meadow plants go to seed and this, combined with the effects of drought, often produces gaps in the matrix which provide opportunities for colonists. Attempts to introduce new species into established meadows, whether by scattering seed or setting out plants from containers, are likely to be more successful in late summer and autumn – provided conditions are not too dry – than in the spring.

Broad-leaved plants growing amongst grasses adopt one of two strategies.

They hold their ground year by year, putting down deep roots that tap nutrients and water at lower levels than the grasses, eventually developing into large, well-defined individuals – such as chicory, hellebores, meadow clary and pasque flowers.

Alternatively, they may infiltrate the grasses, producing crowns horizontally, at or just below ground level, with short, annually renewed roots that extend continuously into new ground. Some examples are erigerons, heleniums, hawkweeds, and moondaisies.

Seed mixtures composed to suit different situations are now widely available, and are likely to be the first choice of most people trying to form a meadow. But these mixtures have limitations.

Plants for fertile, relatively moist meadows

Satisfactory meadow communities are more difficult to set up on fertile, normally moist soils, because the vigorous growth of the grasses in the early years dominates the matrix and overwhelms other plants. It is essential to match the vigour of broad-leaved plants and grasses.

Achillea ptarmica: Limited but effective rhizome development enables this tallish plant with white daisies to infiltrate grasses and hold its own, even amongst dense growth.

Actaea simplex: Does well in very wet situations, even amongst strong-growing grasses. Produces white flowers in late autumn. Unlike some Actaea species, it does not produce poisonous berries.

Aster novae-angliae: A tall daisy with numerous, small purple-blue flowers spreading among grasses by surface rhizomes.

Camassia cusickii: One of several camassias that contribute little to a matrix, but are valued for their beautiful, though short-lived spikes of flowers.

Cardamine pratensis: A rather transient species, which fluctuates in numbers from year to year. Ability to regenerate from leaf bases makes it an excellent gap filler in moist situations.

Cynosurus cristatus: A grass of only moderate vigour, which associates well with many broad-leaved plants.

Deschampsia caespitosa: A clump-forming grass with very decorative inflorescences. Its moderate vigour makes it a good neighbour for meadow flowers.

Eupatorium purpureum subsp. *maculatum:* A tall, vigorous plant, with dense bunches of purple flowers in the autumn, capable of growing amongst vigorous grasses in wet situations.

Festuca pratensis: Another moderately vigorous grass which forms an effective matrix without suppressing neighbouring plants.

Filipendula ulmaria: Capable of holding its own with strong grasses in the wettest meadows. Fragrant sprays of small white flowers produced from mid-summer.

Fritillaria meleagris: A spring-flowering bulb with graceful, broad-mouthed nodding bells. Associated grasses should be mown after seed has matured, and then kept short till autumn.

Geranium pratense: Clump-forming, long-lived perennial, with highly decorative, conspicuous light purple-blue flowers. Expands slowly by short rhizomes.

Helenium autumnale: Late summer, autumn-flowering yellow/orange daisies able to grow in strong matrices in wet meadows.

Heracleum sphondylium: Vigorous, with broad, flat white or light crimson flower heads attractive to many insects. Excellent matrix-former in rough, moderately open swards.

Liatris pycnostachya: One of several blazing stars capable of establishing well amongst herbs and grasses in moist situations.

Lychnis flos-cuculi: Best in perennially or seasonally wet situations in old, well balanced herb-rich meadows where competition from grasses is not too great.

Persicaria bistorta: Grows in moist to wet situations in established meadows, but vulnerable to suppression by vigorous grasses, and likely to need support in recently established meadows.

Ranunculus acris: Another typical established meadow species, able to self-sow in established swards. Liable to fluctuate greatly in numbers from year to year.

Rumex acetosa: A characteristic plant of old damp meadow matrices. Widely tolerant of different situations and valued for its decorative upright spikes of small, red flowers.

Sanguisorba tenuifolia 'Purpurea': One of several sanguisorbas capable of competing with vigorous grasses, chosen for its deep crimson flowers.

Gloriosa daisies transform a dry, sunlit bank in a Russian garden (top left). Native wildflowers encouraged to self-sow produce a dazzling spectacle (right) on dry, impoverished soil in South Africa; while in Devon (bottom left) equally beautiful effects are obtained on a rich, moist loam from North American camassias planted amongst the meadow flowers.

Plants for dry meadows

Numerous, often very colourful perennials grow well in well-drained situations dominated by grasses. Fashion suggests we should use native plants in wildflower meadows, but suitable species from similar habitats anywhere in the world are candidates for these situations.

Actaea dahurica: Grows well in association with rough grasses. Tall spikes of pure white flowers in late autumn.

Anthoxanthum odoratum: A tufted, only moderately vigorous, perennial grass that associates well with other plants. Smells of new mown hay.

Asclepias tuberosa: Produces bright orange flowers, highly attractive to butterflies, from mid to late summer.

Asphodeline lutea: Suitable for very dry situations, such as banks, in association with thin grass swards.

Aster amellus: More or less clump-forming aster which produces clear blue daisy flowers for an exceptionally long season. Best in open swards on well-drained soils on banks.

Cichorium intybus: Deep-rooted, self-sowing perennial with large bright blue flowers produced from spring to mid-summer.

Dianthus carthusianorum. Bright crimson flowers on strong, spiky stems. Does best in very well-drained situations in thin swards.

Dipsacus fullonum: Deep-rooted, self-sowing biennial forming a broad, weed-suppressing rosette the first year and carrying numerous teasels on tall, branching superstructures the following year.

Hordeum jubatum: Attractive, short-lived perennial grass. Best in open swards on well-drained infertile situations where seedlings can find spaces in which to grow.

Lathyrus pratensis: One of a number of *Lathyrus* and *Vicia*

species, mostly with highly decorative flowers, able to grow amongst grasses in open situations. Nitrogen fixers.

Leucanthemum vulgare: The ox-eye daisy is an excellent matrix former. Self-sows actively in many situations and spreads steadily amongst grasses by short surface rhizomes.

Lotus corniculatus: Low-growing, persistent legume with yellow, nectar-rich flowers, associates well with a variety of grasses and other plants. A nitrogen fixer.

Lupinus polyphyllus: A deep-rooted perennial, best in neutral to acid soils in well-drained situations, but tolerant of seasonally wet locations too.

Phleum pratense: Widely cultivated, moderately vigorous grass. A good matrix-former in mixed meadows.

Pilosella aurantiaca: A rapid spreader, producing numerous offsets on short runners. Best in dry, competitive situations that reduce its rate of movement. Decorative, glowing burnt orange flowers during summer.

Plantago lanceolata: Easily grown species, tolerant of a wide range of conditions.

Poa pratensis: Another excellent, persistent matrix-forming grass that associates well with other plants.

Scabiosa columbaria subsp. *ochroleuca:* A pale yellow or ivory version of the pale blue scabious, and a plant for very well-drained, dry situations. Elsewhere, it may produce excessive foliage at the expense of flowers.

Solidago speciosa: One of many goldenrods valued for their yellow flowers in late summer and autumn; inclined to spread over-enthusiastically in some situations.

Trifolium pratense: Red clover is a widespread, tolerant plant that associates well with grasses and other herbs; produces abundant nectar and is a nitrogen fixer.

- Many attractive and desirable plants do not germinate or fail to establish from broadcast seed.
- High proportions of the seed in some mixtures consist of cornfield weeds rather than meadow wildflowers. These germinate quickly and reliably and produce attractive flowering plants rapidly, but disappear within a year or two.
- The species represented are most likely be those that are native to the country concerned, although the seeds will not necessarily be collected from native populations, and many gardeners might prefer to use a broader range drawn from similar habitats in other parts of the world.
- Seedlings that emerge do so in direct competition with the on-site population of weeds and they may find this competition overwhelming.

It may be better to propagate stocks of selected plants from seed under protected conditions, and plant them out in the meadow as young plants. This can be done immediately before sowing a meadow mixture over the whole area.

The mixture of seeds sown will be supplemented by the presence of seeds already in the soil, and what comes up may be quite different from expectations. On dry infertile soils, plants from seed mixtures are likely to establish themselves successfully despite competition from 'weed' species, and the two very often complement each other and develop together into a successful community.

In moister, more fertile conditions, a few vigorous, often 'weedy', species are likely to take over unless precautions are taken to prevent this. The most effective measures include those that reduce the levels of available nutrients: either by mowing closely or scything three or four times a year for several years, removing the cuttings each time, or more radically and often preferably, stripping 5 to 15 cm (2 – 6 in) of topsoil off the surface before attempting to form the meadow. This sounds drastic, but should be no problem now that earthmoving equipment is readily available to tackle operations of any size, from a few square metres to several hectares.

The arrival of a digger is very likely to stimulate ideas about excavating hollows that could be filled with water,

transforming a simple ambition to make a meadow into a much more satisfying garden landscape following the classical recipe of grass, wild flowers and water. The topsoil removed is valuable material that can be used to increase the depth of soil in other situations.

Gardening with tussocks

Tussock grasses can be used in dry locations to form striking and characteristic gardenscapes based on the repetitive patterns of the spaced-out grasses. Wide spacing is essential to give each one room to develop and the size and vigour of the species used should be carefully matched to the situation ranging from the compact tussocks of the glaucous leaved fescues, which can be used effectively in the smallest gardens, to the vast space-consuming mounds of pampas grasses.

Spaces between the clumps of grass can be occupied by other plants, using carpeters like lamiums, acaenas, duchesnias and thymes or, especially in situations where seasonal droughts occur regularly, with seasonal occupants like annuals and bulbs.

Open matrix communities

Swards, in which grasses play a minor role, and broad-leaved plants are the more dominant part of the matrix, occur in some situations. Well brought up gardeners, regarding these as inexcusable examples of neglected, threadbare lawns, instinctively try to remedy the situation with top dressings of marl, peat and any other materials they can lay their hands on to improve the soil, and enable it to retain the water and fertilisers on which well-maintained close-knit swards depend.

Instead of following this instinctive response it is worth considering how these communities might play a more positive part, especially where soils are thin, stony or gravelly, and indirectly, even on heavy clays, in poorly drained situations where lawns remain unapproachably saturated with water during the winter and wet spells. At first sight, these seem totally unsuitable for this kind of planting, but bury the clay beneath a layer of gravel 30 cm (1 ft) deep, and you bury its problems with it. Then the clay, forgotten but not gone, serves a useful purpose as an inexhaustible source of water and nutrients.

Tussock grasses, whatever their
size, contrast excitingly with
their broad-leaved companions.
Elephant grasses (top left)
can dominate even the largest
of borders. Spiky clumps of
tussocks (top right) add diversity
to rich plantings of trees, shrubs
and perennials. A composition
of small plants and paving
(above) in a corner of a garden
is transformed by the presence
of tussocks. Elsewhere, they
make an intriguingly appropriate
setting (left) for a sculptured
figure of the takahe, one of New
Zealand's rarest birds.

A: Festuca glauca planted
40cm. apart. Between them
are creeping Thymes,
Crocus chrysanthus and
Allium narcissiflorum.
B: Carex buchananii
planted 70cm. apart.
They are interplanted with
Acaenas, Tulip kauffmanniana
and Allium karataviense.
C: Stipa gigantea at 2m. centres are interplanted
with Rock Roses and Allium christophii.

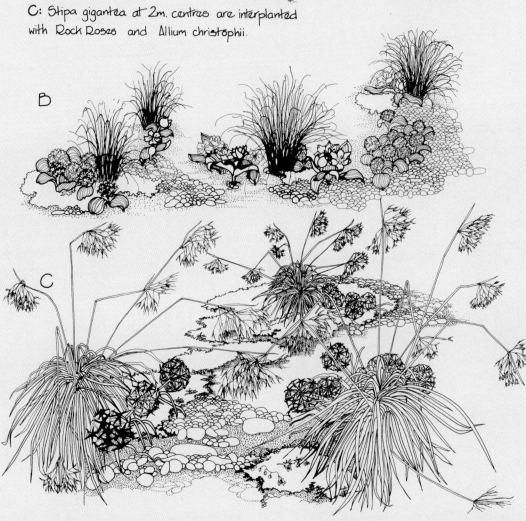

Tussock grasses should be carefully chosen according to the space
available. These three drawings show different tussocks set out at
appropriate spaces and interplanted with broad-leaved plants and bulbs.

Tussock (or bunch) grasses for gardens

Some tussock grasses produce powerful, but often seasonally open, matrices formed by the often strikingly regularly spaced 'citadels' of grasses, between which bulbous and broad-leaved plants grow during seasons when sufficient rainfall is available to provide for their needs.

Andropogon gerardii: This and other species, e.g., *A. ternarius* and *virginicus*, are tall, upright, sometimes distinguished grasses with attractive blue, crimson or rust-coloured foliage.

Arundo donax*: An enormous grass with broad leaves. Most effective as a specimen especially the variety *versicolor.* In mild locations it displays an alarming tendency to colonise beyond the bounds of the garden.

Carex buchananii: Bright copper-bronze foliage and tight, compact tussock form make this ideal for spaced planting with bulbs, etc.

Chionochloa conspicua: An imposing, strikingly handsome tussock with tall, creamy fawn inflorescences, invaluable as a focal point, or where space allows, as part of a community.

Chionochloa rubra: A medium-sized, finely formed tussock with russet-red foliage which provides an excellent setting for bulbs and wildflowers when planted in groups.

Cortaderia selloana: A widely grown South American pampas grass. *C. richardii* and *C. fulvida* from New Zealand are often better choices in gardens and deserve wider recognition.

Dactylis glomerata: A coarse tussock, growing naturally as individual clumps which often form dense matrices in fertile meadows, where it can be difficult to restrain the plant's vigour.

Deschampsia cespitosa: A handsome grass, looking good well into the winter; available in a variety of bronze, gold or rust coloured forms. Best used as a matrix interplanted with bulbs and ground cover.

Elegia capensis*: Probably the most amenable restio for gardens, with architectural inflorescences, and narrow, upright reed-like stems with striking ivory and crimson ligules.

Erianthus alopecuroides: A good specimen plant for light shade. Other species prefer sun and are notable for the colours of their autumnal foliage.

Festuca amethystina: This and *F. glauca* and *cinerea* are represented by numerous narrow-leaved cultivars with steel-blue foliage.

Helictotrichon sempervirens: Excellent blue-leaved tussock when used as a specimen or in groups in well-drained, cool situations. Does not thrive in hot, humid conditions.

Luzula nivea: A dense clump-forming woodrush for semi-shaded situations with unremarkable foliage, but striking ivory-white inflorescences in summer. Self-seeds freely to occupy spare spaces.

Miscanthus sinensis: Giant grasses, best in moist situations with long growing seasons. Numerous cultivars with variegated or crimson-flushed foliage are available.

Molinia caerulea: Excellent in groups interplanted with bulbs and ground cover. Small plants take time to establish.

Pennisetum alopecuroides: Excellent in small groups, or massed for effect. Good ground-holding qualities and associates well with other plants.

Poa labillardierei: Dense, weed-resistant tussocks of narrow grey-blue leaves are effective planted in groups with bulbs, etc.

Sorghastrum nutans: Strikingly effective grass used individually or in groups with statuesque inflorescences from early summer persisting into late winter.

Stipa gigantea: A tall grass with unremarkable foliage but strikingly handsome, mobile, graceful inflorescences. Most effective when planted as a specimen in fertile situations, or in widely spaced groups.

Themada rubra*: Russet-coloured foliage and a tight, but graceful tussock-form provides an excellent setting for interplanted bulbs and flowers.

* Note: plants marked with an asterisk are vulnerable to frost in cold locations.

Carpets of mosses, lichens and scabweeds on a glacial moraine (below left), or ourisias and dracophyllums embedded in mosses high on a mountain (below right top) are examples of single-layered matrices, found only in extreme conditions. Such fragile matrices are vulnerable to invasion by more vigorous plants in gardens, and likely to succeed only in freely drained, infertile settings which discourage weeds. Gravel gardens (below right, bottom) are one way to do this.

Plants for open matrix communities

Open matrices are vulnerable to invasion by weeds unless climatic or other conditions on site prevent their establishment. In most gardens, seasonal drought or free-draining substrates such as gravel, scree or small stones are essential prerequisites for success with such communities.

Acaena novae-zelandiae: This and other species produce mats of close-knit foliage. They are particularly effective interplanted with upright tussocks of small grasses, especially those with glaucous, rufous or copper foliage.

Alchemilla erythropoda: A compact, ground-holding lady's mantle, with distinctive foliage which contrasts effectively with grasses, and prostrate neighbours.

Campanula cochlearifolia: A misleadingly delicate looking little plant with tiny blue, purple or white bells.

Spreads by underground rhizomes to occupy spare spaces, but is not vigorous enough to be a threat.

Crocus chrysanthus cultivars: These are examples of small bulbs which contribute little to a matrix, but add greatly to the attractions of a garden.

Cyclamen cilicium: This cyclamen and other species have attractive flowers, but they are especially valuable for their ground-holding foliage in winter, notably *C. hederaefolium.*

Globularia meridionalis: Tenacious, long-lived, creeping perennials which gradually build up mats of evergreen foliage dotted with spherical heads of bright blue flowers throughout the summer.

Hebe odora var. *prostrata:* Forms a spreading, weed-excluding evergreen mat, with attractive glossy leaves and spikes of small white flowers.

Iris pumila: Excellent for seasonally dry settings, but contributes little to the matrix in competitive situations.

Laurentia (Isotoma) fluviatilis: Builds up into dense, ground-hugging mats of tiny green leaves studded with star-shaped blue or white flowers throughout the summer.

Mazus reptans: Requires perennial moisture in a gravel garden, when its mat-forming woody stems with tiny leaves and comparatively large, deep lilac flowers occupy ground between taller plants well.

Phlox hoodii: This and several species of 'alpine' phloxes, for example, *P. douglasii* and *P. subulata*, can be planted for brightly floriferous small-scale ground cover; they are excellent when planted with the smaller spring bulbs.

Pimelea prostrata*: Moulds itself naturally over rocky outcrops; prostrate forms have good ground-holding qualities and form tough, evergreen, contour-following mats.

Polygonatum hookeri: Unlike any other Solomon's seal, this tiny plant with unexpected lilac-coloured flowers barely above ground level, spreads underground as an infiller and modest coloniser.

Pratia pedunculata: More vigorous than *P. angulata* (better for smaller areas). Its wider ranging mats suit large spaces better.

Raoulia hookeri: This and several other species are mainstays of naturally occurring communities of scabweeds, which provide models for gardens in exceptionally free-draining, but moist, situations.

Saxifraga 'Whitehill': Many saxifrages, including the silvery-leaved encrusteds, can be planted as distinctive ground-holding dot plants in non-competitive settings.

Sempervivum arachnoideum: This and other houseleeks and their cousins, the sedums or stonecrops, can be surprisingly effective ground holders, especially in seasonally dry situations.

Thymus x *citriodorus:* Numerous, moderately vigorous prostrate thymes with fragrant, often colourful, foliage make effective, though sometimes fragile, matrices in well-drained situations.

Veronica prostrata: Forms dense, compact mats of evergreen foliage almost obscured for a brief period each spring with masses of bright blue or pink flowers. Occupies space effectively without being invasive.

Viola hederacea: A vigorous carpet-forming perennial for moist situations with bi-coloured white and blue flowers. *V. cornuta* and other montane species are more suitable for gravel gardens.

* Note: plants marked with an asterisk are vulnerable to frost in cold locations.

Bowing to the Inevitable

The owner's grandfather planted many of the trees in this 1.5 ha (4 acre) garden in the English Midlands, and the last planned changes had been made by his parents in the 1930s when two gardeners, an odd-job man and a garden boy were employed to keep the place in immaculate order. More recently, the owner with the help of a retired farm worker, has struggled vainly to arrest progressive dereliction, and maintain once broad and neatly gravelled paths winding between misshapen Lawson cypresses looming amongst a scattering of senile and dangerously decaying trees. Bindweed threatened to envelop shrubberies surrounding broad moth-eaten lawns, and overgrown hedges encroached on flower beds full of ground elder. The farm worker died shortly before the owner retired from his practice as a solicitor in Derby, forcing serious thoughts about the future. The solicitor has played and worked in the garden since childhood, is physically active for his age and enjoys being in the open air. He has never married, and friends have repeatedly urged him to move to a smaller, more manageable place, but he grew up in it, has always lived in it and loves it. He could not bear the idea even of changing its comfortable familiarity, let alone moving out altogether. Eventually he had to accept the fact that if he wanted to continue living there, something drastic had to be done.

Review

A. This garden, designed when labour was cheap and plentiful, could only be adapted to today's circumstances by fundamental, often distressingly destructive changes. The only way to make these acceptable was as part of constructive improvements which captured the solicitor's interest and imagination.

B. The owner had long grown so familiar with the place he could scarcely imagine it in any other guise, and found it impossible to visualise changes radical enough to solve his problems.

C. The main assets were a number of fine specimen trees; some good quality stone in the tumble-down walls of the kitchen garden, and a generally well-structured, easily worked, though now rather impoverished, light sandy loam soil.

D. He was finally persuaded that one, increasingly elderly, man could look after a garden of this size only by following the principles of matrix planting, and paying a contractor occasionally to do the heavier, more laborious tasks.

Outcome

A. and B.

- Operations started with a survey of the garden, and an assessment of the condition of the trees.

- Following this, a plan, visual impressions of parts of the new garden, and detailed notes about the proposals were presented to the owner and, after discussions and some modifications, these formed the basis for work on a radically different layout.

- Dead, decaying and redundant trees were removed; broken-down walls demolished or in a few cases rebuilt; almost all the hedges were grubbed out, and most of the paths eliminated.

C.

- The patchwork of old paths, lawns and flower beds was dealt with by removing all unwanted plants, filling in many of the paths and spraying the lawns with glyphosate to kill the turf. The whole area was then graded to form a continuous surface. A small area on a terrace constructed close to the house was sown with lawn grass seed. The rest was turned into meadows with mown paths through them, no wider than could be cut by two passes of the mower.

- The best specimen trees were used as focal points, supplemented by new introductions. The latter included native and exotic species, chosen

for their ability to grow with minimal attention, and planted to frame the garden.
- Stone from the walls was used to make a raised terrace along the front of the house, to provide a view over the garden.

D.
- The outstanding innovation was the formation of two small lakes, set amongst the meadows and trees, to form the centrepiece of the garden with grassy meadows in the foreground and trees on a raised bank, made from the excavated topsoil, in the background. The subsoil was used to raise the level of the terrace.

The Plants

The well-structured, free-draining and rather impoverished soil proved to be an ideal foundation on which to set up meadows. Numerous bulbs were planted, with an emphasis on the relatively small hybrid species daffodils, and crocuses, and an attractive balance was produced by planting selected species of wild flowers individually from plugs, immediately before oversowing the whole area with a meadow seed mixture.

The raised bank behind the lakes was planted moderately densely with a screen of trees, chosen for their diverse shapes, foliage and autumn colours and affinity with water. They included: *Alnus cordata* and *A. glutinosa* 'Pyramidalis', *Populus alba* 'Richardii', *P. lasiocarpa* and *P. tremula* 'Pendula'; *Salix alba* var. *vitellina* and its scarlet-twigged form, 'Britzensis', and *Taxodium distichum*. Few wildflowers, apart from *Primula vulgaris*, *Anemone sylvestris*, *Viola riviniana* and *V. odorata* and *Galium odoratum* were planted amongst the grasses in this area, since it would soon become heavily shaded, but bulbs including large drifts of *Narcissus* 'Little Witch', 'Jack Snipe', 'Liberty Bells', 'March Sunshine' and 'Thalia' were planted amongst the trees.

Wild flowers and grasses planted or sown in the more sunlit meadows, between the house and the lakes, included *Galium verum*, *Lotus corniculatus*, *Daucus carota*, *Ranunculus arvensis*, *Silene alba*, *Primula veris*, *Leucanthemum vulgare*, *Centaurea scabiosa*, *Prunella vulgaris*, *Plantago lanceolata*, *Geranium pratense*, *Scabiosa columbaria*, *Rumex acetosa*, *Vicia cracca*, *Lathyrus pratensis*, *Trifolium campestre* and *Achillea millefolium*. Drifts of the large Dutch crocuses and several patches of *Fritillaria meleagris* were planted in these meadows, but no daffodils since the owner, sensitive to hayfever, insisted on mowing just before the grasses came into flower before the daffodil foliage would have died down.

Kiwi Antique Dealer's Blessed Plot

The owner runs an antiques and applied arts business from the ground floor of a fashionable timber house on The Terrace in Wellington, New Zealand. He has had a new house built for himself and his mother on a stony, well-drained, dry section of bush south of Blenheim, to which he commutes at weekends, and often nips home for a day or two in the middle of the week. Formerly covered with bush, it had been a sheep run before being abandoned some years earlier, and colonised by manuka and gorse, with occasional tree ferns in the damper hollows. A few ancient cabbage trees are the only remnants of the original bush. The Marlborough rock daisy *(Pachystegia insignis)* grows in a small, abandoned quarry in the garden and is a source of great pride. He tells everybody it grows nowhere else in the world. The owner's previous perceptions of gardening, derived from wet and windy walks in the Botanic Gardens in Wellington, left him with a decidedly cold attitude towards its attractions. His new acquisition has fired a passion for it, and he not only spends all the time he can spare gardening, but ropes his boyfriends in to help at the weekends.

Review

A. Grass over much of the site maintained a moderately good, but fragile soil structure, due to the low levels of humus. The soil is very free draining, and the small reserves of potash and phosphates it may once have possessed had been lost due to bad management.

B. Despite enthusiasm for his new-found recreation, the section is too large to garden all of it intensively, or for any attempt at rapid overall soil improvement.

C. He expressed an aversion to the only form of extensive gardening he knew – the stilted arrangements of specimen trees and shrubs set out in grass lawns in the Botanic Garden.

D. Annual rainfall is not as deficient as the dessicated appearance of the vegetation during spring and early summer droughts suggests. Water conservation measures, combined with the use of suitably drought-resistant plants, enabled him to make a very attractive garden.

Outcome

A.
- No attempts were made to dig, plough or cultivate the ground as these actions would have destroyed the fragile structure and profile of the soil.
- Intensive planting and management were confined to a small area near the house, and radiating from it to form vistas flanked by more extensively treated settings. One or two of the damper spots, where tree ferns were growing, were also picked out for intensive planting.
- In these areas, the soil was covered with mulches to reduce surface evaporation, and provide a source of humus to boost its water-holding capacity.
- Top-dressings of a general fertiliser were applied on top of the mulches before planting, and repeated annually until a complete cover of plants had developed.

B.
- Elsewhere, invading gorse was sprayed and grubbed out, and broad paths cut between thickets of manuka to form a pattern of clumps separated by more open areas.

C.
- Much of this was planted as 'garden bush', centred on the clumps of manuka. These areas were not mulched or fertilised apart from individual trees and some of the larger shrubs, which were given a generous spread of pea haulm and fed for the first three years after planting.
- 'Garden bush' – mixtures of native and exotic trees and shrubs – was planted to form matrices based mainly on canopy and shrub layers above a patchwork ground cover, including numerous bulbs.
- Steep slopes round the quarry to one side of the house were landscaped with tussock grasses, interplanted with bulbs, perennials and shrubs.

The Plants

Overall, the planting will eventually establish dense, self-maintaining groups of trees and shrubs separated from one another by winding paths – broad in places and narrower in others – forming a pattern of interconnected glades, and providing permanent shade and shelter over much of the garden. The main exception, apart from the 'gardened' areas close to the house, will be the sunlit slope occupied by tussock grasses.

A number of trees, amongst them several members of the pea family chosen for their drought tolerance and/or ability to fix nitrogen, including *Albizia julibrissin* f. *rosea,* were planted in the early stages, as well as *Callistemon citrinus*; *Cornus capitata* and a matching pair of *C. controversa* 'Variegata' flanking a vista from the house; *Dodonea viscosa* and *D.* 'Purpurea'; *Gleditsia triacanthos* 'Sunburst'; several American hybrids of *Lagerstroemia indica* and *L. fauriei*, including the low-growing 'Victor' and the taller 'Acomo' and 'Tonto'. After returning from a visit to Cape Town, the owner insisted on trying *Leucadendron argenteum*, more in hope of enjoying its gleaming silver foliage than expectation of success. *Pittosporum crassifolium*, *eugenioides* and *ralphii* were planted for rapid matrix development, also *Quercus ilex*; *Sophora japonica*, numerous *S. tetraptera* to attract nectar-feeding tui, and *Umbellularia californica*.

Trees in the 'garden bush' were underplanted with tough, self-maintaining drought-resistant shrubs including *Artemisia arborescens* and *Atriplex halimus* for their silver foliage; *Brachyglottis repanda* 'Purpurea' and clumps of *Brachyglottis* 'Sunshine'; several cultivars of callistemon with scarlet or mauve bottle brushes; *Carmichaelia odorata* and *C. williamsii*; *Colutea arborescens*; *Corynocarpus laevigatus* and its cultivar *C.* 'Picturata', to attract pigeons; *Euphorbia characias* subsp *wulfenii*, which seeded itself freely; *Euryops pectinatus*; *Grevillea juniperina* f. *sulphurea* and *G. rosmarinifolia*; *Hebe* x *franciscana*, *hulkeana* and *speciosa*; *Indigofera heterantha* and *I. potaninii*, amongst other nitrogen-fixing members of the pea family; *Olearia albida* and *O. traversii*; *Pachystegia insignis*; *Phlomis fruticosa* and *P. italica*; *Pomaderris kumeraho* despite misgivings about its hardiness; and *Pseudopanax ferox* for its weird form when young, and sturdily independent air when mature.

Chionochloa rubra dominated areas of tussock grasses, supplemented with *Carex buchananii*, *C. flagellifera* and *C. lucida*; the latter planted in patches as ground cover, rather than as tussocks, with *Chionochloa flavicans* and *Cortaderia richardii* individually or in small groups emerging boldly above the general level. A number of perennials were set out amongst the tussocks including *Acanthus mollis* and *A. spinosus*; *Astelia nervosa*; *Eremurus stenophyllus* subsp. *stenophyllus* and *E. isabellinus* 'Shelford' hybrids; *Eryngium agavifolium* and *E. proteiflorum*; and *Phlomis russelliana* to provide contrasting foliage textures and forms or bright splashes of flower. Large groups of phormium cultivars complemented the grasses along one side of the garden and formed a link with the garden bush.

Bulbous plants filled spaces between the tussocks, amongst them crocosmias including 'Firebird', 'Spitfire' and 'Vulcan'; cultivars of *Nerine bowdenii* and *N. undulata*; *Triteleia laxa* 'Koningin Fabiola'; and ixias, sparaxis and tigridias.

Here, and amongst the 'garden bush', transients including *Digitalis* x *mertonensis; Foeniculum vulgare* 'Purpureum'; *Salvia sclarea* var. *turkestanica* and *Silybum marianum* were introduced in the hope they would seed themselves and occupy spare spaces within the developing matrices.

Working Magic in Essex

This is the garden of a cottage surrounded by an old orchard and meadows in a village near Billericay in Essex, England. It is owned by a freelance dubbing mixer, who is single, approaching thirty, and works from home and part-time in a production company in Grays on the Thames estuary. The garden lies in a sheltered position with exceptionally low rainfall, but is exposed on one side to easterly winds. Her predecessor had grown vegetables on most of its 0.1ha (quarter of an acre), apart from the far end where heavier soil borders a ditch, which she had used as a hen run. The owner enjoys her garden, but for weeks or even months is too busy to spend much time in it. Neighbours regard her as an eccentric, arty person with an incomprehensible job. They make knowing comments about her knowledge of herbs, and poisonous plants – one or two have nicknamed her 'the witch'. They are nonplussed by her contention that lawns and conifers are out of place in a country cottage garden.

Review

A. The owner's strong affinities with the rural setting of the garden made her averse to gardenesque approaches which would have set it apart from its surroundings. She preferred an informal design which would make fewer demands on her time.

B. Previous owners had neglected the soil in their pursuit of vegetables, reducing it to an infertile, stony state, apart from the site of the chicken run on a heavier clay loam.

C. The infertility of the soil near the house, combined with low rainfall, thwarted attempts to make a cottage garden with masses of plants crammed into borders.

The soil of the old chicken run encouraged plants to grow lushly and grossly in the spring, before collapsing as the soil cracked open at the first hint of summer drought.

D. Different plants, and a different style of management were necessary to make the most of variations from one part of the garden to another.

Outcome

A.

- Taking a cue from the orchard over the hedge, the owner decided on a simple design of grass and fruit trees for the whole garden. The only path was a 1 m (3 ft) wide strip of mown grass winding between the trees and returning in a broad loop to the house.
- Tests showed that the ground did not need liming, and since the meadow would be easier to establish without it, the owner decided not to apply a general fertiliser. Instead, when planting trees she mixed soil removed from the holes in which they were planted with a few good handfuls of blood, fish and bone before replacing it over their roots.
- Trees were planted early in the winter, almost a year before the first meadow plants, and surrounded by circular sheets of black polythene 1 m (3 ft) in diameter, to preserve a weed-free space round each.

B.

- Half standard apple and pear trees were planted towards the house, with plums in the old chicken run; set out as an open, irregular orchard, and left unstaked to allow the stems to adopt natural, balanced postures as they developed.
- During the first summer the ground between the

trees was sprayed twice with glyphosate to destroy weeds – mainly couch grass in the old vegetable patch, and stinging nettles in the hen run.

C.

- Seeds of meadow species sown in containers in a cold frame in January germinated during the spring, and seedlings were potted into small pots. They were planted out around the trees during the late summer. A few weeks later bulbs were put in amongst them.
- The owner also set out small plants of a number of species growing in plugs and rootrainers obtained from the British Trust for Conservation Volunteers, as well as exotic meadow plants bought from nurseries and garden centres.
- Meadow seed mixtures were broadcast over the whole area the following spring, and gently raked in amongst the plants and bulbs.

D.

- The meadow overlying the old vegetable garden was scythed in late June and again in early September to tidy up for the winter, leaving the cuttings where they fell to recycle nutrients, and as a source of humus. Scything was adopted because the owner found it did her a lot more good than inhaling fumes from noisy mowers or strimmers, and was much kinder to frogs and other wildlife.
- The meadow established on the site of the chicken run was scythed monthly from the end of April to late June, and again in October each year, and the mowings were removed in order to reduce excess nutrients inherited from the chickens.

The Plants

The owner was astonished to discover the range of fruit trees obtainable from a local nursery, many completely unfamiliar to her. She eventually chose the apples 'D'Arcy Spice' (for its local associations), 'Ellison's Orange', 'Arthur Turner' (recommended to her for its beautiful flowers as much as for its fruits), and 'Orleans Reinette'. Plums included 'Cambridge Gage', 'Early Transparent Gage' and 'Goldfinch' and pears 'Beth', 'Louise Bonne of Jersey' and 'Beurré Hardy'.

Plants adapted to relatively heavy, fertile soils were planted in the old chicken run, concentrating on species in flower during mid to late summer and autumn. Grasses used as the basis of the matrix included *Agrostis stolonifera*, *Alopecurus pratensis*, *Briza media*, *Hordeum secalinum* and *Poa pratensis*. Native and exotic wildflowers planted or sown amongst these included: *Astrantia maxima*, *Achillea ptarmica*, *Leucanthemum vulgare*, *Lotus corniculatus* and *L. uliginosus*, *Medicago lupulina*, *Primula vulgaris* (using an 'old-fashioned' perennial strain), *Campanula glomerata*, *Prunella vulgaris* in several colour forms; *Aster amellus*, *A. divaricatus* and *A. lateriflorus*, *Persicaria bistorta* 'Superba', *Gentiana cruciata*, *Geranium sylvaticum* and *G. endressii*, *Centaurea scabiosa*, *Filipendula vulgaris*, *Sanguisorba officinalis* and *Ranunculus repens*. *Cyclamen coum*, *Galanthus nivalis* 'Flore Pleno' and *Erythronium dens-canis* were planted for winter and early spring colour.

Most of the grasses and plants used on the site of the vegetable garden grow naturally on well-drained, calcareous grasslands. These included: *Briza maxima*, *Cynosurus cristatus*, several fine-leaved Festuca cultivars, *Koeleria macrantha* and *Phleum pratense*. Wildflowers included *Anthyllis vulneraria*, *Galium verum*, *Hippocrepis comosa*, *Cichorium intybus*, *Eryngium planum*, *Plantago media*, *Primula veris* (including copper-coloured forms), *Veronica chamaedrys*, several cultivars and colour forms of *Achillea millefolium*, *Aquilegia atrata* and *A. vulgaris* (which promptly hybridised), *Dianthus carthusianorum*, *Geranium pratense*, *Pilosella aurantiaca* and *P. officinarum*, *Ranunculus bulbosus* and *Tragopogon pratensis* (for its vast globular 'dandelion' seed heads).

Numerous bulbs were also planted in this section, including cultivars of *Colchicum autumnale*, and the autumn crocuses *Crocus speciosus* and *C. zonatus*; and *Galanthus elwesii*, several narcissus hybrids such as 'Rip van Winkle' 'Jumblie', 'Bambi' and 'Tête a Tête' for its early and prolonged flowering period; several fosteriana tulips, like 'Madame Lefeber' and 'Yellow Purissima' (chosen for their flamboyant flowers and ability to persist amongst grasses for many years); *Ornithogalum umbellatum* and a few clumps of *Camassia cusickii*.

garden
pools *and* wetlands

MY FIRST WATER GARDEN was a disappointment. I had grasped the principle of a pond as a hole in the ground filled with water, inhabited by interesting creatures. I dug a hole, poured in a couple of cans of water to fill it to the brim, and added a dozen tadpoles out of a jam jar. In the morning I was more than disgruntled to discover that my expectations of a band of happy tadpoles disporting in a limpid pool was no more than a muddy hole dotted with the dead hopes of future frogs.

Many people share my naive belief that a pond is simply a hole in the ground filled with water, including those who sell us bath tub-sized pond formers made of fibre glass. Ponds are not simple. They are amongst the most complex and dynamic of all natural environments and, like meadows, they remove gardeners from a world where control can be enforced with spade, fork or hoe to one where they must depend on their skills to match the needs and aptitudes of different plants with the nature and demands of different situations.

Naturally, ponds are:

Constantly evolving – filling up with silt and debris, eventually becoming swamps that turn into wetlands and end up as meadows.

Repeatedly changing – through the seasons, and even day to day, as water levels, nutrient content and temperatures rise and fall.

Intensely competitive – due to the unlimited availability of water, the constant renewal of nutrients and exposure to abundant sunlight.

Prone to excess – changing conditions allied to ready availability of water, nutrients and sunlight lead to periodic flushes of algal growth, excessive proliferation of water plants and marginals, and other events which disturb the balance of aquatic ecosystems.

Large ponds, usually referred to as lakes by their proud owners, cause few problems, apart from eventually silting up, but by comparison with most natural ponds, garden pools are often scarcely more than puddles. They experience exaggeratedly rapid and large variations in temperature, and the high content of decaying plant material, in proportion to their volume, produces conditions seldom found naturally except during the final stages in the evolution of a pond to a bog. Not surprisingly, small ponds raise fears and doubts about their state of health and suffer from well-meant attempts to 'balance' them. The most common error is to regard green water as stagnant, leading to its removal, vigorous cleansing activity and replenishment with fresh water. But green water owes its colour to photosynthesising algae,

(Opposite) Pools are complex, dynamic garden settings supporting luxuriant growth, in which success depends on careful choice of plants. Here well-matched, mega-powerful herbaceous perennials jostling for space along the banks of a pond have formed a competitive balance. Weaker members are quickly eliminated and forgotten. Take-over bids by stronger members are more of a problem because attempts to remove such tenacious plants seriously damage the banks of the pond.

which maintain a supply of life-giving oxygen, and is healthy water. From the gardener's point of view, plants perform this service more decoratively than algae, and the route to success lies in installing carefully selected mixtures of plants to mop up the nutrients and light on which the algae depend. Until the plants take over, we should be grateful to the algae, and refrain from interfering with the processes through which well-sited, well-designed and well-planted ponds manage themselves.

Siting, design and planting of ponds

Oxygen is the vital force that enables water to support life. The successful management of any pond and, most critically, small ones depends on ensuring a supply of dissolved oxygen in the water. Anything which adds to this supply is good; anything which depletes it is bad.

Siting

Sunlight drives photosynthesis, producing sugars that plants need from carbon dioxide and water and – just as importantly – oxygen, which is released into the water. So, a pond should be sunlit. But small, shallow ponds exposed to the unremitting force of the sun become airless tepid baths in which the inhabitants gasp and die. Shading of some kind must be provided, either by arranging for the surface to become partially covered by foliage, and/or by plants or structures around the edge.

Aquatics with floating leaves, including water lilies and water hawthorns, provide ideal shade; densest in summer, and decreasing to nothing in the winter. Cultivars of water lilies come in a range of sizes capable of matching the needs

Lakes (below left) are easier to manage than ornamental pools (below right). Small volumes of shallow water suffer from variations in temperature and evaporation, and repeated topping-up raises the levels of nutrients. Skilful and varied planting – and a hands-off approach while they find their own balance – is the road to success.

of almost any pond – from an expansive lake to a puddle in a tub – and choosing these is simply a matter of taking care and listening to advice. The water hawthorn survives frost in cold climates provided it is planted at least 60 cm (2 ft) deep, and its vigour is restricted in these cold conditions. Under natural, milder conditions it often grows in shallow pools that dry out during the summer.

Plants sited around the banks of a pond will provide shade for part of the day – on the east, during the morning; on the west, during the afternoon, etc. But if quantities of falling leaves blow into the pond, bacteria may consume all the oxygen during their decomposition, producing the black lifeless brew that is truly stagnant water. Deciduous trees and shrubs make bad neighbours for small ponds and should be used sparingly. Plants whose spent leaves can be more easily removed are bamboos, phormiums, tree ferns, palms and large perennials including rheums, rodgersias, darmeras and ligularias, all of which pose fewer problems. Bridges, summer houses, decking and other structures can also be used to provide shade decoratively, effectively and precisely with no problems from fallen leaves, while making the water more accessible and enjoyable.

Ponds should be sunlit, yet partly shaded. This paradox is resolved by using plants with floating leaves to partially cover the surface (above left), and by growing plants with spreading foliage on the banks (above right).

Moving water is more exciting than water that stands still. Tumbling water (top) or fountains (right) add immeasurably to the atmosphere of a garden.

Design

Being told large ponds are easier to manage than small ones offers little comfort to owners of small gardens in search of a 'Water Feature'. Nevertheless a great many ponds are made unnecessarily puny; a measly couple of square feet gracing the rock garden; a trivial ditch-like moat dividing the patio from the lawn; a dank, dark hole like a dinosaur's lost kidney in the corner of a flower bed. The horizontal lines of ponds interact with the vertical planting around them, just as lawns do. In design terms they can substitute for, or complement, a lawn and do so most effectively when bold enough to make an impression. Ponds as major features in their own right, rather than secondary attributes of something else, would often be easier to look after and be more effective, too.

Still waters proverbially run deep, and depth is a desirable attribute in a pond, however small, though it is seldom necessary to exceed 60 cm (2 ft) in a small pond, or 2 m (6 ft 6 in) in a large one. Still waters also miss out on the sound and play of moving water, which is not only an attractive facet of ponds but also helps to oxygenate their water. Fountains come to mind and

can lead on to grandiose dreams of vast water works, or memories of the simple jets playing into a long canal that relieve the heat of the famous gardens of the Generalife in Granada, Spain. Fountain makers, on whatever scale, invariably contend with problems of water supply and blocked jets. At a modest level, water supply for a small pond is not usually a problem, and pumps of all sizes can be bought to drive any fountains your imagination can devise. But blocked jets will still be a problem, caused mainly by the long strands of filamentous algae, one of nature's most effective devices for clogging small holes. One solution to the problem can be seen at Longwood Gardens, where a clear bourn of limpid water floods over the lip of the impressive spring known as the Eye of the World, and cascades down a gorge into the pond below. This spectacle loses much of its appeal at close quarters where the air is filled with the stench of the chlorine used to destroy any potentially problem-causing life forms. An alternative to a dead pond is a filter system to remove algae and other debris from the water before it reaches the pump and, if this fails you might do better to avoid fountains in favour of less ambitious alternatives.

The simplest is some form of rill through which water flows, or is pumped, into a basin at a higher level than the pond itself, and drops over an edge into the pool below. This creates movement and sound, and oxygen is absorbed from the air by the disturbance of the falling water. It also makes it possible to grow water lilies, whose leaves provide valuable shade in pools of any size, but are averse to the pitter-patter of drops of water from a fountain.

Under natural conditions, ponds are usually part of a system which includes wetlands, reed-beds or marsh, as well as open water. These buffer the system, making it less liable to sudden, short-term changes in temperature, nutrients and water level. Small ponds in gardens are usually contained within impermeable barriers of plastic, fibreglass or concrete which provide abrupt, and most unnatural, boundaries between the pond and the dry land beyond it. When using plastic or butyl rubber sheets, it is usually relatively easy to combine clear water with neighbouring areas of wetland by excavating well beyond the actual area intended to be open water, laying down the plastic and back-filling part of the excavation. When fertile garden soil is used as back-fill, problems can be caused by excessive algal growth in response to nutrients leached from the soil. These can be alleviated by back-filling with mixtures of gravel and soil in the proportions of three to one.

Wetlands adjoining pools reduce fluctuations in temperature and water level, and mop up excess nutrients. Brightly colourful flowers (below left, top and bottom) add to the attractions of a pondscape, and plants with varied and characterful foliage (below right) enhance atmosphere.

Plants capable of growing in wetland conditions

Perennially saturated soil around ponds and in marshy situations supports vigorous communities of plants with strong matrices, resistant to invasion. Only well adapted, robust species can compete and establish themselves.

Aster novi-belgii: Forms persistent, spreading colonies through rhizomes which mix well with grasses.

Astilbe: Numerous cultivars and subspecies are available with plumes of pink, white or crimson flowers in summer. They grow well in light shade, provided the soil remains constantly moist.

Bupthalmum salicifolium: A useful, long-lived plant for moist, sunny situations, producing a long succession of yellow daisies.

Calamagrostis arundinacea: Reed grasses produce feathery heads of flowers on tall stems, and include forms with variegated foliage. Do well in moist conditions and can tolerate light shade.

Carex pendula: Sedges are naturally at home in these situations. This one is a robust, handsome plant with gracefully pendant spikes of flowers. Many species form persistent matrices with grasses and herbs.

Equisetum robustum: Horsetails spread vigorously, often uncontrollably, by underground rhizomes, and are suitable only for large areas.

Filipendula rubra 'Venusta': Flowering in late summer, these Asiatic meadow sweets associate well with strong growing grasses.

Glyceria maxima var. *variegata*: A vigorously spreading but attractive grass, useful where space and competition from neighbours, allows.

Hibiscus moscheutos * 'Southern Belle' hybrids: These herbaceous plants have fine, soft foliage and there are cultivars with pink or white flowers. Grow best in moist, boggy conditions, with high summer temperatures.

Iris sibirica: Upright clumps of narrow foliage combine well with grasses; contrasting with broad-leaved plants.

Matteucia struthiopteris: The shuttlecock fern spreads by underground rhizomes, and provides attractive contrasts to other foliage forms. Colonies occupy large areas.

Osmunda cinnamomea: A vigorous persistent, ground-holding fern forming strong upright clumps of leaves.

Panicum virgatum: A substantial grass with long panicles of flowers on stout stems. Broadly tolerant of a wide range of conditions.

Patrinia scabiosifolia: Tall, branching perennial, with bright yellow flowers in late summer; best when emerging from a ground cover of lower growing plants.

Phormium tenax: Available in different sizes, forms and foliage colours. Tolerant of dry as well as wet conditions, even as a partially submerged marginal plant.

Primula prolifera (*helodoxa*): Many have showy flowers, in a great variety of colours. Do well, provided neighbours are not too competitive. Many appreciate light or partial shade.

Rubus spectabilis: Infiltrates well amongst grasses and herbs, producing spreading colonies of upright stems.

Spartina pectinata 'Aureomarginata': Spreads moderately by rhizomes and may need to be restrained by strong local competition.

Thelypteris palustris: An excellent, spreading ground-covering fern. Creates interesting contrasts when planted amongst perennials and grasses.

Trollius x *cultorum*: Numerous cultivars and subspecies, with brilliant orange or yellow flowers in late spring, all form ground-holding, long-lived clumps amongst grasses and vigorous herbs.

* Note: plants marked with an asterisk are vulnerable to frost in cold locations.

Variations in depth increase the variety of plants that can be grown in a pond, and shallow and deep ends, or broadly defined areas, work better than the narrow shelves seen in so many diagrams illustrating pond construction. These shelves may impart interestingly craggy profiles to pre-formed pools of fibre glass, but plants lodged on them tend to slide gently off their narrow perches into the depths below.

Water levels of ponds in many parts of the world fall during the summer, and it is not unusual for them to dry up completely. Many water-loving plants adapted to this occurrence are widely grown in gardens but have seldom been deliberately grown in this way because until recently most ponds were made with concrete, and this inevitably led to designs intended to maintain a constant water level.

Plastic and butyl rubber sheets allow more flexible approaches but an unchanging water level remains a standard aim of pond construction and management, and the possibility of deliberately providing for changes in level from one season to another is seldom considered. However, doing so opens the way to enjoying different effects at different times of the year; it avoids the need to top up falling water levels in summer with fresh water from the tap – disturbing the balance and replenishing undesirable nitrates and phosphates – and, because it mimics natural events, it makes it possible to do things and grow plants that do not thrive when levels remain constant.

Many plants flourish in these conditions, and even benefit from them because of the elimination of competition from more vigorous, truly aquatic plants and algae. Similarly, amphibians, particularly frogs and toads, with life cycles adapted to seasonally dry pools benefit from the elimination of fish that prey on their tadpoles.

Plants suitable for inclusion amongst communities growing in and around ponds that dry out in summer

Asclepias incarnata: An upright, perennial which contrasts well with low growing plants, grasses, sedges, etc. Grown mainly for its bright pinky-red flowers.

Bulbinella latifolia*: Forms dense weed-excluding colonies, with numerous yellow or pale orange flowers above long narrow leaves, for the margins of seasonally water-filled depressions.

Caltha palustris: A vigorous, ground-occupying perennial with striking bright yellow or white flowers appearing in early spring. Several forms, varying in vigour, are available.

Gladiolus tristis*: An elegant, pale yellow, fragrant gladiolus that makes little contribution to a matrix, but associates well with low-growing plants in situations subject to winter flooding.

Gunnera manicata: Forms a gigantic, weed-excluding mono-matrix. Requires constantly moist soil throughout the summer. A better choice in many gardens would be the smaller *G. tinctoria*.

Iris pseudacorus: Spreading rhizomes occupy ground to form a robust matrix with other equally vigorous plants, topped by brilliant yellow flowers in late spring.

Lysichiton americanus: Forms colonies of plants whose large leaves shade the space between them, and inhibit growth of intruders. Bright yellow spathes are amongst the first 'flowers' of early spring.

Mimulus moschatus: The monkey musk is a small herbaceous perennial, with large brightly coloured flowers in summer. Infiltrates to fill spaces amongst other marginal plants.

Monochoria korsakowii: This east Asian look-alike of pickerel weed (*Pontederia cordata*) produces bold spikes of deep blue flowers for weeks during late summer.

Myosotis scorpioides: Strikingly attractive, early spring flowering forget-me-not; produces a dense growth of short stems and foliage which fills in spaces between taller plants.

* Note: plants marked with an asterisk are vulnerable to frost in cold locations.

'A' The maximum depth of the pool shown here is 1.5 m (5 ft). The hole excavated to accommodate the pool and its associated areas of wetland is encased with a plastic liner. The open water provides the water lily zone.

'B' The area of shallow water was formed by careful shaping during excavation – back-filling with a mixture of gravel and topsoil 3/1 to provide a basin filled with saturated soil 15 cm (6 in) deep.

'C' The wetland area was also back-filled with the gravel/topsoil mix and separated from, but kept in contact with, the pool by an earth bank formed from turves. This was planted with perennials whose interlacing roots will hold the bank in place, but allow water to seep through to maintain bog conditions in the wetland throughout the year.

Key to upper diagram:

a – header pool with small fountain

b – stepped rill – formed to hold water continuously whether the pump is running or not

c – inlet to overflow

d – return pipe from pool to tank containing the filter and pump

e – filter unit and pump

f - feeder pipe for fountain and header pool

g – fountain jet

Osmunda regalis: An exceptionally retentive ground-holding fern with green or copper foliage, which makes a noble focal point, and combines well with other vigorous plants.

*Ottelia alismoides**: A fragile but attractive plant with pale lilac flowers that seeds itself freely to occupy spaces in the matrix.

Ranunculus ophioglossifolius: A rarely grown annual buttercup, native to seasonally dry ponds. More widely grown are the better known and very vigorous marginals *R. lingua* and *R. flammula*.

Salix alba var. *vitellina* 'Britzensis': Potentially a robust tree, responds well to extremely severe annual or biennial pruning which restricts growth and emphasises the scarlet bark of the young shoots.

Schizostylis coccinea 'Major'*: Numerous cultivars are available, with conspicuous scarlet, pink or white flowers in late autumn/early winter. Benefits from mild, frost-free autumns for the flowers to develop.

Spiraea douglasii: Forms dense, weed-excluding thickets within which few other plants grow well.

Typha laxmannii: One of the smaller, less invasive cat's tails. Others may be too robust for all but large-scale situations. All have sharp-pointed rhizomes liable to penetrate and destroy flexible liners.

Veronica beccabunga: Forms dense, weed-excluding masses of stems and glossy foliage in gaps amongst other plants, in shallow water and on wet ground.

Viburnum opulus: An upright water-tolerant shrub, excellent for the upper canopy of a matrix in very wet conditions.

*Zantedeschia aethiopica**: Grows well in seasonally dry pools with the benefit of a covering of water during the winter to provide protection from frost.

* Note: plants marked with an asterisk are vulnerable to frost in cold locations.

Gardeners in parts of the world where winters are relatively mild and wet – such as Britain, the mid-Atlantic states of the USA and New Zealand – take it for granted that pools are flush with water in winter. But many of the wetland or marginal aquatic plants we grow, or would like to grow, come from summer rainfall regions like the Natal Drakensberg; places in eastern Asia with temperate summer monsoonal climates; areas with intensely cold winters like Alaska or Canada, or high altitudes where rainfall is low or water immobilised in ice and snow during the winter. Plants from these places grow in ground that may be saturated with water during the summer but is comparatively dry in winter. These conditions can be replicated by constructing ponds in which water levels are designed to fall in the winter.

Planting

Ponds and their garden surrounds, provide all kinds of opportunities for varied and attractive planting. They also pose dangers and, paradoxically, these often stem from exposure to too much of a good thing. Constantly available water, high levels of sunlight in open, unshaded situations and, increasingly frequently, high levels of nutrients in the water supply, favour very vigorous plant growth. The edges of ponds and the ground around them are battlegrounds in which plants compete vigorously for rootholds, and space for leaves and stems to develop. The matrices formed are extremely dense and persistent, made up of long-lived, robust perennials. Annuals are rarely play significant parts in these communities.

Managing such exuberance successfully depends on understanding the needs of the plants we use, and matching them closely with conditions in the places where we plant them. This matching depends on recognising the ways natural habitats differ from one another.

Wet meadows – occur on heavy loams containing high proportions of clay and silt, or peat. The soil may be water-logged in winter and even in high summer will never dry out completely. Matrices are composed of vigorous perennials and grasses, many of which flower in late summer or autumn; a valuable attribute in gardens. Areas of wet meadows around ponds maintain a reservoir

Plants suitable for inclusion in communities of plants around ponds where water levels fall in winter

Many gardeners would not associate most of the plants on this list with water, though they would be aware of their sensitivity to drought. Only a few of the following actually grow in water; the remainder depend on saturated or near-saturated soil to support growth and flowering throughout their growing seasons, but are likely to suffer from excessive wet in winter.

Acer tartaricum subsp. *ginnala*: An upright shrub, or small tree, useful as a low canopy former in wet, but free-draining situations.

Agapanthus campanulatus*: Spreads by short rhizomes to form extensive clumps of congested, weed-excluding crowns. Can become a vigorous coloniser in places with mild winters.

Cornus alba 'Sibirica': This and other forms of *C. alba* associate well with low growing perennials. All respond well to annual or biennial hard pruning which displays their coloured stems well.

Dierama dracomontanum: This and other species are long-lived perennials which combine well with low growing plants and produce graceful pendant sprays of flowers in the air above their neighbours.

Eupatorium coelestinum: Very late emergence in spring provides good ground cover for bulbs. Produces masses of clear blue, powder puff flowers from late summer into autumn.

of water; their soils remain cool beneath the blanket of foliage above them and the vigorous growth of the plants removes and retains surplus nutrients. All this contributes to the stability and well-being of water in adjacent pools.

When similar features are made in gardens, planting should follow natural patterns and aim to establish a dense, impermeable and permanent plant cover as

Filipendula palmata: The Japanese meadow sweets are long-lived vigorous perennials capable of forming persistent matrices with other plants in rich, moist soils.

Iris ensata: An iris with sumptuously beautiful flowers, with a strong preference for conditions which enable it to grow just below water level in summer, and in drier conditions in winter.

Kniphofia caulescens: This and several other red hot pokers perform well growing in shallow water, preferably circulating in summer, and in drier conditions during the winter.

Leucanthemella serotina: A strongly competitive, late-flowering ox-eye daisy, up to 2 m (6 ft 6 in) tall. Forms a robust matrix with other vigorous perennials.

Ligularia dentata: Numerous garden forms exist, mostly with bright orange or yellow daisy flowers. All are intolerant of drought during the summer.

Lilium canadense: Graceful orange turk's cap lilies are produced on slender stems from wide-ranging underground rhizomes which develop into a dispersed colony.

Lobelia cardinalis: A medium-sized, upright perennial with spikes of velvety scarlet flowers. This and the blue *L. siphilitica* and purple *L.* x *gerardii* 'Vedrariensis' all grow in seasonally wet situations.

Lysimachia clethroides: Short rhizomes form compact weed-excluding clumps topped by twisted spikes of close-knit white flowers. Requires constantly moist soil in summer.

Miscanthus 'Purpurascens': This and cultivars of the species from summer monsoonal locations in east Asia need constantly moist rich soils to achieve maximum growth and development.

Monarda didyma: Easily grown from seed, this attractive perennial, with richly coloured flowers and aromatic foliage, is a decorative addition to communities on moist soils.

Rheum palmatum: A massive, ground-occupying plant with enormous leaves and tall plumes of white flowers. Contrasts well with other plants provided copious water is available.

Rodgersia aesculifolia: Another large perennial with charming foliage and good ground-holding capacity with great decorative value in a matrix.

Sorbaria sorbifolia: A small shrub with short plumes of white flowers flushed with pink over a long season; a useful member of mixed communities in damp conditions.

Spiraea salicifolia: Modestly attractive shrub with pale pink flowers will grow standing in water through the summer, but requires drier conditions in winter.

Vaccinium corymbosum: Another useful member of mixed shrub/perennial communities in wet conditions, infiltrates well to fill gaps between neighbouring plants.

* Note: plants marked with an asterisk are vulnerable to frost in cold locations.

soon as possible. Unoccupied spaces will be rapidly filled by vigorous weeds that are very tenacious, and rapid establishment of the initial planting, and careful removal of unwanted intruders in the early stages, is most important. Later on, it is better to use glyphosate or ammonium sulphamate as spot treatments to control weeds, rather than attempt to dig them out.

Natural communities of plants in wet meadows and bogs are dominated by grasses and sedges. In gardens, the proportion of grasses and sedges can be reduced – or they can be omitted altogether – in favour of mixtures of broad-leaved plants and petalloid monocotyledons. However, these must be capable of developing the dense, vigorous matrices necessary to exclude intruders.

Swamps – swamps occur naturally around the inlets and outlets of lakes and ponds, where water lying just above or just below ground level is colonised by reeds, shrubs and trees, notably willows. They may sound less than instantly appealing as a garden setting but the value of these matrices as water purifying systems is now being recognised in the treatment of effluents from septic tanks. Willow and reed beds can be used effectively and attractively to maintain the balanced conditions that contribute to the wellbeing of the water in ponds and lakes. They are often rich in wildlife, acting amongst other things as nurseries in which young fish and other creatures find cover and readily available food.

Swamps large enough to contain willow trees fit only into large-scale water works, but heavily pruned willows and water loving shrubs including, *Cornus alba*, *Spiraea salicifolia* and *S. douglasii* or *Sorbaria sorbifolia*, are useful substitutes in gardens.

Banks of ponds – the meeting point of water and land is a critical boundary which needs to be stabilised to resist erosion by the action of water, or the dabblings and fritterings of ducks, fishes and other creatures. Concrete or plastic/rubber sheets do this effectively but unattractively; stones or wooden piles more aesthetically. Alternatively, the dense mats of fibrous roots produced by plants in these situations will do the job. Those who doubt the extent and resilience of such root systems should spend an hour or two digging up a long-established plant of gypsywort or royal fern. These water's edge plants produce formidable matrices of roots and rhizomes which are the basis of defence against erosion from water. Once in place they can scarcely be removed without extensive breaches to the defences.

Shallow water – the margins of ponds are home to numerous plants, many of which can spread into moist soil around the water's edge, helping to stabilise banks. Most do not depend on constant immersion in water, and thrive in pools which dry out in summer, provided moisture remains available below the surface. Unlike the plants of wet meadows and pond-side banks, many have exploratory rather than dense root systems, and are comparatively fragile rather than robust, tending

Tenacious, soil-binding plants for banks

Most are suitable for medium-sized, even small, pools and many plants in the previous list fulfil similar roles. Some are tall, vigorous plants more suited to large ponds.

Acorus gramineus: Also a dwarf form – 'Pusillus' and several other cultivars available. All are grass-like and quite low growing.

Astilbe chinensis var. *taquetii* 'Superba': A tall, clump-forming, retentive plant with attractive foliage and flowers.

Athyrium filix-femina 'Victoriae': The dense rhizomes are good stabilisers for shaded locations.

Carex elata 'Aurea' ('Bowles Golden'): Small, upright clump-former with attractively bright foliage, which provides quite low cover along the margins of pools.

Darmera peltata: Vigorous with broad, densely shading leaves and thick rhizomes. Excellent ground stabiliser.

Dryopteris wallichiana: A vigorous, robustly clump-forming male fern, with exceptionally beautiful bright gold-green fronds in spring.

Dulichium arundinaceum: Clump-forming sedge with retentive roots and upright, characterful stems. Provides dense cover around edges of pools.

Eupatorium fistulosum: Garden cultivars of Joe Pye weed, including compact forms, with broad heads of rich purple flowers provide valuable colour in autumn.

Hemerocallis lilioasphodelus (*flava*): This and other vigorous, rhizomatous day-lilies make excellent, soil-binding colonisers with attractive, large orange flowers.

Hosta ventricosa: Strong clump-forming species with purple flowers on long stems. A vast range of hosta cultivars with multi-coloured variegated foliage can be used for similar purposes.

Houttuynia cordata 'Variegata'*: Spreads rapidly by invasive underground rhizomes infilling amongst other plants. Needs to be matched with equally competitive neighbours to discourage attempts to take over.

Iris forrestii: Moderate sized, clump-forming irises provide excellent, non-invasive bank support.

Ligularia przewalskii: This and other subspecies and cultivars make excellent vigorous waterside plants, with decorative foliage and bright yellow or orange flowers.

Lycopus americanus: Small, undistinguished flowers and plain foliage but invaluable in situations where reliable protection from erosion is needed.

Lysimachia nummularia 'Aurea': A comparatively fragile plant, but excellent for creeping cover, either by itself or infiltrating other plants.

Lythrum salicaria: Also *L. virgatum* and many cultivars. Grows up to 2 m (6 ft 6 in) tall, with conspicuous inflorescences of richly colourful crimson flowers from the end of summer into autumn.

Primula japonica: Many other species, notably *P. pulverulenta*, fulfil similar role. Some are short-lived but usually produce numerous seedlings which fill spaces between established plants.

Rodgersia podophylla: Vigorous, large-leaved highly retentive plants fully capable of providing excellent permanent bank support.

Scrophularia aquatica 'Variegata': This tall plant emerges above lower vegetation. Flowers are interesting rather than beautiful.

Spartina pectinata 'Aureomarginata': Upright, moderately tall, clump-forming grass with brightly attractive foliage, and dense mats of soil-retaining roots, for large ponds.

* Note: plants marked with an asterisk are vulnerable to frost in cold locations.

to break apart quite easily. Some are intolerant of frost, surviving only when covered by water during the winter. Their talent for disintegration, combined with a readiness to produce new roots, enables them to spread easily throughout a water system, and their questing, rhizomatous roots exploit the opportunities of new situations when they reach them.

In gardens too, these plants can be used more flexibly than the deeply entrenched plants which stabilise the banks on the water's edge. Marginals are usually easy to propagate and establish, and the disappearance of one or two from a plant matrix, whether intentionally or as a result of unfavourable weather, can quickly be made good by introducing replacements.

Many grow rapidly, and regular reductions to restrict spread may be necessary, in small or even large ponds, and then the choice of species becomes very important. These marginal plants are only partially adapted aquatics, often capable of growing in the saturated soil close to a pond, but not able to embark on a wholly aquatic life-style. Very few are able to grow in water deeper than 45 cm (1 ft 6 in) and takeovers, even by very vigorous species of phragmites, typha and ranunculus, can be prevented simply by ensuring all areas intended to be clear water are too deep for them to colonise.

The water lily zone – Plants with leaves that float on the water, including species of Nuphar and Nymphoides, play such major roles among the communities of plants in ponds that it seems entirely appropriate to use their name as a label for the situation where they grow. Their flowers, and very often their foliage, are not only extremely decorative, but also ecologically dominant in the communities among which they live.

Most aquatics grow in closely defined depths of water. Lotuses (below left) and fringed water lilies (below right) grow in relatively shallow water around the edges of lakes and large ponds. They move towards the middle as the pond starts to silt up.

Marginal plants for shallow water round the edges of ponds

'Marginals' reduce abrupt contrasts between bank and water and form links with wetland communities which amphibious and other wildlife use to enter and leave the water. Most are confined to the shallows and will not invade clear water spaces in deeper, central parts of ponds.

Acorus calamus 'Variegatus': A good 'interface' plant with attractively aromatic foliage, grows equally well in shallow water and wetlands.

Alisma plantago-aquatica: A vigorous, tuberous, self-seeding marginal useful to fill gaps in larger ponds.

Butomus umbellatus: The flowering rush spreads vigorously by rhizomes. Does best in fertile situations with cool summers. Bears open inflorescences of bowl-shaped pale rose-pink flowers.

Calla palustris: An acid-loving marginal that increases by floating rhizomes, then spreads into and forms links with adjacent wetlands.

*Colocasia esculenta**: Enormous deep green or purple leaves provide shade and contrast with other plants. Suitable only for warm water settings.

Hydrocharis morsus-ranae: Similar to a water lily with small, bright yellow flowers. Needs shallow water capable of warming rapidly in summer. Hardy resting buds (turons) sink to mud in winter.

Iris laevigata: Numerous cultivars with pale blue, white or parti-coloured flowers. All are easily grown, moderately spreading, undemanding plants that form links with wetland areas.

Juncus effusus f. spiralis: A shallow water marginal and wetland reed, producing compact clumps of narrowly cylindrical foliage curiously twisted into corkscrew form.

*Nelumbo komarowii**: This and *N. lutea* and *N. nucifera* are attractive marginals for ponds large enough to hold them. The first is capable of overwintering in cold climates when protected from frost beneath water.

*Orontium aquaticum**: A wetland and marginal plant with short, bright yellow 'pokers' that spreads by runners. Winter-hardy only beneath a covering of water.

Peltandra virginica: Best for shallow marginal water; grows slowly unless summer water temperatures are moderately high.

Phragmites australis: Extremely vigorous reed, at home in wetlands or shallow water but only suitable for large areas. Its sharply tipped rhizomes penetrate flexible liners.

*Pontederia cordata**: needs fertile, warm water in summer, and frost protection from a covering of water in winter to enable it to thrive and survive.

Ranunculus lingua 'Grandiflorus': Spreads vigorously by short runners. An excellent, but sometimes disconcertingly spready, coloniser of shallow water and adjacent wetland areas.

Sagittaria sagittifolia: Multiplies by bulb-like organs at the ends of the roots. Distinctive for its attractive arrow-shaped leaves. Spreads only moderately in most situations.

*Sarracenia flava**: For exceptional situations in acid conditions in bogs or shallow water in warm sites on nutrient-poor soils. *S. purpurea* is hardy in colder locations.

*Saururus cernuus**: Lizard's tails spread vigorously with aromatic, creeping rhizomes into adjacent wetland. Only underwater shoots survive cold winters.

Schoenoplectus (Scirpus) lacustris: A sedge that forms close-knit colonies in shallow water. Sharp tips to the roots can puncture flexible liners.

*Trapa natans**: Regenerates annually from nut-like fruits which overwinter in shallow water. Prohibited in the USA.

Typha latifolia: All, apart from *T. minima*, are suitable only for large ponds. Their needle-like root tips easily penetrate liners.

* Note: plants marked with an asterisk are vulnerable to frost in cold locations.

Water lilies (top left) are amongst the most flexible and beautiful plants with floating leaves. The distinctive pads of *Euryala ferox* (above right), and the delicate foliage of water hawthorn (above left) are attractive variations on the theme.

Plants in this zone perform two distinctively different roles.

• Water lilies produce floating pads which shade the water below, reducing over-exuberant growth of algae and submerged aquatics.

• The submerged aquatics oxygenate the water while leaving the surface clear. The ideal is a balance between the two which leaves at least one third of the surface clear, while supporting a healthy but not overwhelmingly abundant growth of plants beneath the surface.

Deep water – when the depth of water reaches and exceeds 2 m (6 ft 6 in) constantly cool conditions at root level, and the distance between the surface of the water and the mud below, defeat even the most vigorous species of Nymphaea and Nuphar. In these conditions, submerged aquatics, including species of Elodea, Myriophyllum and Potamogeton, come into their own, often with undesirable consequences. They grow with their roots in the mud, and their stems and foliage reach up through the water towards the light. Free from competition they can form dense, impenetrable thickets of stems and foliage that choke waterways and increase the rate of silting. When they die in the autumn, they produce masses of dead plant material which overloads the oxygenating capacity of the water, leading to lethal conditions for fish and other pond life. *Elodea canadensis* is one of a number of these plants whose range has been extended by unwise and, later bitterly regretted, introductions.

Others, including *Egeria densa* from South America, species of Lagarosiphon from central and southern parts of Africa: the eel grasses, Zostera subspecies, hornworts, Ceratophyllum subsp. and the berry-bearing *Hydrilla verticillata* have all proved such effective and adaptable colonisers that their presence in gardens is illegal in some countries.

The impression of fragility conveyed by some of the free floaters should be treated with reserve. Even the tiny water ferns Azolla and Salvinia, and the minute pads of duckweeds, quickly become all-pervasive, and are exceedingly difficult to eradicate. More vigorous floaters like water lettuces and hyacinths spread so assertively in favourable conditions that they have become internationally recognised pests outlawed in the few countries, such as New Zealand, where they remain a threat rather than an actual problem. Like the pads of water lilies, they cover the surface and shade the water below, and often do so very decoratively. However, their tendency to escape control makes them dangerous allies for this purpose in comparison with more sedentary alternatives.

Plants for the water lily zone

These truly aquatic plants form a small, but vitally important, minority amongst the communities in and around watery habitats. They depend on constantly available water, they grow best at intermediate depths, deep enough to ensure they are not threatened periodically by falling water levels, but not so deep (in excess of 2 m or 6 ft 6 in) that the distance between the bottom of the pond and the surface is beyond the stretch of their stems.

Aponogeton distachyos*: An aquatic with narrow, floating leaves and white flowers. In mild areas can be planted in shallow, seasonally dry pools. In cold regions plant deep enough to avoid frost.

Azolla filiculoides*: Invasive, but usually harmless, floating fern with attractive crimson-toned foliage. Tender, but like sour-dough, a small starter stock overwintered in a frost-free situation in a bucket can be used to re-populate the water in the spring.

Eichhornia crassipes*: This floating aquatic, with beautiful hyacinth-like flowers, can become dangerously invasive in warm, frost-free situations.

Elodea canadensis: A vigorous submerged aquatic that proliferates too rapidly for all but large areas of water, preferably shaded by a prolific canopy of floating leaves.

Euryala ferox*: This handsome tropical plant with broad, round, floating leaves survives cold winters when planted 45 cms (18 ins) or more deep beyond reach of frost. Needs warm to hot summers to thrive.

Hottonia palustris: Submerged aquatic for slow moving or still, acid water in relatively shallow situations. Produces whorls of attractive pale lilac flowers.

Lagarosiphon major: Submerged aquatic, and excellent oxygenator, grows most rapidly in warm water, but tolerant of cooler situations.

Lemna gibba: Floating duckweed. Usually regarded as an invasive, unattractive nuisance. May serve a useful purpose by providing shading while other floating-leaved aquatics develop.

Myriophyllum aquaticum: Submerged plant for deep water; a good oxygenator which provides excellent nurseries for fish fry and other pond life.

Nuphar japonica: This and *N. j.* var. *variegata* and *N. lutea* are all extremely vigorous plants with floating leaf pads, only suitable for large ponds and lakes.

Nymphaea capensis hybrids*: Produce masses of rounded leaves in warm pools, shading out algae and submerged aquatics. In cold regions can only be grown by overwintering annually produced offsets in a frost-free location.

Nymphaea odorata hybrids: Comprise numerous hybrids of greatly varying vigour. It is important with these and *N. mexicana* and *N. tetragona* to match vigour to space available.

Nymphaea odorata 'Pygmaea' and 'Laydekeri' hybrids: The floating lily pads of small water lilies like these, especially the floriferous 'Laydekeri' hybrids are well suited to the restricted spaces available in small garden ponds.

Nymphoides peltata: This and *N. aquatica* are rather weedy floating aquatics, with attractive clear yellow flowers. Only able to grow in shallow water.

Pistia stratiotes: The water lettuce is a floating aquatic which can become an invasive menace in frost-free, warm locations. Its hanging roots provide good nurseries for fish fry.

Potamogeton crispus: A vigorous submerged aquatic capable of growing too prolifically unless curbed by the shade of water lily leaves. Prefers slowly moving water.

Ranunculus fluitans: Water crowfoots produce masses of pure white flowers in early summer above submerged and floating tresses of deep green, much-divided foliage. Flourishes in flowing base-rich water.

Stratiotes aloides: A rather dull aquatic with unusual habits – surfacing in summer and submerging in winter. Forms dense colonies from offsets in moderately shallow water.

Utricularia inflata: Numerous species of insectivorous bladderworts produce dense growths of submerged leaves and stems with small, often attractively colourful flowers just above the water.

Vallisneria spiralis: Submerged aquatic widely used in aquariums. An undemanding, wild-life friendly plant, tolerant of frost beneath a covering of water.

* Note: plants marked with an asterisk are vulnerable to frost in cold locations.

The Gardens
CASE STUDIES

Exotic Water Gardens in Hull

The 200 sqm (200 sq yds) garden of a house on an estate built by the council on the outskirts of Hull, England was bought a few years ago by its tenant, a car mechanic who recently formed a company to buy the garage where he has worked for many years. He and his wife live here with their two teenage children. Both arrived with their parents in Britain in the 1960s from Uganda where their families had been long-established members of the Asian community. Hitherto, they had grown a few flowers in the garden, and some of the vegetables which they like, but cannot find in the local greengrocers' shops. However, an outing to Fountains Abbey introduced them to Studley Royal and the mechanic returned determined to make a water garden. In direct contrast to his former totally practical and utilitarian use of the garden, he dreamed up a series of ponds, one leading to another, almost hidden amongst the sensationally atmospheric, tropical looking planting that surrounds them.

Review

A. Flights of fancy have been rare on this estate. Until recently, everyone rented their houses from the council, and few trees were planted or much time or money spent on gardens; a situation that has begun to change since most tenants became property-owning democrats.

B. The place has a utilitarian, even drab, atmosphere, and an overall lack of privacy, due partly to its lay-out, partly to its history. This is a place desperately in need of someone to break the mould and do something imaginative and unusual.

C. The conditions offer few impediments to the owner's ideas. The top soil is a neutral, light sandy loam that is easily worked and could be used for almost any purpose.

D. The heavy clay subsoil is almost entirely stone-free, and becomes almost watertight with a little puddling. It makes an excellent base for ponds, using liners to ensure they do not leak.

Outcome
A.

- Action started one bank holiday weekend when a neighbour, who owned a contracting and plant hire business, turned up with his Bobcat and said, 'Let's give it a go!'

B. and C.

- The extended holiday was spent moving the topsoil from one place to another; excavating holes for pools linked by channels; digging out shallow trenches in which to lay paths, and constructing a raised bank at the end of the garden for a screen of shrubs and trees.

- Much of it was done impulsively as no plan had been prepared beforehand, and most of the first day's work was reconstructed during the following few days.

- However, they took great care not to mix the top soil with the heavy clay removed during excavation of the pools. Much of the excavated soil was used to form different levels in the almost flat garden, so that water, circulated by a pump, could drop from one pool to another.

D.

- Heavy gauge, nylon-reinforced polythene sheeting was used to line the excavations, all of it obtained as offcuts or unaccounted surpluses from the contractor's business. The edges were hidden beneath paving slabs, or extended beneath wetland areas adjacent to the pools and channels and disguised by plants growing above them.

- These wetland areas were filled in to about 5 cm (2 in) above the level of the water with a 3:1 mixture of pea gravel and topsoil in which plants were set out.
- The planting was done by plundering local garden centres in a triumphant finale to the operation. They ended with a feeling of having indulged, not wisely but too well, and some of their choices may cause problems as they develop.

The Plants

The owner imagined the garden as a chain of dark, mysterious pools almost lost amongst the surrounding vegetation. In fact, there was little room for trees, and height and shadows were obtained by using bamboos, such as *Phyllostachys aurea* (which died during the first winter), *P. flexuosa* and *Pleioblastus viridistriatus* (not so large, but non-invasive and dramatically beautiful), with *Fargesia murieliae*. These were planted with evergreen shrubs, including *Choisya ternata* and especially *Fatsia japonica* (for the sake of its luxuriant tropical looking leaves), and a few upright deciduous shrubs, notably *Decaisnea fargesii* whose blue beans he found an irresistible prospect. Phormiums, including 'Dazzler', 'Maori Maiden', 'Purpureum' and 'Yellow Wave', were planted in the lower layers of the matrix and, although rather battered by the end of the winter, they did well in the shade and shelter of the bamboos and shrubs.

Several cultivars of *Miscanthus sinensis*, including 'Cabaret', 'Gracillimus', 'Malepartus' and 'Zebrinus', were planted in wetland areas, or on the margins of pools, and grew so well they upstaged the bamboos, and the owner wished he had used them more. Apart from these, touches of opulence were provided by the large leaves of groups of *Darmera peltata*; Hosta cultivars; *Ligularia dentata* 'Desdemona' and 'Gregynog Gold'; and *Lysichiton americanus*. He could hardly resist *Rheum palmatum* 'Atrosanguineum' as a substitute for the obviously Gulliverian *Gunnera manicata* in his Lilliput, but conceded even this was excessively large, and sadly had never heard of *G. tinctoria*. He fell for the ostrich leaf shuttlecocks of *Matteucia struthiopteris* and loaded three onto his trolley, and also took away plants of the copper-toned form of the royal fern, *Osmunda regalis*.

Aquatics were planted in the pools, mostly cultivars of *Nymphaea odorata* 'Laydekeri', with *Acorus calamus* 'Variegatus', *Butomus umbellatus*, *Myosotis scorpioides*, *Myriophyllum aquaticum, Orontium aquaticum*; and *Ranunculus lingua* 'Grandiflorus' around the edges. He was determined to include the red fairy moss *Azolla filiculoides*, not hardy enough to survive outdoors, but at the suggestion of the manager of 'AquaFeatures' at the garden centre, he kept some plants alive in a bucket of water in the utility room through the winter, reintroducing them in the spring.

Cold Comfort for Keen Gardeners

This garden of about 0.5 ha (one and a quarter acres) belongs to a shopkeeper – selling china, glass and craftware – and his wife, in the country north of Concord, New Hampshire, in the USA. They bought it impulsively, after a visit late on a summer's day when the whole place was bathed in sunshine and radiated warmth, after selling their previous house close to Moriches Bay on Long Island. While living there they have discovered their first impressions of a sheltered, wooded valley, with a stream babbling through the garden, were misleading. This can be a very cold place. It faces northwest towards the coldest winter winds, which funnel ferociously down the valley, and bring heavy falls of snow in winter. Late frosts in spring and early ones in the autumn are common as cold air from above settles in the valley, and, in moments of desperation, the owners say their garden might as well be on top of Mount Washington. The soil is a very acidic, poorly drained sand beneath a surface layer of peat, remnants of a bog drained years previously. The couple run the shop between them and have a fair amount of time to spend at home, when they enjoy being in the garden, but their attempts – based more or less on the things that did well on Long Island – have been less than successful.

Review

A. Cold is a feature of this garden and northwest winds, lack of sun and late and early frosts result in short growing seasons that strongly affect the prospects of growing plants successfully. However, heavy winter snowfalls protect plants from extreme winter cold, and summers are warm, moist and very favourable for plant growth.

B. Another problem is wet, particularly when snow melts, and water drains from frozen soil in spring. Then pools of water and mud can persist for weeks on end.

C. Many plants fail to grow well due to the acidity of the ground, but there are others which thrive in these conditions and are well adapted to make the most of the alternations between long periods of dormancy in winter and rapid growth and development during spring and summer.

D. The owners are accustomed to gardens filled with brightly colourful flower beds and trim lawns and hedges. They are adamant in their refusal to 'go back to nature'.

Outcome

A.
- Little could be done to protect woody plants from the cold; only those capable of tolerating it were used.
- Herbaceous perennials, whose tops die down in winter, featured strongly to take advantage of the protective effects of snow – reinforced by a blanket of mulch applied in late autumn.

B.
- Problems with water were traced to the silting up of water channels which had drained the lake before it evolved into a bog.
- An early attempt to remedy this by excavating the old lake bed and supplying water direct from the stream were satisfactory, until a flood washed away most of the plants.
- They now supply the lake indirectly from the stream, using a weir and monk to regulate the flow and the water level.
- They have greatly reduced problems from excess water in spring by lowering the water level in winter, and clearing the bed of the stream and other drainage channels.

C.

- Beds close to the house were raised, and given extra depth by spreading spoil from the dug-out lake over them. Excess acidity in these newly formed beds was reduced by heavy applications of lime.

D.

- Despite the owners' aversion to 'going back to nature', they were persuaded to forego the suburban styles of their Long Island garden in exchange for intensively gardened, brightly planted beds of bulbs and perennials close to the house and a more natural plant matrix composed of trees, underplanted with drifts of perennials around the lake, provided this did not look 'too wild'.

- Some native plants were included for their reliability, and affinity with the surroundings, especially around the lake. Suitably hardy exotics chosen for added brightness were planted around the house.

The Plants

Elaeagnus angustifolia and variegated forms of *Acer negundo* were planted near the house to provide light, bright leaf canopies above polyanthus, *Mertensia virginica* and masses of large-flowered daffodils in spring, followed in summer by hybrid delphiniums, border phloxes like 'Bouvardier', the sunset red 'Charles H. Curtis' and the white 'David', paeonies, and several of the *Papaver orientale* hybrids bred by Countess von Zeppelin, including 'Karine', 'Kleine Tanzarin' and 'Degas', along with numerous other splendidly colourful herbaceous perennials.

Lakeside plantings away from the house were based on native deciduous trees and conifers, several of which were already present, above a well-developed shrub layer, over broad drifts of a relatively few perennials and ferns generously underplanted with bulbs.

The trees included *Acer rubrum* and *A. saccharum*, *Amelanchier arborea*, *Prunus serotina*, *Quercus bicolor* and *Q. palustris* interplanted with *Larix laricina*. A sheltering belt of *Picea mariana* and *Tsuga canadensis* provided a background.

Mixtures of native and exotic shrubs included many chosen for their autumn colours – *Amelanchier sanguinea*, *Aronia* x *prunifolia* 'Brilliant', *Cornus alba* 'Elegantissima' (planted in groups on the edge of the lake for its enlightening foliage and brilliant winter bark), *Corylopsis pauciflora* and *C. sinensis* (for spring flowers). *Fothergilla gardenii* and *F. major*, *Leucathoe fontanesiana*, *Lindera benzoin* and *Symphoricarpos* x *chenaultii* 'Hancock' (as dense groundcover along the margins). *Ilex verticillata*, *Viburnum betulifolium* and *V. opulus* 'Xanthocarpum' were planted close to each other for their contrasting scarlet and translucent orange yellow berries.

Large drifts of *Aegopodium podagaria* 'Variegatum' were planted to light up areas beneath the trees. *Sanguinaria canadensis* and *Cornus canadensis* were also used in large ground-hugging patches with *Alchemilla mollis*, and repeated small groups of the single paeony 'Dainty'. Smaller woodlanders included *Galax urceolata* (for its 'varnished' foliage), interplanted with *Tiarella cordifolia* and *Vancouveria hexandra*. Taller perennials emerging above these and used to reinforce the display of flowers at shrub level included: *Aconitum* x *cammarum* 'Bicolor', *Aruncus dioicus*, *Actea racemosa* and cultivars of *Trollius chinensis*, with *Digitalis purpurea* 'Excelsior' hybrids as gap fillers.

Ferns were freely planted, partly for contrasting effects with broad-leaved plants; partly to reinforce local atmosphere. *Adiantum pedatum* formed flowing drifts interspersed with *Gymnocarpium dryopteris*, *Onoclea sensibilis* using its red form, and the bold evergreen *Polystichum acrostichoides*. Compact clusters of *Osmunda cinnamomea* and *Dryopteris goldieana* were repeated at intervals to create rhythm and visual logic.

Changing Styles in North Carolina

The garden of a small country house south of Raleigh in North Carolina, USA, belongs to the owner of a manufacturing business. After years of hard work and stress, surviving – as the owner puts it 'only by being lean and mean' – the business is running smoothly and profitably. The garden is set in gently undulating countryside on the edge of the Piedmont and the coastal plain, surrounded by old meadows, many now reverting to woods filled with sweet gums, tulip poplars and loblolly pines. A small tributary of the Neuse River runs through the garden which lies on well structured clay, sometimes covered by sandy loam. The owner's wife, who had been almost entirely responsible for the garden, died a while ago. Her 'bible' had been *The Englishwoman's Garden*, and he had always admired the garden while it was in her care, and liked the bright combinations of flowers and foliage in the borders. After her death he made an attempt to take care of it, feeling he owed it to her to do his best. This was not very successful, because he knew little about gardening and, as he eventually had to admit, it was "a woman's garden, really. Not my kind of thing".

Review

A. The garden was too complex and demanding for someone with little knowledge of gardening and only a passing interest in flowers. The hot, humid summers were fatally harsh on the silver-leaved plants so vital to his wife's style of gardening, and he had no idea how to replace them.

B. The site is idyllically set amongst trees with slight but interesting variations in topography that lend themselves to landscaping.

C. Although the owner has more spare time than previously, he has interests other than gardening. A form of gardening which he does enjoy is mowing the grass, which he finds relaxing with a satisfyingly visible end result.

D. The topography, water-retentive clay soil, and a source of water in the form of a stream, lent themselves to the construction of a pond or two.

Outcome

A. and B.

- The garden underwent a fundamental make-over; during which the original layout of borders, hedges and lawns gave way to a more natural, landscaped garden.
- Lawns provided a pattern, and trees were a sheltering, relaxed setting for the house.

- Water replaced borders as major features, in the shape of informal ponds and adjacent wetland areas.

C.

- Maintenance was restricted largely to grass cutting, mowing frequently and leaving the cuttings where they fell. A local contractor was employed when business took the owner away from home.

D.

- Three medium-sized ponds were excavated out of the clay, supplied indirectly by water from the stream. They were not lined, but filled with water naturally. Each was up to 1.5 m (5 ft) deep over the greater part of its area, with broad stretches of shallow water round the margins.
- Associated wetland areas, in which the soil surface was just above summer water levels, were made close to the ponds.

The Plants

The wooded atmosphere was reinforced by planting more trees, mostly native species, with a few exotics. Amongst them were *Asimina triloba* grown as small multi-stemmed trees, *Cercidiphyllum japonicum* for its burnt sugar fragrance and colours in autumn, and *Cladrastis kentukea*; *Diospyros virginiana*; *Hamamelis* x *intermedia* 'Arnold Promise'; *Nyssa sylvatica;* the fragrant snowbell, *Styrax obassia* and *Taxodium distichum*. The owner made space for a fine group of the tall columnar *Magnolia grandiflora* 'Mainstreet', and *Magnolia* 'Galaxy' which has crimson flowers.

Plants with floating leaves planted in the water lily zone included *Nymphaea* hybrids, amongst them *N.* 'Marliacea Chromatella'; *Nymphoides lacunosum* with variegated, mottled leaves; *N. indicum* with masses of short-lived white flowers; and *Aponogeton distachyos*. Other *Nymphaea* hybrids used where the water was less deep, included 'Nivea', 'Rosea' and 'Sunset.

Marginal aquatics included *Acorus gramineus* 'Ogon', several cultivars of *Iris laevigata, Pontederia cordata* and *Sagittaria latifolia*. But by far the most striking effects were produced by large groups of the pale sulphur yellow *Nelumbo lutea* and cultivars of *N. nucifera*, notably the white 'Alba Grandiflora' and deep rose 'Osiris'. All did well in spite of the muskrats' fondness for their tubers.

Wood ducks, black ducks and mallards frequented the ponds, and the banks had to be protected from their feet and dabbling bills by a covering of plants. Bugleweed (*Lycopus virginicus*)

sowed itself naturally and provided effective protection, but its coarse, unattractive appearance was not appreciated and in most places it was destroyed with glyphosate and progressively replaced with vigorous hostas like 'Piedmont Gold', 'Aurora Borealis', 'Francee', 'Aurea-marginata' and 'Royal Standard'. Cultivars of Louisiana iris, including 'Black Gamecock' and 'Gulf Shores', *Iris sibirica* cultivars, *Darmera peltata*, *Ligularia* 'The Rocket', *Gunnera manicata* and forms of *Osmunda regalis* were also planted extensively on the banks.

Wetland areas between and beyond the ponds were heavily planted with robust, summer-flowering perennials, mostly in bold clumps, with infiltrators like *Houttuynia cordata*, *Lysimachia nummularia* 'Aurea', *Myosotis scorpioides* 'Pinkie' and 'Sapphire' and *Phalaris arundinacea* 'Feesey' filling the ground between them. The clumps included *Lobelia cardinalis* 'Royal Robe', *L. siphilitica*; *L.* x *gerardii* 'Vedrariensis', *Sarracenia flava* and some of its hybrids, several species of *Rodgersia* and *Ligularia dentata* 'Desdemona' and 'Othello'. These were set off by colonies of *Matteuccia pensylvanica*, and dramatic clumps of *Miscanthus* cultivars, especially the boldly variegated 'Cosmopolitan', the lax, slender-leaved 'Gracillimus' and 'Kaskade' with clouds of tinted pink flowers.

Scrubberies
and 'the mixed border'

8

DAUNTED BY THE DEMANDS of the herbaceous border and dismayed by the problems of gardening without help, the twentieth-century gardener sought refuge in the shrubbery. This sturdy breed of permanent plants was less intimidating than trees, and less exacting than the sun-loving occupants of herbaceous borders. Shrubs seemed ideally suited to a time and money saving formula. Gardens were reduced to lawns surrounded by borders packed with shrubs. A light garnish of 'King Alfred' daffodils appeared each spring, and a bed or two of hybrid tea roses near the house provided a summer talking point. The result was mindnumbingly humdrum but, while the mower stood ready in the garage and shears hung in the garden shed, the gardener was in command and all was well in the garden.

This mid-century crisis in the life of gardening ended because it sacrifices everything that makes gardening interesting and exciting, not because the system does not work. It is still being practised as bleakly as ever in unimaginatively managed parks and gardens all over the temperate world. Reacting against the lack of variety, the constant demands of the mower, brief phases of flowering, and the deadening impact of dull, overgrown blocks of twiggy greenery, gardeners turned again to perennial plants for inspiration.

Somewhat to their surprise, they discovered life after the herbaceous border. Unsuspected treasures designed by nature to grow amicably side by side lurked behind the ranks of delphiniums, sidalceas, heleniums, phloxes and lupins. Gradually, the penny dropped as gardeners realised that the key to growing perennials successfully was to grow them amongst the plants they associate with naturally. Herbaceous perennials are very seldom dominant members of their communities; they are almost always subordinate to trees, shrubs or grasses.

Perennials have now been found parts in a trinity of gardening styles following – though seldom consciously modelled on – natural associations of plants. The most familiar of these are:

- Meadows – in which perennials and bulbs are combined with long grasses (see chapter 6).
- Spinneys – sometimes in the form of a woodland garden, but much more likely to be found as shaded spaces beneath trees, pergolas and other structures. (See chapter 9).
- Scrubberies – known more elegantly, but less all-embracingly, as mixed borders.

(Opposite) Complex mixtures of shrubs, perennials, grasses and often bulbs provide conditions akin to those found naturally in scrub or along the edges of woodlands. They are not easily managed by employing orthodox gardening methods, which expose them to invasion either by grasses or trees. They are particularly well-suited to matrix-planting in which control depends on the multi-tiered layers of stems and foliage which establish persistent, self-sustaining communities of plants.

Shrubs and scrub

Mixed borders have become rather fashionable. They are often proposed as an alternative to the demanding temperament that has made people wary of exclusive dependence on herbaceous plants, but unless skilfully designed with careful attention to the interplay of different plants, they become even more difficult to maintain than herbaceous borders. Plants in mixed borders often have little in common, apart from the gardener's whim which placed them side by side, and share few patterns of growth on which to base their maintenance. The natural models for these mixed borders are the communities of plants that form scrub, and we should look to these for guidance when trying to create analogous communities of plants in gardens.

Scrub grows in more specialised conditions than woods or grasslands, but is found in many different situations.

Shrubs form heaths covering exposed, acid and often wet mountain ridges in which the predominant plants may be heathers, but, depending on where they grow, may also be rhododendrons, junipers, potentillas, helichrysums, hebes or any of dozens of other species.

Shrubs are the most conspicuous vegetation of patches of gorse, acacia or broom on well-drained, sunny slopes; of the sage brush of semi-desert areas between the Rocky Mountains and the Pacific; of the fynbos in South Africa and the Kwongan in Western Australia; of the evergreen maquis of the

Scrub usually persists only in places which are unfavourable for the growth of trees, or infiltration by grasses. The proteas, restios and heaths of the South African fynbos (above) are vulnerable to invasion by introduced trees and shrubs. Heather (top right) can cover huge areas, but overgrazing tips the balance in favour of bracken or coarse grasses. The pioneer tree ferns and shrubs (bottom right) will one day be replaced by forest as trees take over.

Mediterranean, and the chaparral of California. These varied communities all grow on well-drained, seasonally dry, sometimes infertile soils in situations that experience frequent, often prolonged periods of drought, and/or exposure to wind or low temperatures – often in places where fire is a recurrent element. The places where scrub develops are the antithesis of the fertile, sheltered, well-watered situations which have contributed to the success of so many human settlements and which in turn have become the places where most of us make our homes and gardens.

Consequently, those who garden in rather unusual contexts: on sandy soils, in exposed places, in hot, dry situations or other places where water is scarce – either because there is little of it, it drains rapidly out of reach or is frozen solid for long periods – are likely to find shrubs a satisfying and relatively simple solution to the problems of gardening in conditions which many would describe as difficult, while those who garden in kinder conditions struggle to maintain a balance in their mixed borders.

The 'Mixed Border'! Could any term be vaguer? It leaves maximum freedom for imaginative interpretation by individuals. But since it is impossible to discuss something with no limits, perhaps we can define it by a process of elimination. Evidently, it is not a border planted with a mixture of herbaceous plants, with or without bulbs, or even with or without annuals, because that would be too close to the dear old herbaceous border of late – and seldom lamented memory   to merit a new title. Nor should the name be used for a border in which successive layers of trees, shrubs, and perennials, with or without bulbs, are grown together. Although certainly mixed, that constitutes a garden version of woodland – a spinney. Similarly, borders filled exclusively with mixtures of shrubs are already familiar to us as shrubberies. So we are left with a border containing evergreen or deciduous shrubs, perennials, including grasses as well as broadleaved plants; ferns perhaps and even club mosses: bulbs of all sorts, and – why not? – annuals and biennials. A community of plants, which, as already noted, when found growing together under natural conditions is called scrub.

We are once again confronted by the conflict of interests represented by this kind of planting. The natural matrices of shrubs, perennials, grasses, annuals and bulbs in scrub depend on precarious balances between soil and climate which on the one hand, prevent grasses from taking over; and on the other, ensure trees do not occupy spaces between the shrubs and turn it into woodland. Apparently stable examples of scrub occur in South Africa where different fynbos communities – all based on proteas, ericas and restios – form long-lived, persistent communities across hundreds of square miles of lowland and mountain countryside. Stable, that is, until the arrival of Australian wattles and Mediterranean pines introduced newcomers able to exploit gaps in the matrix and turn fynbos into open woodland. Similarly, the mixture of evergreen shrubs known as the maquis around the Mediterranean had seemed to be the natural vegetation of the area. Now reduced grazing by goats – because goat herders can make a better living tending to tourists – is allowing the stronger members of this scrub to grow up above the shrubs and form dense evergreen woodlands of strawberry trees, oaks and pines, the true climax vegetation of the region.

Matrices in mixed borders are balanced equally precariously, and success depends on finding ways to counter pressures which would turn the border into something else – in natural terms, woodland dominated by trees, or savanna with grasses filling the spaces between the shrubs. Occasional invasions by even the most tenacious trees, such as elders, sycamores, kanukas, birches, eucalyptus and wattles, are seldom a serious problem as they can be removed individually. Grasses are designed to infiltrate and exploit gaps, and very often the natural sub-matrix beneath shrubs, within which broad-leaved plants exist, and so are much harder to exclude.

Unless our gardens are naturally endowed with the qualities that favour scrub, how do we maintain our mixed borders? Meadows are similar anachronisms in most gardens, vulnerable to infiltration by pioneering shrubs and trees, but those are automatically eliminated when the grass is mown; something that is done naturally by fire or grazing animals. We have no such simple, straightforward panacea when we grow mixtures of shrubs, perennials and bulbs together. We cannot lift them and divide and replant every three years like a herbaceous border. We cannot scythe or mow them like a meadow. We cannot fork over the ground between the plants. We cannot set fire to them, even though fire is one of the ways by which natural scrub is maintained. *Buddleja salvifolia* responds to a good blaze like a reviving tonic, but do not expect *B. davidii* to attract many butterflies after being torched. Nor can we smother plants that grow in sunny or lightly shaded spaces between shrubs with an annual blanket of mulch, unlike the woodland perennials that flourish under a winter covering. Mixed borders are a gardening wild card, full of promises but, unless we want to spend our days inextricably immersed in sorting out the problems of a hundred different plants with a hundred different needs, we need to learn how to play the hand.

The complexity of a matrix depends on its situation. In dry, seasonally arid gardens (top), bulbs and annuals grow between established trees and shrubs for only a few months. Under more benign conditions, ground-covering layers of grasses, perennials and ephemerals fill spaces between shrubs and roses throughout the year (bottom).

Elsewhere, problems of this sort have been resolved by analogy with wildflowers in similar situations. But the relatively precise comparisons possible in the previous chapter on water gardens, and the following one on shaded situations, are not applicable to the majority who garden in open, sunny, fertile situations. In these benign settings the habitats in which plants grow naturally become much less relevant. When planting a mixed border we think nothing of putting peach-leaved bellflowers, which grow naturally amongst grasses and shrubs on dry banks, beside Siberian irises from marshy meadows, alongside coral bells, inhabitants of open, deciduous woodlands. These three species would not inevitably form a successful matrix, but we can be confident they would be much more likely to do so in open, sunny, fertile borders than in any of the situations where each individually would find itself at home.

This breadth of choice seems daunting. First impressions may suggest anything goes, leading, when that proves a failure, to bemusement and the defeatist impression that 'nothing goes'. But, as in any other kind of planting, communities of plants in borders play a variety of roles, occupy different levels in the planting, and perform at different seasons, all of which contribute to the development of a matrix. Instead of basing this choice predominantly on the habitats in which plants grow naturally, we should pay more attention to the roles of different plants, placing emphasis on those whose forms and seasons of growth complement each other in the formation of a matrix.

Shrubs – sociable, unsociable and gregarious

Many shrubs grow socially in intimate associations. Their branches grow together, often intertwining or emerging through the undergrowth of grasses and herbs. Smaller shrubs, perennials and bulbs growing close to them are not deprived of light, water or nutrients by their leaves and roots. These sociable shrubs are mostly deciduous and are likely to share one or more of the following characteristics:

Upright shoots – tending to become bare towards the base

and/or easily pruned to make space at ground level for other plants.

Light leaf canopies – formed by open branch structures and small, or widely spaced leaves.

Thongy roots – which draw most of their nutrients and water from the deeper layers of the soil.

Late bud break – enabling neighbouring smaller plants to grow in the shelter of leafless branches in early spring.

Most are inhabitants of open woodland and transitional situations rather than scrub itself, and form complex multi-tiered matrices in situations where water is seldom severely deficient. They find naturally congenial conditions in gardens in Britain, in all but the Mediterranean, montane and northern parts of Europe, in the mid-Atlantic region and Pacific northwest of the USA, and in parts of Japan, New Zealand and southeastern Australia.

Other shrubs are unsociable; a high proportion are evergreen and grow in compact, humped or dome-shaped forms, usually with dense foliage. They may or may not form close matrices. When they do not, each occupies its own ground separated from neighbouring shrubs by spaces which may be filled constantly, but more likely only at certain seasons, with herbs, grasses and bulbs.

This is a pattern frequently adopted by formally-inclined gardeners who plant their shrubs as specimens separated by spaces filled with flowers of one kind and another. Unfortunately, as time passes and the shrubs increase in size, they coalesce and squeeze out other plants, developing into overwhelming masses of close-packed evergreen shrubs. Too often they are shorn mercilessly in ineffectual efforts to restrain them.

Under natural conditions many of these unsociable shrubs grow in places where seasonal drought, often accentuated by infertility, restricts the growth of associated plants. In more fertile conditions in gardens more amply supplied with water, broad-leaved perennials and grasses can quickly fill spaces between them before overwhelming the shrubs themselves, which are ill-adapted to cope with such aggression. Orthodox gardeners restrict such

Sociable shrubs

Many have relatively open branch structures beneath which ground covering perennials can grow, at least when the shrubs are leafless. They tolerate close association with other shrubs and climbers, or light overhead canopies of foliage from trees.

Abutilon vitifolium: An upright shrub or small tree with large, attractive lilac-blue flowers during the summer. The open structure associates well with neighbouring perennials.

Aralia elata 'Variegata': A notable plant with large, pinnate leaves which restrict the growth of other plants in summer, but a sparse superstructure of bare branches in winter favours evergreen undercover plants.

Buddleja davidii: Open structure and hard pruning in spring provide ample light and space for close-planted perennials. Attractive flowers in late summer, greatly enhanced by butterflies.

Chimonanthus praecox: A tall shrub, with fragrant flowers during the winter; easily pruned to provide space for perennials and low-growing shrubs beneath it.

Clianthus puniceus*: Normally low-growing evergreen shrub with trusses of large scarlet flowers, which mixes well with other shrubs, and ground covering perennials. Develops climbing tendencies in shaded situations.

Cornus florida: Large, broadly spreading but open, strikingly attractive shrub which combines well with spring-flowering perennials growing in its shade.

Corylopsis pauciflora: Several species, all with graceful pale yellow flowers in spring, do well in multi-tiered matrices below deciduous trees, with an undercover of woodland perennials.

Euonymus hamiltonianus subsp *hians*: A tall, spreading shrub adapted to light shade, with strikingly conspicuous orange and crimson fruits. Easily pruned to provide space for perennials growing below it.

Fuchsia magellanica*: Grows as a tall shrub, even a small tree, in frost free situations, sheltering smaller perennials and ferns. Cut back to ground level by frost in cold locations.

Hibiscus syriacus: Notable for its large mauve, pink or white flowers in late autumn. The shrub's upright form, and very late bud break, provide excellent conditions for neighbouring and lower plants.

Indigofera potaninii: Small leaves, an open framework of branches, and attractive crimson/purple pea flowers combine well with other shrubs and perennials.

Lonicera tartarica: A tall shrub, providing protection in winter and spring for evergreen, spring flowering perennials. A little dull, but provides excellent support for a clematis.

Magnolia stellata: Usually grown as an isolated specimen, but combines exceptionally beautifully with spring flowering, ground-covering perennials.

Medicago arborea*: Easily pruned to provide space for low growing plants that benefit from its nitrogen fixing bacteria.

Rhododendron yunnanense*: This upright, open-structured species with delicate rose pink flowers is one of a number of deciduous rhododendrons which combine well with low perennials, ferns and bulbs.

Rosa moyesii: The upright, sparsely branched forms of vigorous shrub roses find a natural home planted amongst dense ground-covering perennials and low-growing shrubs.

Spartium junceum: A nitrogen fixer with open growth which casts little shade and provides good conditions at ground level for bulbs, perennials and small shrubs.

Stachyurus praecox: A woodland shrub, with short pendant trails of pale yellow flowers, which thrives in light shade in the company of spring-flowering perennials.

Viburnum plicatum: Numerous forms available – some spreading others upright. All grow well in open woodland and with ground-covering perennials.

Vitex agnus-castus*: Tall shrub, with conspicuous spikes of mauve flowers like a buddleia; tolerant of drought and easily pruned to provide clear space near ground level for perennials and compact shrubs.

* Note: plants marked with an asterisk are vulnerable to frost in cold locations.

Sociable shrubs (top) lend
themselves to varied and
flexible uses in gardens. A
vine can be pruned (middle)
to grow as a sprawling shrub
amongst perennials and
bulbs. Gregarious shrubs like
heathers (bottom) perform
better in blocks than in more
intimate mixtures with other
plants.

Unsociable shrubs

These frequently form extended, rather open communities within which each grows more or less individually, in association with lesser shrubs, perennials, annuals, bulbs, succulents, etc.

*Banksia grandis**: A substantial shrub or small tree with heavy foliage and densely-packed yellow flowers on large, cylindrical infloresence. Intolerant of even moderate phosphorous levels and vulnerable to phytophthora.

Callistemon viminalis 'Little John'*: This compact, broadly amenable shrub has very dense needle-like foliage to ground level and robust, bright scarlet bottle brushes.

Carmichaelia odorata: One of a number of New Zealand brooms containing nitrogen-fixing bacteria in their roots. Produces short spikes of fragrant white flowers on pendulous branchlets in spring.

*Carpenteria californica**: A spreading broad-leaved evergreen, with upright shoots bearing large, pure white flowers in spring.

Cistus argenteus 'Silver Pink': Numerous species and cultivars of sun roses frequently form close-knit heaths naturally, but present better in isolation in gardens.

Euryops pectinatus: Dome-shaped, silver-leaved evergreen, forming compact shrubs dotted throughout late spring and summer with yellow daisies.

Halimium ocymoides: Low-growing twiggy shrub with bright yellow flowers with black centres. Combines well with drought-adapted perennials and bulbs as the ground layer between taller shrubs.

Hebe cupressoides 'Boughton Dome': A natural heath-forming species. This form with a tight-knit individual shape is better grown as an individual.

*Laurus nobilis**: Small tree with large, aromatic leaves and clusters of white flowers in spring. Top growth is killed by frost in cold districts where it usually develops into a large multi-stemmed shrub.

Lavandula stoechas: Species of lavender naturally adapted to acid soils. Produces large spikes of showy deep purple flowers surmounted by conspicuous ear-like bracts.

*Leschenaultia biloba**: Small shrub covered in spring with sky-blue flowers; suitable for seasonally arid conditions. Does not associate well with close neighbours in cultivation.

*Nerium oleander**: A robust shrub with strong straight shoots and long, narrow bright green leaves. Produces showy heads of pink or white flowers throughout summer.

Othonna cheirifolia: Low ground-covering shrubby plant for fully exposed situations in sunlight, with bright yellow daisy flowers.

Phlomis suffruticosa: Drought-adapted shrub with grey-green felted foliage. Grows naturally in dispersed communities, often associated with a rich ground flora of small perennials, annuals and bulbs.

*Pimelea rosea**: Compact, rounded evergreen, with rounded heads of rose-pink flowers. Vulnerable to phytophthora and competition from neighbouring plants in gardens.

*Protea scolymocephala**: Low-growing, drought-adapted shrub with dense foliage and distinctive bowl-shaped heads of greenish-yellow flowers. Intolerant of even moderate levels of phosphorus.

Rosmarinus officinalis: Upright, spreading shrub with narrow, pungently aromatic foliage and masses of grey-blue flowers. Associates well with other shrubs and ground flora in gardens.

Santolina chamaecyparissus: Easily grown, densely-foliaged, small eversilver shrub with bright yellow pompom flowers. Responds to annual shearing after flowering to maintain a compact weed-excluding form.

Sarcopoterium spinosum: The camel thorn is well-named; a low-growing, intensely thorny, rounded shrub. Occurs in open communities in seasonally arid situations.

Thymus vulgaris: Shrub usually grown as a culinary herb, with acutely aromatic foliage and soft purple flowers in summer. Grows naturally in dry, stony situations.

* Note: plants marked with an asterisk are vulnerable to frost in cold locations.

invasions by frequent attention to weeding, something which matrix planting aims to reduce or make redundant. One way of doing this is to grow these unsociable shrubs in a gravel garden, which can be created by covering the ground below with a layer of gravel at least 15 cm (6 in) and preferably 30 cm (1 ft) deep, into which the shrubs are planted.

Sociable shrubs, on the other hand, are naturally adapted to compete with other species, and hold their own in gardens where water is seldom or never a limiting factor, and where fertile soils often support vigorously competitive vegetation. Far from being overwhelmed, such shrubs if left to themselves form robust matrices that resist infiltration by outsiders and develop into interlacing thickets from which most of the ground flora – apart from things like ground elder and other evergreen or semi-evergreen plants whose leaves provide for a winter living – are eliminated. Few intruders can invade such thickets apart from climbers, brambles, old man's beard, woody nightshade and honeysuckles, and pioneering trees like ashes, kanukas and wattles. Left to themselves these eventually grow above the shrubs, shading them out to form a woodland and, at whatever stage of development, invaders of this kind need to be searched for and ruthlessly destroyed.

Roses are amongst the most sociable of all shrubs; amongst the trailblazing species that invade meadows in the first stages of its progression to scrub. Their thorns – prickles may be botanically correct, but the word fails to convey the ferocity many possess – deter grazing animals, and help the plants scramble up into and over competitors. Their roots are long, thongy and deeply penetrating, quickly descending below the surface mats of grasses to draw water and nutrients from lower levels of the soil.

Gardeners prefer to grow their roses apart from other plants in the belief they do better without competition, which is true when success is measured solely by the size of the flowers, but not when the aim is to make an attractive garden. Rose bushes emerging from beds filled with hardy geraniums, violas, euphorbias, crucianellas, pinks and other perennials not only look much prettier, but also mimic the condition in which these plants grow naturally.

Heaths of one kind or another – often growing in exposed, cold, wet, acid conditions – are close-knit plant communities composed of small evergreen shrubs or sub-shrubs growing in a single-layered matrix. Heather (*Calluna vulgaris*) is an extreme example of a species which grows in almost pure stands over enormous areas. Heaths are gregarious, rather than sociable, forming flocks of one or a few similarly disposed kinds, but, unlike sociable shrubs, are less friendly towards outsiders and not good mixers.

Other examples of heath are inhabited by species of Erica; by the closed communities of shrubs, including hebes, cassinias and coprosmas above the tree-line in New Zealand; the mountains covered with dwarf rhododendrons, and other ericaceous shrubs in the Himalayas and western China; or the communities of dwarf myrtles, epacrids, mint bushes and other shrubs in the high cold uplands of the Bogong Plains in Australia. Each consists of well-matched, often relatively few, species of low-growing evergreen shrubs existing as a single tier of plants, often barely 1 m (3 ft 3 in) high. Trees, if any, are widely dispersed or confined to sheltered gullies. Few perennials, bulbs or grasses grow amongst them though they may occupy boggy patches, rocky outcrops and other spaces that shrubs find uncongenial.

Shrubs from these heath communities are seldom suitable for the mixed border, and gardeners use them in other ways. Some are well adapted for easy-care plantings in the garden because of a natural inclination to knit together in weed-resisting phalanxes of self-supporting ground cover.

Gardens composed of heathers combined with low-growing conifers are a widely encountered example of their use in which the polychromatic tones of the foliage of the heathers and conifers combine in long-lasting, often brilliantly colourful effects, which are at their brightest during the winter.

Kurume azaleas provide 'ooh-ahh' spectacles every spring in the National Arboretum in Washington, the Punchbowl at Virginia Water, near London, and the Olinda Rhododendron Gardens among the Dandenong Hills in Melbourne and many other locations. Compact species and forms of hebes can be used equally effectively as weed-excluding, self-maintaining matrices though they lack the technicolour effects of heathers and evergreen azaleas.

Gregarious (heath-forming) shrubs

Many of these grow naturally in extensive communities – sometimes limited to a very few species – that extend over large areas. Familiar examples are provided by heaths (*Erica* and *Calluna* species) on which heather gardens are modelled.

Brachyglottis monroi: One of several shrubby New Zealand daisies with yellow flowers that form dense communities of montane heath in company with other compact shrubs.

Calluna vulgaris: Cultivars provide flowers in all shades of purple, pink and white and often brightly colourful foliage, too. Acid soils are essential for success.

Cassiope lycopodioides: Almost prostrate, dense evergreen shrub with white lily-of-the-valley style flowers, suitable for small scale heaths on acid, peaty soils.

Coprosma repens 'Pink Splendour'*: Bushy shrub with burnished, variegated leaves. Suitable for dry sandy soils and coastal situations.

Daboecia cantabrica: Numerous forms and cultivars. Comparatively large heather-like flowers in white and rich purple. Needs acid soils in gardens, and copes well with poorly drained locations.

*Dracophyllum recurvum**: Grows in mixed communities of alpine shrubs. Relatively drought tolerant.

Erica carnea: This and some other Erica species are small-scale heath-formers ranging from lawn-like ground cover to 3 m (10 ft) high screens. Most of the Cape heaths are more suitable for use as social shrubs.

Euonymus fortunei: Numerous cultivars with variegated foliage. All are tolerant, dense ground covers, even in shaded settings.

Gaultheria mucronata: Vigorous, medium-sized prickly shrubs with short sprigs of pink and white flowers, followed by large pink, white or crimson berries. Form extensive communities in damp, cool, acid situations.

Genista hispanica: An exceptionally dense gorse with prickly stems massed with yellow flowers for a short period in late spring. Needs hot, dry infertile situations.

Hebe diosmifolia: A compact shrub found naturally in alpine shrub communities. Carries masses of small white or pale pink flowers, is one of the progenitors of the series of 'Wiri' hebes.

*Helichrysum splendidum**: Densely packed, upright silver-leaved shoots, prefers abundant summer rainfall and good drainage in winter.

*Kunzea ericifolia**: A low-growing, closely compact shrub with narrow leaves on upright stems carrying numerous small heads of bright yellow flowers during the summer.

Leucothoe keiskei: Low, procumbent shrub with dense foliage and semi-pendant lily-of-the-valley flowers. Tolerant of light shade. Needs acid, cool conditions.

Microbiota decussata: Densely foliaged, extremely hardy ground-covering conifer which combines well with other low, relatively vigorous heath-forming shrubs.

Olearia nummularifolia: Small shrub with upright shoots covered with white flowers in early summer. Grows naturally in mixed alpine heath communities.

Phyllodoce caerulea: Exceptionally hardy, low-growing shrub with pink flowers requiring acid soils, in cool, lightly shaded settings.

Potentilla fruticosa: Numerous forms exist with yellow, white, pink or terracotta flowers. Extremely tolerant, easily established, long-flowering, easily managed shrubs.

Rhododendron fastigiatum: Compact shrub with glaucous foliage and lavender-blue flowers.

Vaccinium vitis-idaea: Small pink and white flowers are followed by bright scarlet berries. An excellent low, dense ground cover for acid soils in cold, wet situations.

* Note: plants marked with an asterisk are vulnerable to frost in cold locations.

Perennials

Perennials – and in this context the term emphatically includes grasses – are the vital components of the mixed border. Unlike a shrubbery, where the eventual aim is a complete cover of shrubs, the mixed border is intended to maintain in perpetuity against all the forces of nature a patchwork of shrubs and other plants. The close cover at ground level produced by perennials is the line of defence against intruders, supplemented to a greater or lesser extent by ephemeral annuals, biennials and bulbs. Annual weeds cease to be a problem as the matrices develop, but several formidably assertive perennial weeds, grasses and trees are adapted to invade communities of perennials and shrubs at seasons when their matrices become temporarily less effective. These invasions can be reduced by skilful planting, but intruders that do appear have to be removed by hand, and at an early stage.

During the formative years, spaces between the plants can be covered with weed-suppressing mulches as a stop gap until the plants in the border knit together. Such matrices depend on mixing together plants with different growth forms. Some are settlers which form ground-occupying fortresses of matted crowns, from which their flowering stems ascend into the air. Others colonise the ground between the settlers, and work their way beneath the shrubs. Yet others can be regarded as explorers seeking out and occupying spaces and plugging gaps in the matrix as they arise.

Settlers

Many familiar herbaceous plants are clump-forming settlers. Oriental poppies, some day-lilies, phloxes and eryngiums display little inclination to spread sideways and are moderately resistant to invasion. Others, including heleniums and Michaelmas daisies, produce crowns close to the surface that spread outwards year by year. As they extend, the crowns separate, leaving spaces open to invasion. Such plants usually need to be dug up from time to time, divided and replanted in fresh soil; they are ill-adapted to situations where intervention is undesirable.

Long-lived, clump-forming settlers are a valuable part of the mixed border, rivalling the shrubs in their permanency and visual impact, and greatly extending the flowering season, the range of textural contrasts and harmonies available, and variety of form. Their impact has been increased in recent years by a general recognition of the value of numerous clump-forming grasses, ranging in size from low-growing fescues to cultivars of the giant *Miscanthus sinensis*. Herbaceous plants contribute most effectively to the matrix during summer and autumn when they fill spaces between shrubs, casting dense shade on the ground below them that inhibits the development of annuals and most perennial seedlings. Even when their tops die down, their roots remain permanently in the ground which deters – although does not totally prevent – invasion by outsiders. However, spaces between them provide entry points through which seedlings can infiltrate the border.

Colonists, explorers and emphemerals

Many evergreen or semi-evergreen perennials grow naturally in association with taller perennials and shrubs, colonising the ground between them. These occupy space, smothering seedling weeds and other would-be invaders, and plugging vulnerable gaps in matrices when the leaves have fallen.

Unlike the settled perennials – which grow from year to year and, hopefully, seldom or never need to be disturbed – these colonists are flexible plants that can be planted, and removed and replanted if necessary as needs arise. Some like lamiums, persicarias and geraniums are easily propagated and large numbers can be produced as and when needed. Conversely, they are easily restrained – if they wander further than they should, just pull them out.

Plants with vigorously intrusive rhizomes, described here as the 'explorers', are amongst the more characterful members of natural plant communities and regarded with justifiable suspicion by gardeners. They can play preparatory parts in the development of a community by helping to stabilise shifting soils, and later can be relied on to fill gaps rapidly and effectively – sometimes too effectively. Plants such as marram grass, fireweed, stinging nettles and creeping thistle – however useful they may be

Ground-holding perennials
are the foundation of many
matrices; whether used in a
modern interpretation of a
perennial border (top left),
as weed-excluding carpets in
sunny, well-drained situations
(top right), or to provide
dense cover in semi-shaded
parts of the garden (left).
They can be equally effective
and decorative on a small
scale (bottom left).

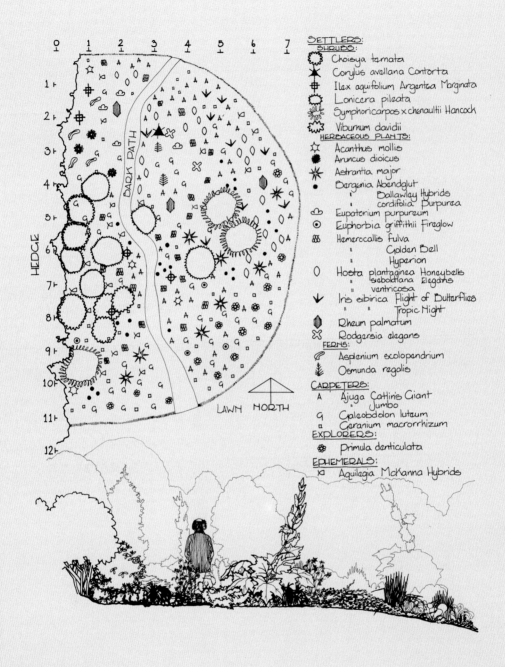

SETTLERS:
SHRUBS:
- Choisya ternata
- Corylus avellana Contorta
- Ilex aquifolium Argentea Marginata
- Lonicera pileata
- Symphoricarpos x chenaultii Hancock
- Viburnum davidii

HERBACEOUS PLANTS:
- Acanthus mollis
- Aruncus dioicus
- Astrantia major
- Bergenia Abendglut
    Ballawley Hybrids
    cordifolia Purpurea
- Eupatorium purpureum
- Euphorbia griffithii Fireglow
- Hemerocallis fulva
    Golden Bell
    Hyperion
- Hosta plantaginea Honeybells
    sieboldiana Elegans
    ventricosa
- Iris sibirica Flight of Butterflies
    Tropic Night
- Rheum palmatum
- Rodgersia elegans

FERNS:
- Asplenium scolopendrium
- Osmunda regalis

CARPETERS:
- A Ajuga Catlin's Giant
        Jumbo
- g Galeobdolon luteum
     Geranium macrorrhizum

EXPLORERS:
- Primula denticulata

EPHEMERALS:
- Aquilegia McKanna Hybrids

Planting plan for a mixed border

This is a large area of planting, approximately 65 m² (700 ft²) in all. It introduces a lush woodland atmosphere into a sheltered garden on a rich clay soil. The garden is bounded by woodland with oaks, ashes, hazels and hollies. The heavy leaf fall from these trees is an added bonus as they supplement the annual mulch from decayed leaves and stems of the garden plants. This annually renewed mulch creates conditions in which the garden thrives. Slugs are not a problem since no pesticides are used and so a healthy population of predators has built up, including frogs, toads, snakes, hedgehogs and birds.

Long-lived, clump-forming perennials

These plants occupy the ground very tenaciously, expanding relatively slowly over the years and producing dense root systems that exclude most intruders.

Acanthus spinosus: Deep-rooted, eternally persistent perennial with handsome foliage and bold flowers, adapted to sunshine but copes with dry shade.

Aconitum napellus: Upright stems produced from clustered tubers. Does best in moist soil, in cool, shaded settings.

Actaea daburica: One of several species of retentive space holders with handsome plumes of white flowers in autumn. Require well-drained, humus-rich soils in light shade.

Amsonia hubrichtii: Numerous upright stems with attractive heads of blue flowers produced from a compact rootstock. Fine foliage colour in autumn.

Astrantia major: Excellent ground-holding perennials with attractive, and very long-lasting, heads of small flowers enfolded by green, pinkish or crimson bracts.

Baptisia alba: Long-lived, tenacious legumes. Other species have yellow or blue flowers. Suitable for sandy, infertile, dry situations.

Cassia hebecarpa*: A perennial with the appearance of a shrub, with trusses of bright yellow flowers. Nitrogen fixing nodules in its roots improve fertility of poor soils.

Dictamnus albus: An almost rock solidly permanent plant for fertile, well-drained soils in sunlit situations. Gradually develops broadly-based clusters of stems.

Eremurus x *isabellinus* Shelford Hybrids: For very well-drained soils in full sun, radiating roots require space around the crowns. Good ground-holding qualities but contributes little to a matrix.

Euphorbia characias subsp. *wulfenii*: Shrub-like perennials which renew themselves annually to form broad weed-excluding 'bushes' topped by splendid heads of green or yellow-green flowers.

Gentiana lutea: Deep-rooted, very long-lived perennial with broad foliage and spikes of yellow flowers carried on strong upright stems.

Helleborus argutifolius: Vigorous and persistent in sun or light shade, hardy in most situations. Produces apple-green bowl-shaped flowers in spring. Self-seeds freely.

Hemerocallis 'Golden Chimes': One amongst innumerable hybrids producing comparatively small, well-formed yellow flowers above closely clustered foliage in early spring from masses of roots.

Hosta sieboldiana: A vigorous, reliably persistent plant which builds dense mats of roots topped by large, brightly glaucous leaves. Excellent for permanent ground-holding.

Paeonia officinalis cultivars: Like other species and cultivars, these are exceptionally long lived, persistent perennials able to hold ground indefinitely.

Salvia x *superba*: Quickly establishes dense root-mats with masses of upright stems topped with spikes of purple flowers throughout the summer; a vigorous ground holder.

Thalictrum delavayi: Gradually grows into a large multi-stemmed plant, in deep, moist humus-rich soil in lightly shaded settings.

Tricyrtis latifolia: Clustered stems above retentive roots. Establishes rather slowly and best in cool, preferably lightly shaded settings and rich, moist soil.

Veratrum nigrum: Establishes slowly but once in place is a perpetual tenant, with handsome, large, pleated leaves and tall spikes of deepest crimson flowers. Grows in sunlit or shaded settings in humus-rich, moisture-retentive soil.

Veronicastrum virginicum: Expands steadily by short rhizomes. Very easy to grow in sunny situations in fertile, well-drained soils.

* Note: plants marked with an asterisk are vulnerable to frost in cold locations.

Interweaving, space-filling colonists

These plants establish rapidly and spread out to fill spaces between the settlers. They are vital in the early stages of the development of a matrix, and plug gaps usefully later on too, as they form the warp to the weave of less mobile ground-holding plants. Many are more or less evergreen; some are short-lived self-seeders.

Alchemilla mollis: A sedentary plant, but one that fills spaces by self-seeding – sometimes to excess.

Anaphalis triplinervis: Spreads moderately, producing tufts of silver leaves on moisture-retentive soils in sun or, unusually for a silver-leaved species, in light shade.

Anemone sylvestris 'Macrantha': For light, humus-rich soil which does not become too dry, among well-spaced perennials or shrubs.

Anthriscus sylvestris 'Ravenswing': This quite recently introduced short-lived, crimson-leaved perennial has brought the common cow parsley into gardens. It fills gaps by self-sowing. Pull out green and pale seedlings.

Asarum canadense: One of the increasingly numerous species of wild gingers which provide excellent evergreen ground-cover beneath taller plants. A few are too temperamental to be useful.

Astrantia maxima: Spreads moderately by underground rhizomes. Fresh, bright green foliage and pincushion heads of pink flowers integrate well with neighbouring plants.

Campanula latiloba 'Alba': Tolerant of drought in sun or shade. The pure white flowers and deep green leaves make a greater impact interplanted with other perennials in fertile, moisture-retentive soils.

Dicentra formosa: This and other species and cultivars develop into excellent, dense ground-cover during spring and early summer between clumps of perennials and shrubs.

Digitalis grandiflora: A reliably perennial foxglove, with soft yellow flowers, which self-seeds freely to occupy spaces between other plants.

Duchesnea indica: Vigorously running strawberry look-alike. A worthy, though less than exciting filler of spaces in moist, lightly shaded settings.

Eryngium planum: This short-lived perennial self-seeds freely on well-drained soils in sunlit situations and is an excellent space-filler, especially the more colourful, of the steel-blue forms.

Fragaria vesca 'Multiplex': This wood strawberry with attractive double flowers produces little fruit, but makes an excellent ground cover, lapping around, but not invading, established plants.

Geranium macrorrhizum: Moderately-vigorous to vigorous evergreen infiltrator with bold aromatic foliage, and rather fugitive pink flowers. Amply fills spaces in sun or shade and tolerates drought.

Lamium maculatum: Numerous cultivars provide easily controllable, vigorous, almost self-sufficient ground cover; especially useful during the formative stages of a matrix.

Persicaria affinis: A moderate spreader which occupies ground very effectively amongst taller plants and at the front of borders in sunlit situations.

Phlox stolonifera 'Blue Ridge': Grows naturally in sunlit spaces along the woodland edge. A vigorous and attractive infiltrator amongst shrubs and perennials on moist, humus-rich soils in light shade.

Phuopsis stylosa: A mat-former with an intriguing, fugitive musky aroma. Good infiller between more upright plants and shrubs in sunlit situations. Responds well to autumn cutbacks.

Sedum spurium: Numerous stonecrops can be used in hot, dry locations as space fillers between clump-forming plants in sunny borders.

Viola cornuta hybrids: Few plants flower over longer periods than these mat-forming montane violets. Hold space tenaciously between more compact plants.

Waldsteinia ternata: Good ground-holding but non-invasive evergreen perennial with unusual foliage and attractive yellow flowers, which fills spaces exceptionally well.

* Note: plants marked with an asterisk are vulnerable to frost in cold locations.

Vigorously spreading rhizomatous perennials

Many of these should be used with great care, matching their potential to the space available and the vigour of their companions. When large spaces are to be filled, several are invaluable and should not be overlooked.

Acanthus mollis: Forms steadily spreading, eventually extensive and extremely retentive colonies, in sun and on dry soils.

Aegopodium podagraria 'Variegatum': Spreads steadily by underground rhizomes and does best in light shade in humus-rich soil that never becomes too dry.

Alstroemeria aurea: Established plants are very retentive, deep-seated colonisers. Best in moist soils in light shade.

Anemone x hybridia 'Queen Charlotte': Like other Japanese anemones this plant forms moderately spreading, almost ineradicable colonies. Few plants do more to enhance shade and poor soils in late summer and early autumn.

Campanula poscharskyana: Low-growing, vigorous evergreen colonist of stony, well-drained sites in sunlit places, and able to cope almost equally effectively with dry shade.

Centaurea hypoleuca 'John Coutts': Good foliage and fine purple flowers, displayed for a long period, combined with a not too invasive nature make a most attractive and serviceable plant.

Convallaria majalis: Spreads vigorously by rhizomes. Valued for its delightfully fragrant flowers as well as its self-sustaining ability to tolerate drought and shade.

Euphorbia cyparissias: Low-growing, rapidly increasing, definitely invasive perennial with good foliage. Use only in company with other vigorous ground occupiers.

Helianthus atrorubens 'The Monarch': Vigorous spreader and occupier of space, more tender than most others of the genus, but with fine yellow sunflowers in late autumn.

Heliopsis helianthoides var *scabra*: Vigorous, but only moderately spreading, yellow daisy for dry, sandy soils especially on well-drained banks.

Hemerocallis fulva: A vigorous spreader capable of occupying large areas, especially on humus-rich woodland soils. Used with caution, this can be highly successful.

Lysimachia punctata: Extremely vigorous plant with conspicuous spikes of yellow flowers. A tolerant and retentive spreader, which rapidly forms colonies in moist settings.

Macleaya microcarpa: Fine plant with superb foliage combining shades of dove-grey and crimson, and capable of occupying whatever space is available in sun on well-drained, fertile soils.

Persicaria campanulata: A moderately vigorous spreader for moist, shaded situations amongst shrubs and tall perennials.

Physalis alkekengi: Another vigorous coloniser, almost uncontrollable in fertile situations. Tolerant of most soils and situations, for use only where occupation of space is the primary objective.

Podophyllum peltatum: Spreads steadily, but rather remorselessly, to form large colonies, particularly amongst grass in partial shade.

Romneya coulteri: May be reluctant to establish, but once happily settled it spreads vigorously in hot sunny positions on fertile, free-draining soils.

Solidago 'Golden Wings': A comparatively modest member of a genus notable for vigorous species and cultivars capable of taking over considerable areas.

Tanacetum vulgare: Beguiling, deep green, dissected foliage can blind gardeners to the plant's ability to spread vigorously and tenaciously in sunny situations on any but sodden soils.

Thalictrum minus 'Adiantifolium': Forms dense, extremely retentive colonies of short stems covered with attractive foliage, from almost ineradicable roots.

---

* Note: plants marked with an asterisk are vulnerable to frost in cold locations.

Space-filling ephemerals and short-lived perennials

These include annual and biennial species, either deliberately planted out or sown *in situ*. They vary greatly in their aggression and vigour, but all are relatively easily controlled by removing them or dead heading to prevent or reduce seed production.

Ajuga reptans: Numerous cultivars of this mobile perennial exist, most with richly colourful foliage. The plants seldom stay put, but spread erratically by short stolons.

Angelica archangelica: An imposing biennial for fertile, moderately dry, sunny situations. Self-seeds where there is space.

Aquilegia atrata: A moderately long-lived woodland perennial for lightly shaded situations on base-rich soils. Self-seeds readily when happy, but hybridises with other columbines.

Commelina tuberosa coelestis group: A perennial in frost-free situations, but a self-seeding annual in cold areas. Prefers fertile, moist soils in sun or light shade.

Dianthus plumarius: A short-lived perennial for dry, sunny, well-drained situations on base-rich soils where it produces occasional seedlings.

Digitalis purpurea: Stately biennial, available in a number of different forms, for light shade or sun on moist, humus-rich soils. Freely self-seeding in open spaces on neutral or acid soils.

Eryngium giganteum: Biennial for free-draining, fertile soils in sunlit locations. Regenerates from seed even amongst established perennials.

Foeniculum vulgare 'Purpureum': Large, short-lived perennial with fragrant, ferny, richly colourful foliage, and a very free self-seeder in hot, dry, sunny situations.

Glaucium corniculatum: Unreliable, but sometimes moderately long-lived, imposing perennial. Self-seeds in dry, very stony situations.

Hesperis matronalis: Short-lived perennial with fragrant lilac or white flowers freely self-sowing, even amongst established plants. Does well in light shade or sunny situations on moisture-retaining soils.

Lunaria annua: Several forms of this biennial seed themselves reliably in gardens; sometimes to excess and thinning may be necessary.

Malva moschata f. alba: An attractive short-lived perennial, often maintains itself from seedlings growing in gaps in sunny borders.

Meconopsis cambrica: Not always easy to establish, but once installed, likely to become a freely self-seeding species. Valued for its long succession of bold, bowl-shaped yellow flowers.

Myosotis sylvatica: Self-seeds in gaps in light woodland, but seldom maintains itself beyond the initial stages of matrix formation.

Oenothera glazioviana: A rather coarse biennial with large, showy yellow flowers that readily naturalises in sunny, open situations on free-draining, base-rich soils.

Onopordum nervosum: The so-called 'Scotch Thistle' is a massively formidable biennial, inclined to self-sow moderately freely, often in unexpected places.

Papaver rupifragum 'Flore Pleno': Freely self-seeding, short-lived perennial with fine semi-double tangerine flowers, for dry, sunny banks and other well-drained situations.

Salvia sclarea var. *turkestanica*: A biennial with fine foliage and imposing flower heads – especially when in bud – for fertile, free-draining, base-rich soils.

Silybum marianum: Biennial thistle with broad green leaves veined with white; tolerant of a wide range of light to medium, well-drained or humus-rich soils.

Verbascum olympicum: Short-lived perennial with majestic branching stems illuminated with yellow flowers; freely self-seeding on warm, dry, sandy or base-rich soils in sunny situations.

* Note: plants marked with an asterisk are vulnerable to frost in cold locations.

as members of communities of wildflowers – carry a warning that gardeners ignore at their peril. Some are valued, useful and, in most situations, trustworthy members of the garden community, even in small gardens. But gardeners with little space, looking for intricate rather than bold plantings should avoid most of these rhizomatous plants and look for other, more controllable space-fillers.

Many emphemerals perform a useful and decorative function during the early stages of matrix formation. As matrices take shape, they are likely to be replaced by perennials, but may continue to play a part by self-seeding to fill occasional or seasonal gaps.

Plants that self-seed may do so too enthusiastically while gaps are spacious, and may need a little curbing. However, in the later stages of development of a matrix they take on the role of explorers; finding and filling incidental

Bulbs seldom contribute materially to the strength of a matrix, but can be used liberally for decorative impact without prejudicing the success of their neighbours. Many alliums (top) associate well with plants in sunlit settings. Lilies (bottom) provide brilliant, though short-lived, displays amongst shrubs and perennials in light shade.

spaces. Then the unplanned appearances of love-in-the-mist, foxgloves, rose campion and other annuals and short-lived perennials add colour and spontaneity to the planting.

Bulbs

Gardeners become so carried away by the attractions of the stems, foliage and flowers of trees, shrubs and perennials, they sometimes forget about the roots. But try to plant beneath established trees and you will soon discover what a formidable deterrent the subterranean parts of plants can be to the entry of newcomers, and what a critical part of the matrix they are. Alliances with roots are an important part of matrix management and some of the most attractive of these allies are those plants that retreat into resting organs below the ground for part of each year. Bulbs, tubers, corms and rhizomes are all refuges against adversity, from which the plants sally out when drought or cold or shade or whatever other threatening danger has passed, and more agreeable growing conditions return.

This ability to survive difficult conditions makes it possible for bulbs to thrive in situations where other plants would struggle. The woods in the river valleys where I live are filled with snowdrops in February, when little else is stirring. Later the dense canopy of the trees produces so much shade, the ground is almost bare. In other, hotter parts of the world alliums flower on naked stems after summer drought has withered their leaves, and the colours of the spring display of most bulbs and annuals has faded away. Some bulbous plants like the Italian arum and cyclamen add to the variety and interest of plant communities by occupying space above ground when other plants are leafless. Wherever possible, bulbous plants should be planted before, or at the same time, as other permanent plants are being put in position, rather than afterwards.

The Gardens

C A S E *S T U D I E S*

Brigadier in Seaside Retreat

The 300 sq m (350 sq yd) back garden of a Georgian house in the south coast seaside town of Sidmouth in Devonshire, England. Winters are mild with few nights when temperatures fall below -5°C (23°F) and, although westerly gales may buffet it at any time of the year, the garden is far enough from the sea to escape serious problems from salt spray. In common with many long-established gardens in towns, the soil is almost black, free-draining and easy to work. The owner, a retired brigadier who never married, is an assistant bursar at a local boarding school and his part-time duties leave him plenty of time for the garden. He is a pedantic, rather pernickety, self-confessed old buffer with strong views about the value of appearances, and frets at the least hint of untidiness. He takes great pleasure showing his garden off to his friends. He does not pretend to be knowledgeable about plants, and is a stalwart supporter of 'good old-fashioned flowers', being particularly cool towards those known only by their Latin names.

Review

A. The Brigadier is less active than he used to be. It was time for changes to be made to reduce the demands of the garden while still offering scope for him to continue to enjoy working in it.

B. As is often the case in long-established town gardens, the dark, easily managed soil was less fertile than it looked. It needed a nutrient boost, and treatment to enhance its water-holding capacity and structure.

C. Plants, including weeds, grew more vigorously as a result and would have added to the brigadier's problems if changes in planting styles had not been adopted.

D. The owner's pleasure in sitting out in the garden has decreased as his blood thins, and he feels the effects of the sea breezes and gales more keenly. Increased shelter was a high priority.

Outcome

A.

- A path of pavers was laid from the house along one side of the lawn to make a safer all-weather route through the garden.

- When the paths were excavated, the spoil was spread over adjacent beds, and replaced by gravel, kept weed-free by annual applications of 'Pathclear' containing diquat, paraquat and amitrole for immediate effects, plus simazine as a pre-emergence weedkiller.

B.

- Borders were regularly top-dressed in late winter with a proprietary garden fertiliser (N:P:K 7:7:7) at the rate of 100 g/sq m (3 oz/sq yd).

- Early each winter, a mulch of mushroom compost or spent hops was spread under the trees and shrubs, more or less submerging the perennials beneath them.

- The owner was finally persuaded to scatter the mowings from the lawn in a thin layer over the back of the borders instead of dumping them at the end of the garden where they had formed a putrid, greasy pile.

C.

- Very reluctantly and with great misgivings he accepted advice to replace his regimented parade of well-spaced plants, isolated from one another by bare earth, with less defined groupings in which shrubs and perennials formed weed-excluding matrices under trees.

Scrubberies and 'the mixed border' 147

The brigadier insists on an orderly garden, but the necessity of reducing work has introduced him to styles and methods of planting he would never have previously considered. To his surprise, he is delighted by the effects following his use of matrix planting, and his beds now look much more lively for longer periods than before. The garden is more sheltered in the winter and also more interesting – the groups of new trees are attractive in themselves and provide shelter not only for neighbouring plants but also for numerous birds that were seldom seen before.

- This cost very little as, apart from trees, he was able to obtain most of the plants he needed by propagating those already in the garden, or by buying one or two from garden centres as stock plants for cuttings.

D.

- The matrices of trees and shrubs around the lawn sheltered the garden, making it much more enjoyable for relaxation and reducing his work.
- A high hedge along one boundary, previously clipped precariously from rickety wooden steps, was removed and replaced by a stout trellis-work fence, covered with climbing roses, honeysuckles, clematis and ivies, etc. This was safer for him to look after and provided more interesting and effective shelter.
- A small greenhouse made a warm, sheltered place to work, where he could grow plants from seeds and cuttings, including replacements for the tender perennials that make such a bright display during the summer.

The Plants

The only trees planted were seedling birches, including *Betula albosinensis* and *B. utilis*, and *Acer rufinerve*, *A. davidii* and *A. grosseri* var. *hersii*. Two to four of each were closely grouped to emphasise the effects of their stems. A close-set trio of *Cupressus macrocarpa* 'Goldcrest' was planted in an exposed corner for shelter and colour in winter.

The sheltering effects of the trees were reinforced by underplanting with evergreen shrubs, concentrated towards the boundaries as backgrounds for deciduous shrubs and perennials. These included *Ceanothus* 'Delight' and 'Italian Skies'; groups of solid cover from *Hebe* 'La Séduisante', 'Marjorie' and 'Watson's Pink', with the bright, glossy foliage of *Pittosporum tenuifolium*

'Irene Paterson' and 'Wharnham Gold' like shafts of sunlight. *Rhododendron* 'Praecox' was included for an early taste of spring, and – the Brigadier's favourite – *R.* 'Pink Pearl'.

Other shrubs planted around the lawn and alongside the paths included *Abelia* x *grandiflora* and the tall, fragrant *A. triflora*; *Cestrum parquii*, *Coronilla valentina* subsp *glauca* in sunlit places; *Kerria japonica* 'Golden Guinea', because bachelor's buttons used to grow in the Brigadier's granny's garden; *Fuchsia magellanica* vars. *molinae* and *gracilis* and 'Dollar Princess', which grew into large shrubs in the mild conditions; *Hydrangea* 'Madame Emile Mouillere' and 'Générale Vicomtesse de Vibraye', although the Brigadier confessed himself baffled by the lady's military pretensions. *Hypericum* 'Rowallane' was added for late summer colour, and the easily controlled *Weigela florida* 'Foliis purpureis' for its purple leaves.

The owner insisted on numerous roses – 'not those dreadful blowsy old-fashioned things that always look so untidy' – but kinds like 'Alec's Red', 'Arthur Bell', 'Peace' and 'Silver Jubilee', which were kept apart from the trees and shrubs in beds underplanted with *Geranium macrorrhizum* and *G. renardii*, *Viola cornuta* hybrids, *Lamium* 'Beacon Silver' and *Acaena* 'Blue Haze' and 'Copper Carpet' among other low-growing perennials.

Perennials planted amongst the trees and shrubs, in the less accessible places, were encouraged to grow into a complete weed-excluding ground cover. Closer to the lawn and along the paths, spaces were planted annually with osteospermums and marguerites, snapdragons, Canterbury bells, Coltness hybrid dahlias, nemesias, petunias and scarlet salvias grown by the Brigadier in his glasshouse – an achievement of which he is immensely proud.

Gardening Editor's Crisis of Confidence

The owners of this garden, at the back of an old house in Saffron Walden in East Anglia, England are the editor of a gardening magazine and his wife. High walls on three sides make it a sheltered, warm and tranquil place. The editor's post was a commercial decision, and does not reflect a deep interest in gardening or knowledge of plants. He prefers to spend his spare time sailing, but is not averse to a little fair-weather gardening; cruising, glass in hand, showing it off to colleagues and friends. His enjoyment of this little pleasure has been rather spoilt on several recent occasions by aromas from the neighbour's barbecue drifting over the wall. His wife loathes cold water, hates sailing and loves gardening. The garden owes everything to her work and imagination, and she looks on it as hers – a claim unacknowledged by her husband, whose barbed comments to guests about her efforts grow snider under the influence of the party spirit. He has been uneasy about the garden, feeling it falls short of the well-groomed statement he would like to make as editor of a prestigious gardening magazine. From time to time, he affronts and enrages his wife by launching into a weekend of furious tidying and pruning.

Review

A. This garden, enclosed foursquare by walls in the centre of a town, would seem to many people, as indeed it does to the editor, an automatic choice for a formal lay-out. His wife's decision to treat it informally is at the root of his ambiguous attitude towards it.

B. The site is a very favourable one. The pH of the soil is too high for rhododendrons to grow, but otherwise imposes few restrictions on the choice of plants. In other respects the soil is in good condition, with a well-maintained structure, adequate fertility and reasonable water-holding capacity.

C. The editor's appetite for gardening is entirely saturated within the limits of his job, and he would be the first to object if called upon to commit himself to any prolonged creative or consistent effort in the garden.

Outcome

A.

- The informal layout provides a relaxing contrast to the hard lines of neighbouring buildings, and the noise and activity in the surrounding streets.
- In particular, it sets the scene for an abundant, free style of growth which creates shelter, shade and privacy in a variety of places, and provides attractively secluded 'hide-outs' at different times of the day.

B.

- There is no lawn, but a gravel garden forms an open, irregularly shaped sunny area in the centre. This was made on a base of about 20 cm (8 in) of broken bricks and mortar, covered with 10 cm (4 in) of Cerney gravel, consisting of flat, rounded fragments of limestone that are comfortable to walk on.
- The warm, sheltered site and especially the walls have been used for an interesting collection of shrubs, predominantly roses. There are only a few trees – with a variety of perennials beneath them.

C.

- Recently, the garden featured in a chic homes and gardens glossy magazine with flattering photographs and appreciative comments about its originality and style. The editor now feels less defensive about the impression it creates; is less given to criticism, but even more inclined to claim it as his own.

The Plants

Trees were carefully sited to provide shade and seclusion while leaving an open space in the centre of the garden. Most were naturally small, or could be kept small by judicious pruning, and several were chosen with pinnate leaves for their light and airy effects. They included *Acacia dealbata*, planted against a wall; *Albizia julibrissin f. rosea* and *Gleditsia triacanthos* 'Rubylace'. Also planted were *Magnolia* 'Iolanthe' – a Felix Jury hybrid that not only flowers precociously, but produces a succession of buds which enable it to recover flower power after a frost; *Parrotia persica; Sorbus aria* 'Chrysophylla' and *Xanthoceras sorbifolium*.

The sunshine and warmth in the centre of the garden were accentuated by the free-draining, base-rich gravel garden, which provided a home from home for many plants with fragrant foliage native to limestone around the Mediterranean. The planting formed an open matrix of shrubs and woody perennials amongst which were *Ballota pseudodictamnus*; *Caryopteris* x *clandonensis* 'Kew Blue' with *Indigofera potaninii* and *Perowskia atriplicifolia,* for later colour; several sun roses included *Cistus* 'Paladin', C. 'Peggy Sammons' and *C.* x *skanbergii*. Also included were *Convolvulus cneorum*, *Daphne cneorum* 'Eximia', *Genista hispanica*, *G. lydia* and *Hyssopus officinalis*. Lavenders included 'Loddon Pink' and 'Munstead', with the woolly leaved *Lavandula lanata*. There were *Phlomis chrysophylla* and *P. italica* and several rosemaries, including the tender *Rosmarinus* var. *prostratus*; 'Jackman's Blue' rue as well as *Ruta graveolens* 'Variegata'; and cotton lavenders, 'Edward Bowles' and *Santolina pinnata* subsp *neapolitana*.

Perennials amongst the shrubs were planted to form mats overlying bulbs, capable of resisting a little foot-wear. These included *Antennaria dioica* 'Nyewoods Variety', *Aethionema* 'Warley Rose'; several colour forms of *Campanula carpatica* and *C. cochlearifolia*, *Dianthus crinitus*, *D. gratianopolitanus* and 'La Bourboule', *Erysimum* 'Jacob's Jacket' and 'Moonlight'; *Euphorbia myrsinites*, several different colour forms of *Geranium cinereum* and a variety of low-growing thymes. More upright, spiky contrasts were provided by *Asphodeline lutea*, *Iris pallida* subsp. *pallida* and 'Florentina'. These were supported by grasses including *Bouteloua gracilis,* a bronze form of *Carex comans;* and the curiously malformed 'Frosted Curls'; also *Festuca amethystina*, and *F. glauca* 'Elijah Blue' and 'Blue Fox', with background effects from clumps of the tall, mobile *Stipa gigantea*.

Flower Arranger's Garden Showpiece

The managing director of a company selling cars in Folkestone in southeast England is the owner of this garden of nearly a hectare (two-and-a-half acres). It faces northeast at the foot of a chalk hillside a mile or two inland, and is exposed to cold winds. The soil is a base-rich, putty-coloured boulder clay heavily laced with flints; intractably sticky in winter; dry as a brick and riven by cracks in summer. The rainfall is quite low. The owner took over the car business on the death of her husband, and has since come into her own, both financially and personally. She has a reputation as a perfectionist, who spares neither effort nor expense in keeping her garden looking like a showpiece. The founder and president of a local flower arranging group, she is an outspoken participant in the national flower arranging society NAFAS; she opens her gardens to groups for visits and meetings several times each year. She employs a full-time gardener but does a great deal of gardening herself. The previous gardener departed rapidly after a worldly-wise member of a visiting NAFAS group pointed out that unfamiliar plants growing amongst the vegetables were cannabis.

Review

A. The pale, unattractive appearance of the soil is misleading. It is intractable and difficult to work, but is much more fertile than it looks.

B. The garden's position on a northeast slope, accentuated by exposure to cold winds, is a more serious disadvantage.

C. Employing a gardener to mow lawns, trim hedges and edges, and cultivate vegetables, gives the owner time and energy to think creatively and try out new ideas; something she does with great verve, and little compunction about dismantling last year's grand scheme.

D. The garden is a source of material for flower arranging, and this is an important function of the planting, which is generously deployed to satisfy her friends' needs as well as her own.

Outcome

A.

- The best way to enhance the appearance of this soil, and make it easier to work, would be to cover it with a mulch. However, the owner considers mulches untidy. First attempts to persuade her to give the idea a try using 'Forest Bio-mulch', chosen for its appearance, came to nothing when its suppliers failed to arrange delivery. She continued to insist on regular applications of compost or farmyard manure dug in, or forked between established plants, and timely use of the hoe.

- Recently she was persuaded to invest in a shredding machine, and its practicality and economy is beginning to persuade her to use its products directly as a mulch, rather than composting material.

B.

- Parts of the garden have been terraced, with walls of flint and brick, to convert cold northeast slopes into level surfaces, which warm up more rapidly in spring and drain freely during the winter.

- Yew hedges, planted years ago for shelter, have grown excessively broad, and a programme of drastic reduction was necessary. The first year, every branch on one side was cut back to the main stems, followed by similar treatment to the other side the next.

C.

- Terraces and hedges form sheltered compartments planted to create different effects.

- The owner spurns the contemporary fashion of narrowly defined colour theming in favour of effects obtained by thoughtful compositions of foliage and texture, reinforced by well coordinated repetition, following the flower arranger's precept of 'Repetition makes Rhythm'.

D.

- A flair for arrangement makes it natural for the owner to combine plants of different kinds in the multi-tiered fashion of matrix planting, but she has little inclination to surrender control of any kind to the plants.
- The result is a highly dynamic, constantly changing, labour-intensive version of matrix planting. The extremely attractive and varied compositions of flowers and foliage, beautifully graded from the ground upwards, which this produces never have time to develop into self-sustaining communities before being replaced.

The Plants

Hybrid tea and floribunda roses are grown mainly in the cutting borders alongside the kitchen garden, and the owner relies almost entirely on shrub roses elsewhere. These include numerous 'old-fashioned' gallicas, albas and hybrid perpetuals, but she has been converted to David Austin's 'English roses' and every year tries a few new ones; keeping some, rejecting others. She liked the drooping glowing crimson heads of 'The Squire' for arrangements, and amongst others, also grows the yellow 'Graham Thomas', 'Abraham Darby' and 'Leander', and has high hopes for 'Brother Cadfael', a modern version of the classic, bowl-shaped, pink rose.

The roses are grown in intricately mixed borders with shrubs, perennials, bulbs and annuals. The latter are varied year by year and play a major part in the appearance of the border, where they are planted wherever there is space for them between other roses, paeonies, hard-pruned *Hydrangea paniculata* 'Praecox' and 'Grandiflora', *Syringa* x *persica* and its white form 'Alba', *Ligustrum ovalifolium* 'Argenteum' and 'Aureum' (cut back hard each spring), *Philadelphus* 'Avalanche' and 'Beauclerk', and other shrubs.

Some annuals, and other transients, tried recently include the tall florists' forms of ageratums and snapdragons; *Ammobium alatum* 'Grandiflorum'; *Beta dracaenaefolia*; the bright oranges and yellows of *Calendula* 'Early Nakayasu', 'Orange Shaggy' and 'Radar'; the special Matsumoto florists' forms of the China aster, and *Celosia* 'Fire Chief'; 'Stock Flowered' and 'Imperial' larkspurs; *Euphorbia marginata* for the bright contrast of its variegated leaves; *Helichrysum orientale*; *Helianthus* 'Taiyo' and other small, branching sunflowers. Also *Helipterum manglesii*, *H. roseum*, *Limonium sinuatum*, *Molucella laevis* (having discovered how to germinate its seeds), *Papaver nudicaule*; *Rudbeckia* 'Gloriosa' hybrids, *Tithonia speciosa*, *Xeranthemum annuum*; and strains of *Zinnia elegans* with green or white flowers.

She grows some annual as well as perennial grasses, including the hanging lanterns of *Briza maxima*; *Coix lachryma-jobii,* which seldom flowers but is grown for its hummocks of broad leaves; *Hordeum jubatum* and the fluffy tufts of *Lagurus ovatus*.

Recently, she has become enthralled by the possibilities of several very large, broad-leaved grasses including *Sorghum bicolor* and *S. dochna* var. *technicum* (broom corn) which grows to nearly 3 m (10 ft) in a warm summer, as well as clumps of *Zea mays* 'Harlequin' and 'Quadricolor'.

Bulbs, especially daffodils and tulips, play a major part in the border in spring, and are thickly planted amongst the perennials and shrubs. The daffodils are lifted and divided every third or fourth year; the tulips every year. Later *Allium cristophii*, *A. giganteum* and other decorative onions are grown for their dried heads, and *Crocosmia* 'Citronella', 'Jackanapes' 'Norwich Canary' and 'Firebird' for their bright colours after midsummer. She is also fond of *Galtonia candicans*, finding its conspicuous white spires invaluable for effective repetitive use, and *G. viridis*, because of its silken, light olive-green tubular bells.

counting
the *blessings*
of shade

9

TREES ARE GREAT ASSETS, but these giant vegetables are not always welcome in gardens. Torn between admiration and apprehension, we miss opportunities to use them and the spaces beneath them creatively, and the shade they cast is seen as a problem. They are lopped and mutilated in half-baked attempts to keep them within bounds, instead of being pruned constructively.

Most gardeners today compose their gardens with mixtures of perennials, shrubs and bulbs. These are the natural associates of trees, whose presence should simplify – not complicate – management. There is an attitude problem here. which seems to be a peculiarly British affliction. Elsewhere more relaxed attitudes to trees prevail, particularly in parts of New England and Western Canada, and in Holland, Germany and France too, where trees are more likely to be prized for their shelter, and valued for the ways their upright stems and spreading tops provide settings for houses.

The forest in the garden

Few people make gardens within a natural wood; more often, trees are less obviously at home. Newly planted trees make little impact. Badly managed mature trees in older gardens create deserts of dry shade in which few plants are comfortable. Gardens of all kinds contain ornamental trees, chosen on an assurance they will not grow too big, whose stems, seldom even 2 m (6 ft 6 in) high, are crowned by densely foliaged, rounded tops which interrupt every vista and deprive plants beneath them of light. These are situations where muddled thinking has led to problems.

Good management limits the unfavourable aspects of trees, and instead makes use of the benefits they offer by:

Maintaining, and if possible increasing levels of organic matter beneath the trees – Fallen leaves should not be removed; heavy dressings of organic mulches should be applied before planting, and repeated annually as long as possible. Perennials growing under trees can be blanketed in early winter with mulches, through which they will emerge the following spring.

Reducing shading effects while maintaining shelter – The height of the canopy is a critical part of the system: in most situations, the higher the better. Stems occupy little space at ground level, and a long, clear reach to the lower branches raises the canopy high enough to allow light to reach plants growing below.

(Opposite) Shade, so often looked on as a problem in a garden, can be used to create some of the most attractive and relaxing of garden settings. Shade-tolerant ferns, hostas and other broad- or narrow-leaved perennials combine to fill spaces on the ground amongst trees in a restful and enticing mix of shapes and textures, based almost exclusively on variations of the colour green.

Benefiting from the woodland edge effect – The margins of forests and the perimeter of established trees are sheltered settings, where wildflowers, shrubs and climbers grow naturally. Most gardens contain examples of a 'woodland edge'. Every isolated, or well-spaced tree provides such areas; they appear beneath pergolas, along hedges, around the edges of large shrubs in mixed borders, and in the shadow of buildings.

Choosing suitable trees – Shrubs and plants combine more easily with trees with light canopies and deeply penetrating roots than with densely foliaged, surface-rooting kinds. Apples, thorns, plums, many cherries and other popular ornamental trees are not true canopy-formers in forests. They occupy lesser positions in woodland or grow in savanna where trees are widely spaced, or amongst scrub. Their low, densely twiggy and heavily foliaged, rounded crowns lack the long clear stems that provide views through the garden and allow light to reach plants beneath them.

Pruning intelligently – Trees that become noticeable, which is inevitable in most gardens, too often suffer from unskilful, thoughtless pruning. They are lopped to reduce their spread, often enthusiastically rather than skilfully. Far from curbing exuberance, this short top and sides treatment stimulates vigorous renewed growth below the cuts, and a reversion, within a few years, to an even more densely twiggy and heavily foliaged version of the original

Large and small trees, shrubs and perennials (top left and right) form strong multi-tiered matrices, especially when they include evergreens. A bird's eye view of birches amongst heathers (bottom left) shows how little space the trunks of trees occupy at ground level.

problem. It is almost always better practise to lift the crown by removing lower branches, and thin out rather than cut back the upper branches.

Planting in appropriate ways – Isolated trees suffer from exposure. Planted in groups, and thinned out as they grow, each benefits from the shelter of the others. The repetitive vertical accents of trees is particularly effective when acers, birches and others with conspicuous bark are planted in groups. Even trees intended to develop as specimens grow best amongst sheltering, faster growing kinds which are progressively removed to make space. This provides woodland effects with all its benefits early on, and encourages the formation of long clear stems on those that are left.

Relevant management – Instructions for choosing trees almost invariably start with injunctions to match the anticipated size of the mature tree to the space available. There is wisdom in this when trees are intended to grow to maturity, but that day may be so far away it is almost irrelevant. Often, it is more rewarding to plant for the foreseeable

future and, when necessary, restrict the growth of the trees by managing them in ways that are used by foresters as a matter of course but largely ignored by gardeners. Foresters thin out trees, and gardeners should be less reluctant to take them out before they become derelict hulks, taking advantage of the rapid growth of some and the youthful beauties of others, in situations where full-grown specimens would be out of place. Many broad-leaved trees, and a few conifers, can be coppiced before they become too large by cutting them off at ground level and letting them shoot again. Others can be pollarded – gum trees, ashes and willows respond particularly well – by cutting their main stems several feet above ground level and establishing a head of strong branches, which can be repeatedly cut back over the years.

It is particularly important to follow these guidelines in small gardens, where there is little space for specimen trees to spread their branches, and for which a stereotyped range of offerings are repeatedly proposed that take little account of the enormous variety available. Some alternative deciduous trees are introduced below, and others in a list of evergreen species a few pages on.

Deciduous trees for small gardens

Many more trees are suitable for small gardens than are usually considered, such as the ubiquitous cherries, crab apples, magnolias and rowans. Some grow naturally as small trees, others more usually tall shrubs can be trained into a tree form.

Acer palmatum: Numerous very beautiful cultivars are available but the too often neglected green form also makes an excellent, characterful small tree.

Aesculus parviflora: A large shrub that can readily be pruned to form a graceful, small multi-stemmed tree.

Amelanchier asiatica: This and *A. canadensis* form attractive flowering and fruiting trees, often with multiple stems and the added benefits of magnificent autumn colour.

Asimina triloba: Small tree with purple flowers followed by edible fruits. Revels in rich, moist, acid soil and high

summer temperatures. More successful in the USA than in the UK.

Broussonetia papyrifera: Easily established, fast-growing tree which responds well to repeated cutting back to keep it within bounds in small gardens.

Cercis canadensis: Also the Judas tree, *C. siliquastrum*. Excellent small trees for moist, well-drained, fertile soils in full sun with considerable drought tolerance. Striking purple flowers in early spring.

Chionanthus virginicus: Large shrub-like form develops with maturity into a tree with attractive, white, feathery flowers. Needs moist, acid soils in sun or light shade.

Clerodendrum trichotomum var. *fargesii*: Usually grown as a large shrub, but easily trained into a characterful, multi-stemmed small tree with broad heads of crimson and ivory flowers in late summer.

* Note: plants marked with an asterisk are vulnerable to frost in cold locations.

Cornus kousa var. *chinensis*: An elegant small tree covered in large white 'flowers' in spring. Prefers sunny positions on fertile loam soils. This variety is able to grow on moderately base-rich soils.

Cydonia oblonga: Quinces are versatile and attractive small trees, with beautiful spring foliage and shell-pink flowers. Retain leaves late and break into bud early.

Diospyros kaki: This and other species of persimmon only fruit and grow well on rich, moist soils. Need warm to hot summers to do well.

Elaeagnus 'Quicksilver': A very hardy, olive-like tree with bright silver foliage and fragrant,though tiny, yellow flowers. Excellent in cold and exposed situations, provided they are sunny.

*Fuchsia excorticata**: Distinctive tree with characterful peeling, rufous bark for mild situations. Combines well with plants and shrubs in its shelter.

*Lagerstroemia fauriei**: This, and hybrids with *L. indica*, produce luxuriant bunches of flowers even when immature. Thrive on humus-rich, fertile soils in full sun and warm/hot summers.

Morus rubra: A mulberry with attractively variable foliage. Like *M. nigra* and *M. alba*, produces edible fruits, but needs warm to hot summers and fertile loamy soils to do well.

Ptelea trifoliata: Notable for its long-delayed bud-break in spring, intensely fragrant flowers and elm-like fruits. Needs a sunny site on fertile, free-draining but moisture-retentive soil.

Rhus typhina 'Dissecta': An outstandingly graceful tree with large pinnate leaves and glorious autumn colours. Damage to roots leads to prolific production of suckers.

Salix exigua: A small upright, slender willow with exceptionally bright, narrow, silver foliage. Extremely hardy, and amenable even in relatively dry situations.

Staphylea colchica: A hardy, characterful tree with fine foliage and attractive form. Inconspicuous flowers are followed by nut-like fruits, enclosed in curious green Chinese lanterns.

Syringa reticulata: Hardy, densely foliaged small tree with masses of fragrant, creamy-white lilac flowers, for sunny situations in places with warm summers.

Problems with trees

Mature trees pose hazards that need to be taken seriously. Senile trees collapsing on cars, or dropping limbs on peoples' heads, cause more than embarrassment, and can lead to expensive litigation and claims for damages. It is important to check that trees intended to play major parts in the attractions of a garden are healthy and have a future. Fortunately, most trees display evidence of problems before these lead to structural frailty, and those that are mature or beyond maturity should be examined from time to time to check their health.

Signs that all may not be well include:

Rotten wood – underlying flaking bark on the trunk or major limbs.

Badly healed wounds – showing signs of decay, after large limbs have broken, or been pruned back.

Thin canopies – carrying sparse foliage, and the presence of numerous dead twigs and small branches.

Bracket fungi – on main stems, or cankers girdling major limbs.

Pockets of water – in the angles where stems divide, leading to fungal infections and splits.

Cavities – and decaying wood between the root buttresses close to ground level.

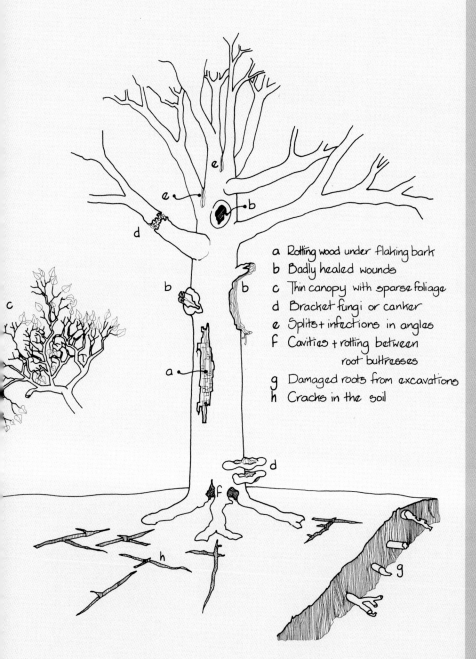

Trees are too large and heavy to take risks with, so it is important to watch out for signs of instability and decay in elderly individuals and take action promptly if necessary. Symptoms of possible danger are illustrated here.

a Rotting wood under flaking bark
b Badly healed wounds
c Thin canopy with sparse foliage
d Bracket fungi or canker
e Splits + infections in angles
f Cavities + rotting between root buttresses
g Damaged roots from excavations
h Cracks in the soil

Damaged roots — due to excavations, such as a trench dug close to the tree.

Cracks in the soil — and other signs of instability caused by movement of the roots.

Any of these justify calling in expert help. Sometimes tree surgery will provide a new lease of life. Sometimes what you see is due to deep-seated problems with poor prospects for survival, and a high risk of catastrophic collapse. Felling is then the only responsible and economic course of action. Sad though the loss of a large and characterful tree may be, its departure from the scene opens the way for new developments. Often these turn out to be even more interesting and enjoyable than the presence of the tree.

Woodland plants in gardens

Trees and other plants establish balances by sharing resources (see Chapter 2) and the matrices formed by these woodland communities are exceptionally robust, constructed of successive tiers in which trees, shrubs, climbers, perennials, ferns, mosses and bulbs not only exist as successive layers, but often form secondary tiers within themselves. Young trees grow up amongst older ones, evergreens may reinforce the seasonal matrices of deciduous species, Solomon's seal arches over dicentras, which in their turn grow above violets, beneath which grow mosses and liverworts.

Deciduous woodlands form diverse, colourful matrices that provide

Trees in groups enjoy mutual shelter and grow up with long clear trunks which display their bark attractively (left). Hostas, like many woodland perennials (middle), benefit from the shade and shelter of trees. Progressively removing the lower branches (right) opens up views across gardens and reduces the shading affects of canopies.

attractive models for our gardens, and in many parts of the world grow in company with evergreen trees and shrubs which reinforce the matrix when deciduous plants are leafless. In gardens, especially in mild areas, the foliage – and often flowers – of evergreens add interest in winter, and in their turn provide more sheltered conditions for lesser plants at ground level.

Evergreen trees and shrubs give the impression they are so well able to endure frost and snow they do not need to drop their leaves before the onset of winter; an impression confirmed by the great northern forests of Siberia and Canada, in which conifers capable of enduring the coldest winters are prominent. But this impression is misleading. The hardy spruces and pines in these northern forests are exceptional. The broad-leaved evergreens and conifers in the forests of New Zealand, southern Chile and the Pacific northwest of the USA, and the maquis vegetation of the Mediterranean, Western Australia and California are more typical. These are places where photosynthesis can continue throughout the year due to moderate winter temperatures, and many of the most interesting and attractive evergreens are not very hardy, as evidenced by the liberal sprinkling of asterisks in the following list of evergreen trees.

Forests of evergreens can be so dense that scarcely anything grows at ground level, and the closely spaced trees of conifer plantations is a forbidding model few gardeners would want to emulate. As they mature, conifers and broad-leaved evergreens develop long clear stems often with compact, rounded canopies. The intimate contact between trees is lost and light penetrates the spaces between them, providing sheltered, humus-rich, humid and more or less brightly lit conditions in which a great variety of plants, especially ferns, evergreen shrubs and perennials thrive.

Evergreen trees suitable for shelter and shade

Evergreen trees grow naturally both in hot, often arid, situations, and in humid locations with cool winters and summers. The diametrically opposed requirements of the two groups imply very different roles in gardens.

Acacia dealbata*: Deep-rooted, fast-growing tree with light overhead canopy for well-drained soils in warm situations. Fragrant mimosa-like flowers in spring.

Acca sellowiana*: Densely foliaged round-headed, small tree with succulent fruits (feijoas). Needs a warm, humid site on moist fertile soils.

Agonis flexuosa*: Fast-growing, deep-rooting, drought-resistant shade tree with trailing branches for warm situations.

Arbutus unedo*: Densely foliaged, slow-growing tree with attractive bark, eventually developing extremely characterful form. White lily-of-the-valley flowers followed by insipid, gritty fruits.

Cordyline australis*: Several cultivars available. Sturdy stems are topped by exuberant heads of long, narrow leaves in striking contrast to broad-leaved plants.

Embothrium coccineum*: Fast-growing pioneer species for moist, acid soils in humid, high rainfall locations. Notable for its abundant orange-scarlet flowers.

Eucalyptus caesia 'Little Silver Princess'*: A small, weeping gum tree, with a light canopy of narrow, intensely silver foliage; tolerant of dry soils in hot, exposed situations.

Eucalyptus coccifera: An upright, compact, hardy gum tree with silvery grey leaves, suitable for exposed situations.

Fremontodendron 'California Glory'*: Very showy, upright tree with broadly bowl-shaped ochre-yellow flowers throughout spring and summer. For hot sunny positions on well-drained soils.

* Note: plants marked with an asterisk are vulnerable to frost in cold locations.

Genista aetnensis: Hardy small tree, developing from shrubby form. Yellow pea flowers in late summer. Light canopy, and deep roots favour underplanting.

Ilex aquifolium: Numerous cultivars and species varying greatly in vigour. Deep, fertile moisture retentive soils in sun to moderate shade.

Laurus nobilis*: In frost-free conditions develops into a small tree with a clear stem and heavy canopy of aromatic, broad leaves. Trees cut down by frost develop multiple stems.

Lomatia ferruginea*: Attractive fern-like foliage needs mild, humid conditions and moist, humus-rich soils.

Luma apiculata *: Multi-stemmed tree, notable for its cinnamon bark and white myrtle flowers. Needs sheltered moist, humid conditions and humus-rich, acid soils.

Myrsine australis*: A tall shrub or small tree up to 6 m (20 ft) high. Small flowers clustered along the shoots are followed by black, spherical berries.

Nothofagus dombeyi: Fast-growing, large tree for any good garden soil, preferably with shelter for the first few years. Eventually forms an impressive specimen.

Olea europaea*: Olive trees have grace and beauty when young and great character with age. Tolerant of hot, dry summers.

Olearia virgata*: A small multi-stemmed tree, with sinuous main stems; sage-green leaves and masses of white flowers clustered in the axils of every leaf.

Pittosporum obcordata*: Narrowly upright, extremely twiggy tree so densely foliaged it is reminiscent of some forms of Lawson's cypress. Olive-green leaves have an attractive lustre.

Pittosporum eugenioides*: A broad-leaved, fast-growing species with fragrant bark and greeny-yellow flowers, for mild humid situations, on moist soils in shelter of other trees.

Pseudopanax ferox*: Small tree with extraordinarily gawky, upright shoots and exaggeratedly long saw-toothed leaves when young. Slowly transforms itself into a dense rounded lollipop form as it matures.

Quercus coccifera*: An oak with prickly leaves like a holly. Shrublike when immature, it gradually develops a tree form. Tolerant of hot, dry situations.

Rhododendron arboreum*: Large shrub with heavy foliage and trusses of pink to deep crimson flowers, developing into a broadly rounded tree on acid, moisture-retentive soils in sheltered sites.

Sophora tetraptera*: Upright open-canopied tree with deep roots and hanging trusses of nectar-bearing, butter-yellow flowers, that associates well with plants set out beneath it.

Climbing shrubs, vines and lianes

These can be the most difficult of all the members of the woodland community to use in gardens in the ways they grow naturally. Roses scrambling through ancient apple trees have become something of a garden cliché and, provided the tree does not collapse too soon and the vigour of the rose has been accurately judged, can be very effective. But visitors confronted at Kiftsgate in Gloucestershire by the archetypal rose of that name learn a salutary lesson about the vigour and ferocity with which a powerful climber can infest even full-sized trees, let alone ancient apples. Climbers are naturally adapted to climb and climb they do. Hydrangeas in Chile almost

Climbing roses, vines and lianes grown over trellises, pergolas and other structures provide shade and shelter effectively and decoratively far more quickly than trees.

Vines and climbers for pergolas and trellises

Climbers combine well with other climbers. They can be planted close together to extend flowering times, and diversify foliage effects, including the use of evergreens for winter cover.

Actinidia deliciosa 'Hayward' and 'Tomuri': A very vigorous dioecious climber (both male and female plants are needed to produce kiwifruit). Sunny, sheltered situation.

Aristolochia macrophylla: Vigorous large-leaved climber, with curious looking but insignificant flowers; for partial shade or sun on fertile, humus-rich moist soils.

Celastrus scandens 'Indian Brave' and 'Indian Maiden': Vigorous dioecious climber on any fertile soil, in full sun. Males and females should be planted together for fruit.

Clematis cirrhosa var. *balearica**: Innumerable clematis species and cultivars are available. Vigour and other qualities should be matched to situation.

Eccremocarpus scaber*: Short lived, moderately vigorous plant with colourful orange, cinnamon or red flowers; easily raised from seed and useful for rapid effects in newly planted gardens.

Gelsemium sempervirens*: Twining, moderately vigorous evergreen with deep yellow flowers for open sunny situation or light shade. Inclined to be rampant.

Hardenbergia violacea 'Happy Wanderer'*: Moderately vigorous, hard to control, evergreen climber with masses of crimson/purple pea flowers, for warm situations on well-drained soils.

Hedera helix: Numerous cultivars and species varying in vigour, leaf size, colour and variegation. For dense ground cover or as a climber. Excellent in heavily shaded sites.

Humulus lupulus 'Aureus': Vigorous, herbaceous climber with bright yellow foliage. Establishes rapidly and is useful during early stages of a planting.

Jasminum nudiflorum: Evergreen climber with bright yellow flowers throughout the winter. Very tolerant of shade from other plants or buildings.

Kennedia coccinea*: Moderately vigorous evergreen climber with scarlet pea flowers, for warm situations on well-drained soils in light shade or sun.

Lapageria rosea: Moderately vigorous evergreen with large rose-pink or white flowers, for humid, shaded situations on water-retentive, free-draining soils.

Lonicera sempervirens 'Cedar Lane': Evergreen honeysuckle for lightly shaded or sunny situations, associates well with other climbers.

Passiflora caerulea*: The hardiest species amongst many. Needs a warm site in sun with shelter from cold winds. Responds well to regular pruning.

Rosa 'Zéphirine Drouhin': Innumerable climbing and rambler roses are available. Absence of thorns makes this one easy to handle.

Schizophragma integrifolium: Vigorous, self-clinging climber with broad heads of whitish flowers, suitable for spacious situations, rich loam soils and ample moisture.

Solanum laxum 'Album'*: Moderately vigorous climber with a misleadingly fragile appearance. Produces jasmine-like white flowers throughout the summer. Ideal for trellises and screens.

Trachelospermum jasminoides*: This with the hardier *T. asiaticum* are twining evergreens with heavy foliage and fragrant flowers, for warm, lightly shaded situations.

Vitis vinifera 'Purpurea': A moderately vigorous vine, easily controlled by pruning, with leaves suffused with crimson and magnificent autumn colour, for sunny situations on any well-drained soil.

Wisteria frutescens: Less vigorous, more controllable than *W. floribunda* or *W. sinensis*, and flowers over a longer period; full sun on well-drained, fertile soils.

* Note: plants marked with an asterisk are vulnerable to frost in cold locations.

overwhelm evergreen laurels 30 m (100 ft) high, and bridge gaps between the trees to form dense, light-excluding tangles. Cables thicker and more sinewy than forearms hang from trees in the Appalachians and the Sikhote Alin mountains overlooking the sea of Japan; the shoots of the vines they sustain lost from sight amongst the tops of tall tulip trees and Korean pines. In gardens, wisterias, *Clematis montana* and *Vitis coignettiae*, not to mention *Chusquea quila* (should anyone be foolhardy enough to plant it) can infiltrate, invest and overpower trees, defying all efforts – short of outright destruction – to control them.

Nevertheless, climbers are invaluable in even the smallest garden. Unlike many woodland shrubs and perennials, they are not shade-tolerant. They climb to reach the sun, and when planted over trellises, pergolas, arches and arbours form fast-growing screens and suppliers of shade, adopting the role of flexible trees. In a few years they reproduce the effects of a forest canopy that trees would take far longer to produce, and in a form and at a level that can be maintained within pre-defined limits by pruning.

Some, like wisteria, flower on their older wood, which becomes increasingly floriferous with the passing years. Others, like the hybrids of *Clematis viticella*, produce flowers on the current season's growth. The former develop a permanent, or at least semi-permanent, framework of branches which grows ever heavier and more extensive and needs the support of large and robustly built structures, unless very severely pruned to restrict growth and development. The latter can be cut back year by year, removing the greater part of the previous year's growth, and are easily kept within the bounds of small, lightly built structures.

Perennials

The crucial role of perennials in the matrices of the mixed border has already been described. These plants are just as important in woodland settings, where successful matrices are equally dependent on occupying ground effectively. Some woodland perennials are evergreen, others produce leaves precociously early, and both take advantage of the protection of the trees while making full use of the period when they are leafless. Dense shade in summer reduces prospects of making a living at ground level, and some woodland perennials like dicentras and aconites lose their leaves and retreat below ground; others including pulmonarias and primroses retain their leaves but merely tick over, scarcely growing at all. Plants which are in leaf at different seasons can be used to create communities in which different kinds play active roles at varying times, ensuring as complete a cover as possible at ground level throughout the year.

Dry shade beneath mature trees is repeatedly cited as one of gardening's more intractable problems. Often, problems arise only because the wrong species have been used, and little has been done to improve the soil, or make it easier for young plants to establish themselves. That said, sycamores, beeches, griselinias, horse chestnuts and other trees with dense canopies and vigorous surface roots create conditions in which few flowering plants can thrive, even when crowns have been raised to let in light, and copious amounts of organic matter have been spread to make the soil more receptive. Mosses may then be the only answer, supplemented perhaps by some of the tougher more drought-resistant ferns including forms of *Dryopteris filix-mas* and *Polystichum aculeatum*.

The woodland edge

Marginal partially shaded, partially sunlit areas between forest and scrub, or woodland and meadow, are unusually complex, changeable and competitive. Temperatures, light intensity, effects of drought and exposure to wind all vary intricately over short distances, and plants need to be tolerant and adaptable to make the most of the opportunities on offer. Conditions change progressively as trees thrive or decline, and grasses or shrubs infiltrate or are excluded. It is not enough for plants just to be able to hold their own; they must also be equipped to move about and establish themselves in new locations.

Not surprisingly, plants of the woodland edge tend to be easily grown, tolerant and amenable under garden conditions. The combination of persistence and mobility possessed by many of them makes them particularly useful as space fillers during the early stages of matrix formation, and pluggers of gaps as matrices develop. Evergreen forms, in particular, like bugles, strawberries (including duchesnea) and self-heals can often be used to provide a carpet of foliage in winter beneath taller perennials and shrubs.

Bulbous perennials

Bulbous perennials, particularly those that appear during the winter or spring, are another group with distinctive roles in communities of plants. They survive beneath overshadowing vegetation by retreating below the ground, and in that state occupy no space at all, though their roots may hold ground effectively below the surface. Even when in leaf, daffodils, scillas and others with narrow upright leaves contribute little to the density of the aerial matrix, but arums, colchicums, cyclamen and some others with broad leaves hold space effectively at times of the year when most perennials, deciduous trees and shrubs are leafless.

Ferns

Optimistic assertions in articles in gardening magazines have been telling us for years that 'ferns are coming back'. Perhaps so, but judging by what I see in gardens, and on visits to garden centres, the tide comes in excessively slowly. These plants are seldom prominent, and it is rare to find nurseries that supply more than a handful of different kinds.

Ferns are remarkable plants, the possessors of primitive sexual procedures which were superseded aeons ago first by conifers then, apparently conclusively, by flowering plants. These apparent improvements should have led to

Shrubs and perennials to grow under trees

Many of the following grow naturally on the woodland floor beneath deciduous trees or in open evergreen forest. They are invaluable in gardens for shaded settings, whether beneath trees or structures, or in the shadow of buildings. Many are evergreen or partially evergreen and flower in late winter or spring when trees are leafless.

Asarum europaeum: Ground level, with glossy evergreen leaves; capable of growing even in deep shade beneath deciduous perennials on moist soils

Aster divaricatus: Modestly rhizomatous, medium-sized plant with white daisies, for light to moderate shade on humus-rich soils in open woodland-floor communities.

Chasmanthium latifolium: One of comparatively few grasses that thrives in woodland, contrasting well with hostas, tellimas, etc.

Clivia miniata*: Glowing orange flowers. Excellent even for deeply shaded situations on moist soils, where it is tolerant of seasonal drought.

Cornus canadensis: Spring-flowering, ground-carpeting, stoloniferous perennial topped by pure white flowers for cool, moist humus-rich soils.

Desfontainea spinosa: Fine medium-sized evergreen, sociable shrub for humid locations on persistently moist, preferably acid soils.

Elatostema rugosum*: Vigorous, ground-covering rhizomatous perennial with characterful, rugged foliage infused with crimson, for moist soils in warm, shaded sites.

Epimedium perralderianum: Numerous species and cultivars available, almost all forming dense, steadily expanding, powerfully persistent clumps of evergreen shoots over matted rhizomes.

Galax urceolata: Hardy evergreen with spikes of creamy flowers and brightly burnished leaves, for cool, moist humus-rich acid soils.

Geranium nodosum: Vigorously self-seeding perennial in flower throughout the summer, capable of thriving on dry soils in heavy shade.

Heuchera americana: Several forms, all with attractive leaves, good ground-covering, clump-forming species for heavy shade. Respond well to heavy annual mulching in late autumn.

Kirengeshoma palmata: Steadily expanding clump-former with many stems and elegant butter-yellow flowers in late summer for acid, moist soils. Very susceptible to spring frosts.

Lamium galeobdolon 'Florentinum': A vigorous – though potentially smothering – perennial runner, grown for its brightly silver-variegated foliage. Should be planted amongst competitive neighbours.

Mertensia virginica: Attractive spring-flowering woodlander with sky-blue flowers. Leaves decline in mid summer. For cool, humus-rich, lightly shaded sites.

Milium effusum 'Aureum' (Bowles' golden grass): Golden-leaved grass grows well in moderate shade on moist humus-rich soils. Will self-seed freely.

Mitraria coccinea*: A sprawling, sometimes semi-epiphytic shrub with vermilion flowers, growing amongst thick cover in humid situations on constantly moist, humus-rich soils.

Pachysandra procumbens: Fairly vigorous coloniser with attractively mottled leaves. Tolerant of moderately deep shade in humus-rich woodland.

Rhododendron 'Praecox': Many early-flowering rhododendrons grow well, and benefit from some frost protection, in light shade beneath deciduous trees on acid soils.

Sanguinaria canadensis: Precociously early perennial with large pure-white flowers in spring. Strong rhizomes just below the ground form slowly expanding colonies on damp humus-rich soils.

Tellima grandiflora 'Purpurea': Excellent woodland ground cover, forming broad, domed clumps of attractive foliage, flushed with crimson in winter, topped by open spikes of fringed, green, flowers.

Tiarella cordifolia 'Echo Red Heart': One of several forms of the foam flower. All are spreading, moderately vigorous plants useful for filling spaces between other plants in shaded situations.

* Note: plants marked with an asterisk are vulnerable to frost in cold locations.

Perennials and shrubs of the woodland edge

Plants in these places are able to survive in shifting, unstable matrices where opportunities and problems change continuously. In gardens, similarly challenging conditions occur in semi-shaded situations close to buildings, along fences and hedges, close to trees and beneath shrubs.

Arthropodium cirrhatum*: Develops moderately dense colonies of broad leaves in warm sites in light shade on moisture-retentive, free-draining soils.

Aruncus dioicus: A splendid plant as a specimen or in groups, with tall plumes of ivory-white flowers. Widely tolerant of soils and situations; will repay good treatment.

Camellia x *williamsii* 'Donation': Upright, floriferous, broadly tolerant, evergreen shrub with outstandingly reliable and abundant pink flowers for cool, moist situations on humus-rich soils.

Daphne mezereum: Excellent, early flowering shrub with pink or white flowers for lightly shaded positions on humus-rich, free-draining, base-rich soils.

Gaultheria shallon: Medium-sized shrub, with pink flowers followed by purple berries. Forms dense evergreen thickets in mild, humid locations on moist, acid soils.

Geranium x *magnificum*: An 'old-fashioned' almost indestructible, clump-forming perennial for intermittently shaded settings. Tolerant of most soils.

Helleborus x *hybridus*: Very long-lived perennials with outstanding flowers in early spring. Form dense mats of crowns on heavy, moisture-retentive soils.

Itea virginica: Hardy deciduous shrub with fragrant creamy-white catkins. Fertile, moist soils.

Lamium maculatum: Numerous cultivars with attractive evergreen foliage. All fill spaces well and are especially valuable during the early stages of matrix formation.

Lunaria rediviva: Perennial form of Honesty with lilac-purple flowers. Long-lived in intermittently shaded situations on fertile soils.

Lychnis coronaria: A short-lived, silver-leaved perennial, with pink, white or velvety magenta flowers. Self-sows freely on dry, base-rich soils in light shade.

Macropiper excelsum*: Dense, evergreen shrub, thriving in light to moderate shade in humid situations on moist soils.

Ruscus hypoglossum: Short, upright, prickly shrub, with inconspicuous flowers followed by large scarlet berries. Tolerant of dry shade and extremely persistent once established.

Sarcococca hookeriana var. *digyna*: One of a number of sweetly fragrant winter boxes, in flower during the winter. Excellent low-growing evergreens for deep or moderate shade on most fertile, not waterlogged soils.

Skimmia japonica: Compact evergreen shrubs, notable for their scarlet berries. Tolerant of summer drought in lightly shaded situations on fertile soils.

Spiraea japonica 'Goldflame': Easily propagated, small domed shrub with striking yellow and apricot leaves for short-lived or permanent positions in sunlit spots or light shade.

Tolmiea menziesii 'Taff's Gold': Useful, brightly foliaged, ground-covering, evergreen perennial. Spreads steadily. Drought-tolerant but does better on moist soils.

Tradescantia virginiana: Persistent clump-forming perennial with blue, pink or white flowers, for sun or light shade close to trees. Broadly tolerant of variety of soils.

Vancouveria hexandra: Forms densely clustered stems with pendant yellow flowers above short, creeping rhizomes. Very hardy and shade-tolerant once established.

Vinca major: Evergreen, vigorously trailing shrub with large periwinkle blue or white flowers. Exuberant ground cover where space allows, and can be invasive. Plant *V. minor* where space is limited.

* Note: plants marked with an asterisk are vulnerable to frost in cold locations.

Bulbous plants for shaded and semi-shaded situations

It is a rare garden which is so filled with bulbs there is no room for more. Although many make only a minor contribution to matrix development, they can add enormously to the visual attractions of plant communities.

*Allium triquetrum**: This onion with pendant white flowers can be an almost ineradicable coloniser in light shade amongst deciduous trees and shrubs in mildly temperate parts of the world.

*Anemone apenina**: The foliage of this, *A. blanda* and *A. nemorosa* form an attractive and useful part of the cover of a woodland floor before more vigorous perennials come into leaf.

Arisarum proboscideum: Broad, deep green leaves, enhanced by curious looking flowers, form steadily expanding colonies in shaded, moist situations.

Arum italicum 'Marmoratum': One of the best plants for winter ground cover. Produces broad, attractively variegated foliage as other plants die down in autumn.

Cardiocrinum giganteum: Unpredictable, usually temporary matrix in mild, wet locations, more valuable for its magnificent spikes of flowers than its leaves.

Clintonia borealis: Moderately ground-holding from mats of roots in moist, cool, acid soils. Most notable for its gleaming purple-blue berries.

Cyclamen hederifolium: A very significant provider of winter ground-cover, with leaves to be prized. Tolerates deep summer shade under deciduous shrubs.

Eranthis hyemalis: Brief spring eruption of yellow flowers and foliage provides early ground-cover in spaces between woody plants.

Erythronium dens-canis: Foliage of several species and cultivars provides early, nearly rabbit-proof interim foliage cover in sites that later become deeply shaded.

Galanthus nivalis: Can develop into large colonies in clusters dotted over the ground but narrow short-lived foliage forms a weak matrix.

Hyacinthoides non-scripta: With *H. hispanica* form dense colonies able to hold ground between woody plants until midsummer.

Iris foetidissima var. *citrina*: Broad evergreen leaves form persistent, retentive clumps. A plant able to cope with the driest, least promising shaded spots in the garden.

Lilium martagon: Colonises well in light shade amongst grasses and herbs where it forms an effective part of the matrix up to mid-summer.

Narcissus pseudonarcissus: This and other daffodil species and cultivars provide outstanding spring flowers, but are not great contributors to matrices.

Nectaroscordum siculum subsp. *bulgaricum*: Will colonise moderately in light shade on well-drained soils. Plays little part in matrix formation

*Oxalis pes-caprae**: Even more than most species of oxalis, inclined to excess, but in competitive situations can provide useful early cover.

Ranunculus ficaria: A useful, though rather ephemeral matrix-former amongst dense planting. Too invasive for fertile non-competitive situations.

*Sandersonia aurantiaca**: A colourful plant for lightly shaded woodland margins in warm situations on warm free-draining soils.

Scilla bifolia: Forms widespread colonies below deciduous woody plants with bright blue, sometimes dirty pink, flowers. Attractive but only a minor contributor to spring matrices.

Trillium grandiflorum: An excellent, true woodland species, with most attractive white flowers and broad foliage which plays a useful role in the forest floor matrix before trees develop leaves.

* Note: plants marked with an asterisk are vulnerable to frost in cold locations.

the rapid extinction of the ferns, but never did. Their archaic lifestyle, with its alternating 'generations' and fragile dependence at critical stages on delicate tissues and freely available water, appears to be laborious, chancey and inefficient, but it is combined with extraordinary tenacity. Once established, ferns tend to be long-lived, self-maintaining, self-sustaining plants distinctly disinclined to surrender their space.

Ferns evolved in wetter and warmer conditions than those generally found in temperate parts of the world today and, although many have adapted to cope with cold, the consummation of their sexual routines still depends on saturated atmospheres and freely available water. They grow most abundantly in the forests of the wetter and warmer parts of the world where they flourish on levels of nutrients and light which would be starvation rations for more

Deep beds of moss form decorative and effective matrices with acers and azaleas in this version of a Japanese garden (left). Mosses and ferns (right) form an almost complete ground layer in moderately deep shade beneath trees in a naturally humid setting.

Ferns for lightly and deeply shaded situations in gardens

The great majority of ferns grow naturally in the shade of trees, other plants or rocks, and do well in similar situations in gardens. Few thrive in consistently dry soils, or in fertile sunlit borders amongst other plants, but in the right settings they make reliable, easily grown, immensely long-lived garden plants.

Adiantum pedatum: A hardy and graceful maidenhair, dense rhizomes and wiry stems form steadily expanding clumps.

*Asplenium bulbiferum**: Broad, arching, ground-shading fronds for humid, mild situations in light or moderate shade.

Athyrium filix-femina: Numerous forms available, thrive in light shade on moist, free-draining acid or neutral soils.

*Blechnum capense**: A vigorous pioneer species that spreads by surface rhizomes, even in situations with thin soils, provided they remain moist.

*Blechnum discolor**: Clump-forming shuttlecock fern, spreading by rhizomes to form colonies in moist to wet conditions in light to moderate shade.

Blechnum spicant: Hardy, enduring fern, broadly tolerant of a range of conditions, but always in shade on humus-rich soils. Associates well with broad-leaved woodland perennials.

*Cyathea dealbata**: A tree fern for mild, humid situations on generally moist soils. Has a measure of drought tolerance.

*Dicksonia antarctica**: A relatively hardy tree fern for mild humid sites, preferably in light or intermittent shade. Like most tree ferns grows most rapidly when young in moderately well-illuminated settings.

Dryopteris wallichiana: One of the most striking of the male ferns, with glorious golden-green, immature fronds in spring. Most species are broadly tolerant and capable of thriving even in relatively dry sites.

Gleichenia cunninghamia: Branching, creeping rhizomes colonise thin soils and rocks, producing tiered umbrellas of gracefully distinctive fronds.

*Marattia salicina**: A majestic fern capable of thriving even in deep shade, in warm humid situations on wet soils.

Matteuccia struthiopteris: Spreading rhizomes produce colonies of gracefully beautiful shuttlecock fronds in sun or light shade, on wet humus-rich soils.

Onoclea sensibilis: A hardy woodland fern producing masses of upright fronds from spreading rhizomes in shaded, moist sites.

Osmunda claytoniana: Relatively large, robust fern, producing fronds in clusters from spreading rhizomes in light shade on humus-rich, moist well-drained soils.

Phegopteris connectilis: Slim underground rhizomes produce numerous individually disposed, lightly attractive fronds, on moist, humus-rich acid soils.

*Phymatosorus diversifolius**: Leathery, very broad fronds produced from creeping rhizomes provide excellent ground-cover in shade.

Polypodium vulgare: Capable of colonising thin soils, or growing epiphytically on rocks, as well as the trunks and branches of trees. Once established is markedly tolerant of periodic seasonal drought.

Polystichum aculeatum: Vigorous, clump-forming fern for lightly shaded, well-drained sites; established plants are tolerant of periodic drought.

Polystichum munitum: Evergreen species developing into large, long-lived clumps of fronds in humid situations in shade on moist, acid soils.

Polystichum setiferum: Semi-evergreen; numerous forms available, tolerant of infertile, heavily shaded situations.

* Note: plants marked with an asterisk are vulnerable to frost in cold locations.

(Left) The possibilities of lichens, liverworts and club mosses have scarcely been explored. The former produce decorative, colourful but fragile matrices naturally which are difficult to maintain in most gardens. By comparison, club mosses (above) are relatively robust plants which could contribute forms and textures seldom seen in gardens.

active, more evolved and more demanding higher plants.

Few ferns can compete with flowering plants in the feather-bedded conditions of the mixed border, or the luxuriantly competitive battlefield of a rich meadow, but beneath trees, in damp, dank corners amongst buildings, in cool, wet upland gardens, and even in crevices in walls, ferns can answer any gardener's needs – unless that need includes flowers as essential, and bright colour a prerequisite. Ferns produce no flowers and are almost always green. The grace of form and texture of their foliage compensates for lack of flowers, and makes an entirely individual and irreplaceable contribution to a garden. They are colourless only to those whose prejudices blind

them to tones of green – not because they cannot see green, but because it is so abundant they have become accustomed to ignoring it.

Perhaps the predictions that ferns are coming back into favour will prove to be accurate, and we can look forward to seeing these beautiful plants play more conspicuous roles in gardens. There is even a possibility of a return of the ferns on a scale that would transform the garden landscapes of Britain, and the more oceanic parts of Europe and North America wherever winter temperatures do not fall too low. Gardening is most vigorously pursued in many places where winters are at present too cold for tree ferns to survive, frequently by a margin of only a degree or two. If global warming proceeds as predicted, an early effect could be the possibility of introducing these plants to gardens where they cannot be grown today.

This would be all the more dramatic because where tree ferns lead, cycads, agaves, cordylines and the hardier palms would not be far behind. Small increases in minimum winter temperatures would allow millions of gardeners on mainland Britain, the oceanic borders of
Europe, and many cool temperate parts of the United States to play variations on gardening themes which have never before been possible in these places.

Mosses

The dry sterility beneath mature beech trees, which plants and gardeners both find so discouraging, has already been mentioned. But not even the most extreme of these places is a lost cause. Flowers fail, ferns find the conditions too spartan but mosses can cope and, free from competition at ground level, thrive. Western gardeners have barely explored the possibilities of mosses and know them only as intruders to be raked from lawns, and as disturbing indicators of damp on roofs and paths. We hear of their use, and see pictures of the results in gardens in Japan. We see them used in Japanese-style gardens constructed in the West and, almost invariably, move on to think about other things.

Mosses play a part in many natural matrices formed by communities of wildflowers. They move into our lawns and can be almost impossible to expel, especially in poorly aerated, badly drained swards where they can grow more luxuriantly and abundantly than grasses. Along with their two-dimensional cousins the liverworts, they are conspicuous amongst ferns and woodland plants in damp woods, and in dry shade they have little competition.

Anyone who repeatedly uses paraquat or glyphosate to kill weeds on shaded paths or between shrubs in borders discovers that mosses colonise the bare surfaces, often making them as green as they would be if covered with more familiar plants. This opens the way to gardening with mosses without the expertise, patience and attention that we associate with their culture in Japanese gardens. All we need do to encourage them is to destroy other plants by spraying them with weed killers; and the first place where this knowledge can be put to good use is in the dry shade beneath mature trees.

We should look more closely at mosses and their place in matrices of plants growing elsewhere too – especially those that are wet and cold; on moorlands and mountains; as part of the vegetation of the forest floor, and often on trees in damp forests, and beside springs and streams. Mosses, liverworts, filmy ferns, lichens and club mosses, comprising between them a vast section of the plant kingdom, possess forms and textures all their own, and many thrive in places that gardeners despairingly label 'difficult'. Yet we pay scarcely any attention to them when we plan and plant and, in our role as casting directors, provide virtually no parts for them to play in our gardens.

The Gardens
CASE *STUDIES*

A new life on Vancouver Island

This garden by a sheltered sea inlet surrounds a recently built house near Victoria, on Vancouver Island in Canada. The well structured neutral loam soil, adequate rainfall (the greater part during the winter), and temperate conditions are very favourable for gardening most of the time. The area is old Douglas fir/western hemlock forest with numerous big leaf maples and a few madrones. Trees left standing in the garden rather intimidated the owners and they had to learn how to garden beneath them. They lived previously near Regina in Saskatchewan, and had little experience of trees or gardening. Now, in a kinder climate and with the children at school during the day, the wife spends much of her spare time gardening. She regularly buys *The Island Grower*, which has helped her develop ideas, and discover which plants grow well on Vancouver Island. She recently paid a visit to Phoebe Noble's garden, leaving it a convert to the principles of 'layer-cake' gardening, and convinced of the benefits of mulching.

Review

A. The construction of a timber house had avoided serious disturbance to the ground, and a number of fine specimen deer and sword ferns as well as vanilla leaf, shallon and other forest-floor plants still grew beneath the trees. Huckleberries and rattlesnake plantains sprouted naturally on old rotting stumps.

B. The presence of the mature trees had major effects on preparations for planting, the plants chosen, and subsequent management and, once attended to, the trees became valuable attractions.

C. The advantages of the mild winters, when temperatures seldom fall below -5°C, (23° F) and the rarity of spring frosts, are offset by occasional short interludes of savagely severe weather. Similarly, periodic droughts during the summer have to be reckoned with when choosing plants.

D. The garden is not large, and the wife has time, energy and enthusiasm to spare, enabling her to pay attention to the individual needs of plants.

Outcome

A.

- The structure and profile of the soil were practically intact, built up over many years beneath the forest trees – assets which would have been destroyed by digging. Surface treatments were used instead.

- Numerous surviving wild flowers suggested a rather natural style of planting, using native species supplemented with woodland plants from other parts of the world.

B.

- The trees provide shelter rather than shade because their canopies are high above the ground. The only attention required was the removal of a few of the lower branches to lift some of the crowns a little higher.

- All areas to be planted were mulched before planting, with a 7.5 cm (3 in) layer of composted bark, infilling between the plants afterwards with a 4 cm (1.6 in) layer of chipped bark.

- Fertility was boosted with a top-dressing of 125gm/sq m (4 oz/sq yd) of blood, fish and bone manure, incorporating rock potash, scattered over the surface of the bark to help the young plants become established.

C.

- The trees, shrubs and the more permanent perennials were chosen with due regard for the occasional very cold spells during the winter.
- The warm, dry summers are ideal for many short-lived, or dubiously hardy but easily replaced, colourful perennials, and these were used liberally in sunlit areas to follow the spring display of the woodland plants.

D.

- The wife very soon set up a small propagation unit with a greenhouse and cold frames and a standing out area for plants in containers. She used this to grow plants not readily available from nurseries from seed, and to propagate tender perennials needed for beds near the house, and in troughs and hanging baskets.

The Plants

The absence of spring frosts, and the sheltering canopy of the trees enables plants with flowers or young leaves sensitive to frost to be grown. These included *Acer circinatum*, and cultivars of *A. palmatum*, including 'Bloodgood', 'Margaret Bee' and crimson and green forms with dissected leaves; several of the Kosar-DeVos magnolia hybrids, including the deep pinky purple 'Ann' and rosy lavender 'Ricki', as well as *Magnolia* x *soulangeana* 'San José; *Styrax japonica* 'Carillon' and 'Pink Chimes' also grew well. Other shrubs, some quite low-growing, were used to thicken the lower parts of the matrix and provide sheltered, humid conditions for ferns. Amongst them were *Amelanchier alnifolia*, *Nandina domestica* 'Fire Power' and *Aronia* x *prunifolia* 'Brilliant' for their autumn foliage. *Holodiscus discolor* introduced itself to the garden, and other natives planted included *Mahonia aquifolium* 'Apollo' and *Philadelphus lewisii*. Also used were *Ribes laurifolium*, *Pieris japonica* 'Daisen' and 'Pink Delight', *Stephanandra tanakae*, and *Vestia foetida*.

She adopted the idea of layer-cake planting for the perennials, mixing them with bulbous plants and ferns, starting with a scattering of upright or moderately tall plants using clumps of *Aruncus dioicus*, *Filipendula palmata* and *Aconitum* x *cammarum* 'Bicolor', amongst ribbons of *Maianthemum racemosum* and *M. stellatum* and the giant Solomon's seal, *Polygonatum biflorum*. Other, taller emergent plants included *Lilium columbianum* and *L. pardalinum*.

Below these was an intermediate layer, with compact hummocks of foliage for much of the year with taller spikes of flowers. Hostas and hemerocallis were prominent, and also *Agapanthus campanulatus* 'Isis' and 'Castle of Mey', and *Arisaema speciosum*. Several eastern North American plants were used too, including *Heuchera americana* 'Molly Bush' (with bronze and purple foliage), *H.* x *brizoides* 'Widar' (with brilliant red flowers), and *Mitella breweri* and *Tellima grandiflora* 'Purpurea'. Other clump-forming plants included *Erythronium oregonum* (which self-seeded freely), and *E. 'Pagoda'* and *E. revolutum* 'Rose Beauty'. She tried *Cypripedium pubescens* and *C. reginae* without much success.

The lowest level of the matrix consisted of ground carpeters and infiltrators including the deeply shade-tolerant *Asarum canadense* and *A. shuttleworthii* 'Callaway' (with glossy, silver marbled leaves), and *Arisarum proboscideum*. *Cornus canadensis* was interplanted with *Clintonia borealis* and *Maianthemum bifolium*, and there were several patches of the runnering *Duchesnea indica* and *Saxifraga* 'Cuscutiformis'. She also planted drifts of *Tiarella wherryi* and *T. cordifolia*, including 'Oakleaf' and 'Echo Red Heart' (with crimson centred leaves).

Ferns became a notable feature of the planting, including drifts of *Adiantum pedatum* and the copper form of *Onoclea sensibilis*, numerous plants of *Blechnum spicant*, and fine individual specimens or groups of the crimson-flushed *Dryopteris erythrosora* and *D. goldieana*, and *Polystichum aculeatum*, *P. munitum* and *P. vestitum*.

London 'Barrister's' Suburban Play-pen

This garden round a mock-Tudor villa in Northwood in the western suburbs of London lies on heavy clay; claggy in winter, brick-hard and riven by cracks in dry summers. Comparatively large for the neighbourhood, its owner habitually claims it is 'two acres' – in fact at 0.4 ha, it is exactly half that. He is the recently retired clerk of a barristers' chambers in the Temple, sometime divorced, who spends much of his time at a local golf club, where he is angling for election as chairman of the Greens Committee. He employs a gardener, but is not averse to pottering about in the garden, and has strong ideas about how it should look. A collection of hybrid tea roses in formally laid-out beds is his pride and joy. He is pernickety about his lawns, hates ivies in any form, anywhere, has no use for ferns and appreciates the well-groomed, sexy shapes of dwarf conifers in bed with brightly-foliaged heathers. In retirement, he throws a popular line in barbecue parties at which he enjoys playing the chef, and for which he has built a 'Barbecue Garden'. These affairs with secluded seats, and shelter from showers and cold night airs, have become much sought after by his pals at the golf club, who appreciate opportunities for a little partner swapping to revive jaded appetites in their declining years.

Review

A. The Barbecue Garden was an urgent priority, demanding 'instant' shelter and seclusion.

B. It had to provide a visually exciting setting for his parties, and protection and cover from the elements while retaining an alfresco atmosphere.

C. The clay soil was a particularly unsuitable substrate for party shenanigans. When wet, its cloying properties guarantee it sticks to anything it touches, and climbs up anything that moves.

D. The planting had to take account of the effects of numerous feet, not always well controlled, and the probability of party horseplay, while providing secluded nooks and arbours for more intimate communications.

Outcome

A.

- A pergola-like framework of timber, fronting on to the lawn, and enclosed on two sides by trellis-work, provided shelter and also formed arbours and secluded corners.
- Solid round-wood pillars supporting the pergola were a feature of the design, simulating the effects of tree trunks rising to the overhead canopy of this synthetic forest.

B.

- Spaces between the cross members of the pergola near the house were glazed with polycarbonate acrylic to reinforce overhead cover. Further out these were left open.
- Vines and other climbers grown over the timber framework and on the trellises provided a quick solution to the need for a sheltering canopy.

C.

- The clay soil was excavated to a depth of 15 cm (6 in) and replaced with hardcore and quarry rubble, over a woven polypropylene membrane, forming a well-drained, level surface on which a pattern of brick pavers and nonslip, reconstituted stone slabs was laid. Spaces for plants were left at the foot of the pillars and along the bottom of the trellis.

- A small, raised ornamental pool and fountain, with submersed lighting, was built in a space open to the skies in the centre of the garden as a focal point.

D.

- In spring and early summer, when parties took place at midday, and the vines and climbers cast little shade, woodland perennials and bulbs planted in spaces between the paving and in containers provided colour.
- Later, parties tended to be held after dark, and plants at ground level became too vulnerable to damage. Colour was provided by plants specially grown in large containers, and by the foliage, flowers and fruit of the climbers.
- A lean-to greenhouse against a high south wall was used as an 'orangery' in which to overwinter tender plants in containers.

The Plants

The first climbers planted were cultivars of *Wisteria floribunda* and *W. sinensis*, rigorously pruned to encourage spurring and control their size. *Vitis vinifera* 'Purpurea' was grown on the trellises, and the small sweet 'Himrod', and 'Baco Noir' were trained as rods across the pergolas, the latter for its innumerable bunches of grapes, which though colourful were rather sour and not too tempting to party goers. Numerous clematis were planted, amongst them *Clematis florida* var. *sieboldiana* which did well under cover by the house, 'The President' for its double flowering season; late flowering 'Madame Julia Correvon', 'Madame Edouard André' and 'Huldine' pruned to about 60 cm (2 ft) from the ground early each spring. Honeysuckles, golden hop, *Ipomoea purpurea* and jasmine were planted on the trellises, but thorns on climbing roses made them so unpopular with guests they had to be removed, replacing them with the thornless 'Veilchenblau', 'Zéphirine Drouhin' and 'Kathleen Harrop'. Several

bougainvilleas, amongst them the salmon 'Miss Manila', bright glowing red 'San Diego Red' and pink 'Blondie' were grown in pots and pruned annually to a narrow upright framework, providing dramatic late summer colour amongst the vines.

Spring-flowering woodland perennials planted in narrow beds and spaces at the base of pillars included *Corydalis flexuosa*, which was too fragile to survive trampling, *Arum italicum* 'Marmoratum', several pulmonarias, *Mertensia virginica*, polyanthus hybrids, *Dicentra* 'Langtrees' and 'Luxuriant' and wallflowers. These were supplemented by bulbs grown in large containers, particularly large and flamboyant ones like the Darwin hybrid tulips 'Apeldoorn's Elite', 'Gordon Cooper' and the multi-hued 'Gudoshnik' with 'Blue Parrot' and 'Flaming Parrot'; a selection of orchid-flowered daffodils included 'Baccarat' and 'Lemon Beauty' and, his favourites, the doubles 'Tahiti', 'Texas' and 'Acropolis'. *Fritillaria imperialis* 'Aurora' and 'Maxima Lutea' produced suitably impressive flowers, accompanied by a distinctive odour which aroused suspicions of defective personal hygiene, creating some embarrassing moments between guests, before its source was traced. They were not used again. Later on, plants in containers contributed much of the colour, using cultivars of argyranthemum and pelargonium, including those with fragrant foliage, supported by other aroma contributors like *Heliotropium arborescens*, *Calomeria amaranthoides*, *Lilium regale* and *Nicotiana* 'Evening Fragrance'. Large Chinese dragon pots filled with *Zantedeschia aethiopica* and the cultivar 'Green Goddess' featured round the fountain. Height and a 'tropical atmosphere' were contributed by several half barrels containing the giant, brightly silver-edged reed *Arundo donax* var. *versicolor*, *Phormium tenax* 'Purpureum' and the brilliant scarlet, yellow or orange flowers of cultivars of *Canna indica*, including 'Purpurea' and 'Variegata'. The superb *Brugmansia* 'Grand Marnier' was tried one year, but took up too much space, and had scarcely started to flower before the partying season was over.

New Zealand Politician's Haven from Divisions

The garden of a former farmer and politician and his wife, on the slopes of Mount Taranaki in New Zealand. The annual rainfall is very high, and the climate mild, and in many winters virtually frost-free. The garden of about two hectares (five acres), containing remnants of the original evergreen bush, is on gently sloping ground a couple of hundred metres above sea level, with fine views to the snow-clad cone of the volcano and across the Tasman Sea. Numerous lahars (hillocks of clay, stones and ash) which are the left-overs from ancient eruptions, make the topography of the garden extremely variable. The owner and his wife both delight in gardening, and he wryly regrets frustrating, and finally disillusioning, years as a politician which could have been better spent gardening. They regularly visit the Hollard gardens, and enjoy renewing acquaintance with the large brindled cat, who accompanies them cradled in their arms. To their great joy, they discovered the garden made by Gordon and Annette Collier at Titoki Point at an early stage in their own gardening development, and found its combination of informality and intention so exciting they returned several times, finding it an inspiration for their own garden. On their first visit they were amused to be greeted near the gate by two small dogs, who escorted them courteously up the drive but, unlike the Hollard cat, left them to make their own way round the garden.

Review

A. The evergreen bush was a crucial asset. Although damaged by logging, domestic cattle, wild goats, pigs, possums and hurricane Bola, enough remained to provide the nucleus of the new garden.

B. The natural vegetation is an extreme example of a temperate forest matrix, and the mild winters, abundant rainfall and fertile, reddish topsoil (known as Egmont ash) appear to impose few limits on gardening. The main challenge was finding ways to control exuberant growth which could quickly make the garden almost impenetrable.

C. The husband had been brought up to appreciate well-regulated, ordered styles of garden. Their discovery of Titoki Point has made him more appreciative of subtle styles of coordination and design; a change much appreciated by his wife who has been contending with his preference for regimentation for years.

D. The benign conditions made it possible to combine trees and other plants, with a remarkable diversity of form and texture, offering opportunities that are still being developed.

Outcome

A.

- The first years were spent sorting out the bush; fencing out grazing animals, identifying the trees and tree ferns, and noting those most worth preserving; forming paths and more open areas; trying to control the possums, and giving the vegetation time to heal itself.

B.

- Control depended on creating effective matrices within which plants could develop in mutually balanced ways.
- This was done by identifying different settings within the garden suitable for a variety of plant communities, and by carefully balancing the vigour and other attributes of the plants themselves.

C.

- The highly controlled patterns of the Hollard garden were not applicable to this situation, and although the topography more closely matched Titoki Point, other conditions were too different to make that an easy model to follow.

- In the end they used central cores of native bush to provide backgrounds and shelter for broad paths flanked by rhododendrons and other shrubs and perennials, based on what they saw at the nearby Rhododendron Trust Gardens at Pukeiti.

D.

- The husband was uneasy at first with the lack of formality and definition; he was feeling insufficiently in control of the garden and the way it was developing.

- These feelings were, at least partially, relieved by careful attention to visual logic. Harmonies and contrasts within the planting were very carefully devised – the former to create quiet areas, the latter to emphasise transitions from one part of the garden to another. Repetition was used to establish patterns emphasising design, and linking different areas. Routes through the garden were defined by using plants and shapes to signal approaches to steps, viewpoints and transitions from one setting to another.

The Plants

The bush, battered but regenerating, is an increasingly impressive part of the garden. Tall trees, their upper limbs crowded with epiphytes, loom above densely-foliaged layers of evergreens. These tall, emergent individuals are wind-blown and decayed; their crotches stuffed with pubic astelias, their superstructure of branches draped with lichens, ragged, with clustered foliage at the tips of some branches – others reduced to gaunt dead limbs pointing grotesquely towards the sky. The evergreen foliage below is a dense green, amorphous mass, relieved only by the striking forms of the cabbage trees and tree ferns, or the bright

white splash of a clematis in flower. Only scattered ferns, fallen astelias, mosses, liverworts and filmy ferns can make a living in the constant, almost unrelieved shade on the dim, humid floor of the forest.

A 'hedge' of ancient *Phormium tenax*, and a windbreak of gnarled and contorted *Cupressus macrocarpa* provided shelter near the house and a setting for a small, more ordered, more formal garden in which the upright grass tree *Dracophyllum latifolium* and the spiky foliage and giant inflorescences of *Beschorneria yuccoides* stand out in exotic contrast to a ground-covering matrix of perennials, composed of broad, mounded clumps of ligularias, hostas, astilbes, rodgersias and hellebores, enlivened by the vertical accents of Siberian iris and arching Solomon's seal. Japanese anemones, epimediums, Spanish bluebells, dicentras, navelwort and a variety of candelabra primulas occupy spaces between them; and, in recent years, the imposing spikes of white trumpet lillies on self-sown *Cardiocrinum giganteum* seedlings have become one of the glories of the garden. The crimson, purple or variegated foliage of ajugas, and the bright blue pea flowers of *Parochetus africanus* fill whatever room is left at ground level.

The most impressive trees in the remnant of bush were conifers like *Dacrydium cupressinum*, *Phyllocladus trichomanoides* and *Prumnopitys ferruginea*, all fruitful supporters of the native birds. Broad-leaved trees included titoki, a small glade of the deciduous *Fuchsia excorticata*, *Griselinia lucida*, a number of tall, upright *Knightia excelsa* (regenerating vigorously in gaps in the canopy); the brilliant *Metrosideros robusta* (spectacularly covered with crimson flowers in the years when it bloomed well), and *Pittosporum crassifolium* with numerous *Weinmannia racemosa*, most of which provided nectar for the birds. Contrasting forms and foliage were introduced by palms, including several long-established and mature *Rhopalostylis sapida* (nikaus), and numerous slowly developing juveniles, and the tree ferns *Cyathea medullaris* (with its glossy

Native woodland, bush or spinney can provide very friendly conditions in which to make a garden. Here, existing trees, shrubs, climbers and ferns have been used as the foundation of the garden. Other native and non-native trees and shrubs have been planted, and numerous woodland herbaceous perennials introduced.

Native trees and shrubs include pittosporums, fuchsias, rimus, rewarewas, celery pines, cabbage trees and clematis. Perennials planted below include hostas, Siberian iris, Solomon's seal, bugles and primulas – highlighted in places with bromeliads growing epiphytically on tree stumps and branches.

Spiky-leaved plants are repeatedly used as a contrast to the heavy evergreen leaves of many of the native trees and shrubs – sometimes to highlight routes through the garden, sometimes to emphasise changes of atmosphere within it.

black rachises), the silver fern *Cyathea dealbata*, and *Dicksonia squarrosa*.

Shadowed areas beneath the tree canopy were already occupied by ferns, especially the unpalatable *Polystichum vestitum*. They were careful to add several plants of the giant *Marattia salicina*, which had been exterminated by wild pigs in search of its starchy tubers, and the large, graceful *Asplenium bulbiferum* which had been similarly reduced by goats. The Prince of Wales's feather established well in some of the cooler, moister gullies in company with the almost monotone, slightly glaucous fronds of *Histiopteris incisa*, and ribbons of the kidney-shaped fronds of the filmy fern, *Trichomanes reniforme*.

Bromeliads planted to create foliage contrasts amongst ferns, in semi-shaded, partially sunlit glades included the rare *Ochagavia carnea* (found naturally only on Juan Fernandez Island), *Nidularium rutilans* (with deep crimson bracts in the centres of the rosettes), and *N. innocentii* 'Striatum' whose variegated leaves suggest dappled sunlight.

conclusion

I THOUGHT THE TERM Matrix Planting had occurred to me spontaneously till I came across an article by an old friend, and fellow student at Wye College, E. C. M. Haes, in the quarterly bulletin of the *Alpine Garden Society*. He employed it to describe alpines growing in intermingled mats in a corner of his garden. Long forgotten though it was, perhaps the name had lurked hidden in a corner of my memory to be recalled when I needed a concise way to describe a method of gardening in which plants are intended to meld together in more or less self-sustaining communities.

Some may argue this is just another term for ground-cover – an attempt to revive an image tarnished, a little unfairly I think, by too many examples of unimaginatively chosen plants in uninspired settings masquerading as ground-cover. Many of the principles, and the plants used, on which the success of one depends, apply to the other. But matrix planting is concerned with successive layers of vegetation, one above the other, through which plants form multi-dimensional communities. Few would refer to the stratified vegetation of a wood as ground-cover (though seen from a bird's-eye view the cover is most effective), or the complex mixtures of grasses and herbs that form long-lived, self-sustaining communities in meadows. The growth patterns of the plants that grow in and around ponds would not form part of a dialogue on ground-cover, but communities like these are models for matrix planting.

More recently we have learnt about habitat planting that also has much in common with matrix planting. Both adopt as models the natural behaviour of plants, the places where they grow, and the ways they use the opportunities and cope with the problems of different situations. Some garden settings are inextricably linked with habitats where plants grow naturally. For example, in the shadow of trees and buildings, success depends on a close match between the setting and the nature of the plant. But that is not always so. Mixed borders in open situations on neutral soils, amongst the commonest of all garden settings, are undoubtedly habitats, but they would accommodate with equal prospects of success plants adapted to a variety of different situations and conditions in nature. In such settings the natural origins of garden plants become less significant; their ability to form self-sustaining matrices of stems, foliage and roots becomes critical. In some situations, careful matching of habitat and setting is the key; in others, it is attention to the compatibility between members of the community.

Many gardeners will feel that empowering plants reduces their own power to control what goes on in their gardens. Calendars, books, magazines and television present us with picturebook gardens filled with beautifully posed, meticulously selected plants. Sometimes, in carefully controlled groups,

(Opposite) If you could be content with a garden where a discarded olive stone would pass unnoticed, you might find matrix planting a rewarding path to follow.

sometimes in more natural looking communities – but all still clearly under control in a framework of weed-free borders and paths, mown grass and clipped hedges. They convey the message that, whatever the way we garden, we should all obey the commandment that 'Thy garden shall be immaculate'.

These reassuring signs of control are part of our defences against nature, and our attempts to dominate everything that goes on around us. It seems to me that such attempts increasingly take the form of obsessive attention to tidiness and order, aimed at the elimination of anything that interrupts this order, often at the expense of individuality, atmosphere and sense of place. Matrix planting depends for its effects on imagination rather than tidiness. Clear-cut distinctions between weeds and garden plants are less easily made; it is better to leave insects alone and rely on natural balances between predator and prey than attack with poisonous sprays; dead leaves are a source of humus and part of the natural cycle of growth and decay on which success depends.

Some time ago a friend of a friend invited me over for a tour of his garden. Later, sitting on a chair on his impeccably maintained lawn, chatting over a drink, I automatically flicked the stone from an olive into the nearest border, where it landed on the finely tilled soil between the perfect dome of a dwarf rhododendron and a carefully combed clump of irises. It lay there reproaching me for my sluttishness, seemingly the only unintentional object in the immaculate order of the garden. A calling card left by my dog on my host's lawn would have been only marginally more shaming.

If you are dedicated to gardening as a form of housework, matrix planting is unlikely to appeal as an alternative. If you prefer more relaxed styles where happenstance plays its part, if you do not measure the success of your gardening by the regimentation of your plants, if you could be content with a garden where a discarded olive stone would pass unnoticed, you might find matrix planting a rewarding path to follow.

appendix

gardens and *plants* featured in the *photographs*

Page 2: *Hosta* cvs, *Aruncus dioicus*, irises, *Digitalis purpurea*, *Primula pulverulenta*, *Acer palmatum* var. *dissectum* Atropurpureum Group cv. Betty and Charles Moore's garden, Doctors Point, Waitati, New Zealand. Photo: Gil Hanly.

Page 6: Includes *Stachys byzantina*, *Ammi majus*, *Paeonia* cv. (single, blood red), *Papaver somniferum*, *Rosa* 'Iceberg', *Phuopsis stylosa* 'Purpurea'. Elizabeth Kerfoot's Garden, North Saanich, Vancouver Island, Canada.

Page 8: *Dicentra eximia* (bleeding heart), *Polygonatum biflorum*, *Viola* sp. Brandywine Conservancy Wildflower Garden, Chadds Ford, Pennsylvania, USA.

Page 10 (bottom): *Paeonia mlokosewitschii*, *Geranium* spp., *Bergenia cordifolia*, *Aucuba japonica* 'Variegata', *Iris sibirica* cv. East Lambrook Manor, Somerset, England.

Page 10 (top): *Dryopteris wallichiana*, *Meconopsis cambrica*, *Lamium galeobdolon* 'Florentinum' Red Lion House, Horderley, Shropshire, England.

Page 11: *Aloe arborescens*, *Agave* spp., *Aeonium* sp. The Abbey Gardens, Tresco, Scilly Islands, Cornwall, England.

Page 12: *Iris pseudocorus* 'Variegata', *Meconopsis grandis*, *Primula prolifera*, ligularias, hostas, tree ferns, *Dryopteris* spp., *Pseudopanax ferox*, *Acer palmatum* cvs.Titoki Point, Taihape, New Zealand. Photo: Gil Hanly.

Page 13: Numerous herbaceous perennials, including *Sisyrinchium striatum*, *Stachys byzantina* 'Silver Carpet'. De Kempenhof Garden , Domburg, Zeeland, Holland.

Page 14 (top): *Eucalyptus accedens* (powderbark wandoo). Coomallo Creek, near Eneabba, Western Australia.

Page 14 (middle): *Dacrydium cupressinum* (rimu), *Astelia* sp., *Rhododendron* cvs., *Cordyline* cv. Mark & Felix Jury's garden, Titirangi, New Zealand.

Page 14 (bottom): *Jovibarba heuffelii*. Mount Olympus, Greece.

Page 15: *Leschenaultia macrantha* (wreath flower), *Glischocaryon aureum*. Canna, Mullewa, Western Australia.

Page 16 (top left): *Lilium* cv., *Hydrangea arborescens*, *Streptocarpus* cv., *Onoclea sensibilis*. Red Lion House, Horderley, Shropshire, England.

Page 16 (right): *Dianthus* 'Mrs Sinkins', *Arctotis* x *hybrida*, *Artemisia pontica*, *Othonna cheirifolia*, *Convolvulus cneorum*, *Linum flavum* 'Compactum', *Senecio cineraria* 'White Diamond', *Fremontodendron* 'California Glory', *Cistus* x *purpureus*. Powys Castle, Welshpool, Powys, Wales.

Page 16 (bottom right): *Stachys byzantina* 'Silver Carpet', *Allium christophii*, *Achillea* 'Moonshine', *Verbascum* 'Silver Spire', *Dianthus* cv. Red Lion House, Horderley, Shropshire, England.

Page 16 (bottom left): *Aquilegia vulgaris*, *Iris orientalis* 'Variegata'. Stourton House, Mere, Wiltshire, England.

Page 18 (top left): *Dahlia* cv. Decorative. Godspiece Leaze, Norton St Philip, Somerset, England.

Page 18 (bottom left)): *Rosa* 'Dioressence' hybrid tea. Regional Botanic Garden, Manurewa, Auckland, New Zealand.

Page 18 (right): *Grevillea eriostachya* (flame grevillea). Between Dongara and Mingenew, Western Australia.

Page 19 (left): *Lupinus* Russell hybrids. Lake Tekapo, New Zealand.

Page 19 (right): Candelabra primulas. Achnacloich Gardens, Taynuilt, Argyllshire, Scotland.

Page 20: *Bergeria* cvs, *Matteucia struthiopteris*, *Hosta seiboldiana*, *Phalaris arundinacea* 'Picta', *Iris pseudacoras*, *Phormium tenax* Purpureum Group, *Primula prolifera*. Titoki Point, Taihape, New Zealand. Photo: Gil Hanly.

Page 21 (left): Rambling roses. Roseraie de l'Hay-les-Roses, Paris, France.

Page 21 (right): Herbaceous perennials. Oxford University Botanic Garden, Oxford, England.

Page 23 (top right): *Osmunda claytoniana*, *Aegopodium podagraria* 'Variegatum'. Weston , Vermont, USA.

Page 23 (left): *Dacrydium cupressinum* (rimu), *Monstera deliciosa*, *Astelia* sp., bromeliads. The Jurys' Garden, Waitara, New Zealand.

Page 23 (bottom left): *Leucadendron strobilinum* 'Waterlily'. Regional Botanic Garden, Manurewa, Auckland, New Zealand.

Page 23 (bottom right): Various plants, including *Cordyline australis* cvs, *Astelia* spp. The Anthony's Garden, Kauri, Whangarei, New Zealand.

Page 24 (top left): *Hippophae rhamnoides*, *Betula* sp., *Hosta* cv., *Ligularia* cv. Van Dusen Botanical Garden, Vancouver, British Columbia, Canada.

Page 24 (top right): *Rosa* cvs., *Taxus baccata*. de Kempenhof, Walcheren, Holland.

Page 24 (bottom left): Includes *Lunaria annua* 'Variegata', *Hydrangea macrophylla* cv., *Fuchsia magellanica* var. *gracilis*, *Aquilegia vulgaris*, *Alchemilla mollis*. The Davisons' Garden, Auckland, New Zealand.

Page 24 (bottom right): *Trillium grandiflorum*, *Rodgersia aesculifolia*, *Hyacinthoides hispanica*. Savill Garden, Windsor Great Park, England.

Page 26: Includes *Euphorbia characias* subsp. *wulfenii*, *Bergenia* cv., *Tanacetum parthenium*, *Hosta sieboldiana*, *Alchemilla mollis*. George Radford's Garden, Victoria, Vancouver Island, Canada.

Page 27: *Kniphofia uvaria* 'Nobilis', *Galtonia candicans*, *Agapanthus* 'Blue Imp', *Agapanthus* 'Castle of May', *Hemerocallis* 'Lexington'. Savill Garden, Windsor Great Park, England.

Page 29 (top): *Canna indica* cv., *Senecio cineraria* cv., *Salvia splendens* cv. The Quarry Garden, Shrewsbury, Shropshire, England.

Page 29 (bottom): Various herbaceous perennials. Tedstone Court, Bromyard, Worcestershire, England.

Page 34: *Euphorbia amygdaloides* 'Rubra', *Myosotis sylvatica*, *Anthemis punctata* subsp. *cupaniana*, *Helleborus argutifolius*. Red Lion House, Shropshire, England.

Page 35: *Erica* cvs., mosses. Knightshayes Garden, Devon, England.

Page 36 (top left): *Malus domestica* cvs., *Geranium macrorrhizum*, *Paeonia* cv. The Noble Garden, Sidney, Vancouver Island, Canada.

Page 36 (middle left): *Malus domestica* cvs. Heale House, Wiltshire, England.

Page 36 (bottom left): Gardenscape. Newby Hall, Yorkshire, England.

Page 36 (right): *Dicksonia squarrosa* (wheki), *Fuchsia excorticata*, *Lunaria annua* var. *albiflora*, *Blechnum capense*. The Wallaces' Garden, Taumarunui, New Zealand.

Page 39 (left): *Galax urceolata*. The Garden in the Woods, Framingham, Massachusetts, USA.

Page 39 (top right): *Rodgersia aesculifolia*. Abbotsbury Gardens, Dorset, England.

Page 39 (bottom right): *Echinocactus grusonii*, *Aloe* sp., *Cereus* sp. Le Jardin Exotique, Monte Carlo.

Page 50 (top left): *Rhododendron* cvs., including azaleas. Hergest Croft, Kington, Herefordshire, England.

Page 50 (middle left): *Magnolia sprengeri*. The Arboretum, Westonbirt, Gloucestershire, England.

Page 50 (bottom left): *Protea reflexa* 'Chittick Red'. Regional Botanic Garden, Manurewa, Auckland, New Zealand.

Page 50 (right): *Telopea speciosissima* 'Sunburst' (waratah). Regional Botanic Garden, Manurewa, Auckland, New Zealand.

Page 52 (top left): *Cistus creticus*. Powys Castle, Welshpool, Powys, Wales.

Page 52 (top right): Dianthus pink single, *Osteospermum jucundum*. Godspiece Leaze, Norton St Philip, Somerset, England.

Page 52 (bottom left): Iris bearded, white, *Osteospermum ecklonis*, *Osteospermum* pink cv., *Anthemis punctata* subsp. *cupaniana*, *Salvia officinalis*. Powys Castle, Welshpool, Powys, Wales.

Page 52 (bottom right): *Buddleja* 'Loch Inch', tortoiseshell and painted lady butterflies. Red Lion House, Horderley, Shropshire, England.

Page 56: Shrubs of the Kwongan. 'The Wildflower Way', Perenjori, Western Australia.

Page 58: The Dillon Garden, Ranelagh, Dublin, Ireland.

Page 60: *Acer palmatum*, *Ligularia* sp. Chateau Courances, Essonne, Fontainebleu, France.

Page 61 (left): *Petrea volubilis*. Ayrlies, Whitford, Auckland, New Zealand.

Page 61 (top right): *Hosta* cv., *Adiantum pedatum*, *Hydrangea aspera*, rambling rose cv. The Noble garden, Sidney , Vancouver Island, Canada. Page 61 (bottom right): *Clematis* 'Rouge Cardinal'. Godspiece Leaze, Norton St Philip, Somerset, England.

Page 62 (left): *Euphorbia amygdaloides* 'Rubra', *Geranium* x *oxonianum* 'Wargrave Pink', *Anthriscus sylvestris*, *Primula veris*. Red Lion House, Horderley, Shropshire, England.

Page 62 (right): *Impatiens walleriana* (busy Lizzie 'elf mixed'), *Hedera helix*, *Dryopteris filix-mas*. Red Lion House, Horderley, Shropshire, England.

Page 64 (top left): Gardens under construction. Godspiece Leaze, Norton St Philip, Bath, England.

Page 64 (top right): Various trees grown as standards. Speight Gardens, Arrowtown , New Zealand.

Page 65 (bottom): Vegetables of various kinds, including peas, lettuces,

onions and courgettes. The Noble Garden, Vancouver Island, Canada.
Page 65 (left): *Narcissus* 'Tête a tête', *Primula vulgaris* subsp. *sibthorpii*, *Valeriana phu* 'Aurea', Lottie the dog. Red Lion House, Shropshire, England.
Page 65 (right): *Viola cornuta* 'Lilacina', *Digitalis purpurea* (foxglove), *Saxifraga* x *urbium* 'London Pride'. Red Lion House, Shropshire, England.
Page 66 (left): Includes *Grielum humifusum, Lampranthus comptonii, Heliophila* sp. white. Skilpad Wildflower Reserve, Namaqualand, South Africa.
Page 66 (right): Includes *Osteospermum pluvialis, Ursinia cakilefolia*. National Botanical Institute, Kirstenbosch, Cape Town, South Africa.
Page 67 (left): *Verbascum* 'Silver Spire', *Achillea* 'Moonshine', *Diascia barberae* 'Ruby Field', *Buxus sempervirens* 'Latifolia Maculata', *Geranium psilostemon*, Roland the cat. Red Lion House, Horderley, Shropshire, England.
Page 67 (right): *Digitalis purpurea* 'Sutton's Apricot', *Osteospermum jucunda*, *Geranium* x *magnificum*. Red Lion House, Horderley, Shropshire, England.
Page 76: *Artemisia* 'Powis Castle', *Celmisia* spp., *Cortaderia* spp., *Echium candicans*. Ormonds Nursery & Garden, Havelock North, New Zealand. Photo: Gil Hanly
Page 77: *Matteucia struthiopteris* (shuttlecock fern), *Meconopsis betonicifolia*. Longstock Water Gardens, Stockbridge, England.
Page 79 (top): *Pilosella aurantiaca*, Grim the collier, *Leucanthemum vulgare* (ox-eye daisy), *Hieracium* sp. (hawkweed). Inverewe Gardens, Polewe, Scotland.
Page 79 (middle): *Astelia nervosa, Chionochloa rubra, Celmisia coriacea, Hebe pinguifolia*. Jack's Pass, Hanmer Springs, South Island, New Zealand.
Page 79 (bottom): *Themada triandra*. View across the Orange River, Fort Hartley, Near Quthing, Lesotho.
Page 83 (top): *Agrostemma githago* (corncockle), *Papaver rhoeas* (poppy), *Centaurea cyanea* (cornflower). South of Riano, Castille, Spain.
Page 83 (bottom left): Includes *Senecio aquatica, Lychnis flos-cuculi, Dactylorhiza incarnate*. Piedrasluengas, Picos de Europa, Spain.
Page 83 (bottom right): *Viola graeca, Iberis sempervirens, Ranunculus* sp. Mount Olympus, Greece.
Page 86 (top left): *Rudbeckia hirta* (gloriosa daisies). Botanic Garden, Khabarovsk, Ussuriland, Russia.
Page 86 (right): *Ursinia* sp., *Gazania* sp., *Lampranthus* sp., *Carpobrotus* sp. and other wildflowers in a garden on the Sandveld. Silver Seas, Noordhoek, near Cape Town, South Africa.
Page 86 (bottom left): *Camassia quamash, Ranunculus acris* (buttercup). Dartington Hall, Totnes, Devon, England.
Page 89 (top left): *Arundo donax* var. *versicolor, Miscanthus floridulus, Verbena* scarlet cv. Arboretum, North Carolina State University, USA.
Page 89 (top right): Matrix of trees, shrubs and grasses. Misty Hills Hotel, Muldersdrift, Gauteng, South Africa.
Page 89 (bottom left): *Chionochloa rubra*. Speight Gardens, Arrowtown, New Zealand.
Page 89 (bottom right): *Festuca glauca, Plantago media*. de Kempenhof, Walcheren, Holland.
Page 92 (left): *Raoulia* spp. (scabweeds), *Festuca novae-zelandiae*. Tasman Glacier moraine, Mount Cook National Park, New Zealand.
Page 92 (top right): *Ourisia vulcanicola, Dracophyllum recurvum*, moss, lichen. Mount Ruapehu, above Ohakune, New Zealand.
Page 92 (bottom): Includes *Pimelea prostrata, Raoulia* sp., *Androsace* sp. Larnach Castle, Otago Peninsula, New Zealand.
Page 100: *Rodgersia podophylla, Rheum palmatum, Filipendula ulmaria, Podophyllum peltatum, Hosta* cvs, *Aruncus dioicus, Betula albosinensis, Zantedeschia aethiopica, Gunnera manicata*. Trotts' garden, Ashburton, New Zealand. Photo: Gil Hanly
Page 102 (left): Canada geese with goslings. Stourhead, Wiltshire, England.
Page 102 (right): *Iris pseudacorus* 'Variegata', *Darlingtonia californica, Nymphaea* cvs. Stourton House, Mere, Wiltshire, England.
Page 103 (left): *Gunnera manicata, Dicksonia* spp. (tree ferns), *Nymphaea alba*. Rapaura Water Garden, Tapu, Coromandel. New Zealand.
Page 103 (right): Pool with densely planted margins. The McRae Garden, Chindie, near Otorohonga, New Zealand.
Page 104 (top): Waterfalls amongst coprosmas, chionochloas and other native New Zealand plants. Ayrlies, Whitford, New Zealand.
Page 104 (bottom): Fountains in the Patio de la Acequia, in the Generalife, Grenada. The Generalife, Granada, Andalucia, Spain.
Page 105 (top left): *Iris sibirica* hybrids. Regional Botanic Garden, Manurewa, Auckland, New Zealand.
Page 105 (bottom left): *Zantedeschia aethiopica, Primula prolifera*. Ayrlies, Whitford, New Zealand.
Page 105 (right): *Iris* hybrid, *Gunnera manicata, Juniperus* x *pfitzeriana* 'Aurea', *Lavandula angustifolia* cv., *Anigozanthos* sp. Rapaura Water Garden, Tapu, Coromandel. New Zealand.

Page 112 (top): *Hosta sieboldiana, Primula japonica, Hosta ventricosa, Primula* sp, *Mimulus luteus, Nymphaea alba*. Longstock Water Gardens, Stockbridge, Hampshire, England.
Page 112 (bottom): *Primula* sp., *Hosta* cvs., *Dicksonia* spp., *Gunnera tinctoria*. Titoki Point, Taihape, New Zealand.
Page 114 (left): *Nelumbo komarovii*. Near Lesozavodsk, Ussuriland, Russia.
Page 114 (right): *Nymphoides peltata, Monochoria korsakowii, Phragmites australis*. Lake Khanka, near Gayvoran, Far Eastern Region, Russia.
Page 116 (top left): *Nymphaea alba*. Ayrlies, Whitford, New Zealand.
Page 116 (bottom left): *Aponogeton distachyos* (water hawthorn). Knysna Forrest, Knysna, South Africa.
Page 116 (right): *Euryala ferox, Monochoria korsakowii*. Near Lesozavodsk, Ussuriland, Far Eastern Region, Russia.
Page 126: *Magnolia* x *soulangeana, Chamaecyparis lawsoniana* 'Lanei', *Rhododendron* cvs, *Camellia* cvs. Titoki Point, Taihape, New Zealand.
Page 128: *Erica corifolia, Leucadendron gandogeri* and other plants of the fynbos. Boskloof, Napier, The Overberg, South Africa.
Page 129 (top): *Calluna vulgaris, Fagus sylvatica*. The Long Mynd, Shropshire, England.
Page 129 (bottom): *Cyathea* spp., *Dicksonia* spp. Waitakere Forest, Auckland, New Zealand.
Page 130 (top): *Aloe dichotoma, Pachypodium namaquense*. Hester Malan Nature Reserve, Springbok, Namaqualand, South Africa.
Page 130 (bottom): *Rosa* 'Bloomfield Courage'. Greagh, Three Mile Bush Road, Whangarei, New Zealand.
Page 134 (top): *Eucalyptus* sp., *Rhododendron* cvs. The Gerdiman Garden, Yachats, Oregon, USA.
Page 134 (middle): *Eryngium* x *tripartitum, Vitis vinifera* 'Purpurea'. Godspiece Leaze, Norton St Philip, Somerset, England.
Page 134 (bottom): Cape heaths, *Erica* spp. and cvs. Wittunga Botanic Garden, Adelaide, South Australia.
Page 139 (top left): *Arundo donax* var. *versicolor, Hibiscus moscheutos, Iris ensata* white cv., *Allium* sp. Arboretum, North Carolina State University, USA.
Page 139 (top right): *Persicaria affinis* cv., *Bergenia* cv., *Sedum* sp., *Lamium maculatum* 'White Nancy', *Geranium* x *cantabrigiense, Eryngium giganteum, Heuchera* 'Palace Purple'. Red Lion House, Horderley, Shropshire, England.
Page 139 (middle): *Camassia quamash, Lunaria annua, Galanthus nivalis, Geranium nodosum, Pulmonaria* cvs, *Dryopteris filix-mas*. Red Lion House, Horderley, Shropshire, England.
Page 139 (bottom): *Aconitum lycoctonum, Ajuga reptans* 'Burgundy Glow'. Iford Manor, Bradford on Avon, Wiltshire, England.
Page 145 (top): *Allium christophii, Sedum sieboldii*. Great Dixter, Northiam, Sussex, England.
Page 145 (bottom): *Lilium* 'African Queen', *Lilium* orange cv., *Macleaya cordata, Coreopsis verticillata*. Little Norton Mill, Somerset, England.
Page 154: *Hosta* cvs, ferns. Titoki Point, Taihape, New Zealand.
Page 156 (top left): *Betula alba, Phormium* cv., *Dicksonia fibrosa* (ponga), *Cordyline australis, Cynara carduncellus*. Titoki Point, Taihape, New Zealand.
Page 156 (right): Matrix of trees and shrubs in bushveld garden. Pieter de Jager's Garden, Monument Park, Pretoria, South Africa.
Page 156 (bottom left): *Betula pubescens, Erica* cvs, *Calluna* cvs. Royal Botanic Gardens, Kew, London., England.
Page 160 (middle): *Dicksonia fibrosa, Cordyline australis* (cabbage tree), *Hosta* 'Frances Williams'. Titoki Point, Taihape, New Zealand.
Page 160 (left): *Acer* sp., *Rhododendron* sp., *Betula albosinensis*. Newby Hall, Ripon, Yorkshire, England.
Page 160 (right): Several mature trees. Hillside, Connecticut, USA.
Page 163 (top): *Macfadyena unguis-cati*. The Stacey Garden, Bal-yana, Te Puke, New Zealand.
Page 163 (bottom): *Rosa* 'Francis E Lester'. Hestercombe, Somerset, England.
Page 165 (top): *Trillium grandiflorum*. Oaks Overlook, Shenandoah National Park, Virginia, USA.
Page 165 (bottom): *Pinus* sp., *Blechnum* sp. Hillside, Connecticut, USA.
Page 170 (left): *Acer palmatum* cv., *Polytrichum commune*. Tatton Park, Knutsford, Cheshire, England.
Page 170 (right): *Blechnum spicant* (deer fern), *Rhytidiadelphus loreus*, moss. Bloedel Gardens, Bainbridge Island, Washington, USA.
Page 173 (left): Mosses and lichens. Parque Nacional Queulat, Puyuhuapi, Aisen, Chile.
Page 173 (top right): *Isotachys lyallii* (red moss), mosses, liverworts, ferns. Wilmot's Pass, Otago, New Zealand.
Page 173 (bottom right): *Lycopodium anotinum*. Kutusova, Ussuriland, Russia.
Page 182: South Island garden, New Zealand. Photo: Gil Hanly

index of plants

This index includes the names of plants referred to in the main body of the text and accompanying lists, and provides the Latin equivalents of all vernacular names used.